Father *Songs*

Also by Gloria Wade-Gayles

Rooted Against the Wind:
Personal Essays

Pushed Back to Strength:
A Black Woman's Journey Home

My Soul Is a Witness:
African-American Women's Spirituality

Anointed to Fly

No Crystal Stair:
Race and Sex in Black Women's Novels,
1946–1976

Father Songs

Testimonies
by African-American
Sons and Daughters

Edited by

Gloria Wade-Gayles

BEACON PRESS • BOSTON

BEACON PRESS
25 Beacon Street
Boston, Massachusetts 02108-2892

BEACON PRESS BOOKS
are published under the auspices of
the Unitarian Universalist Association of Congregations.

03 02 01 00 99 98 97   8 7 6 5 4 3 2 1

Text design by Elizabeth Elsas
Composition by Wilsted & Taylor

Library of Congress Cataloging-in-Publication Data
Father songs : testimonies by African-American sons and
    daughters / edited by Gloria Wade-Gayles.
        p.   cm.
      ISBN 0-8070-6214-6
      1. Fathers—United States—Literary collections.
    2. Fathers and daughters—United States—Literary
    collections.   3. Fathers and sons—United States—
    Literary collections.   4. Father figures—United States—
    Literary collections.   5. Afro-American families—Literary
    collections.   6. American literature—Afro-American
    authors.   I. Wade-Gayles, Gloria Jean.
    PS509.F34F375   1997
    810.8′03520431—dc21   96-47802

Contents

3. Praise-Songs

4. Fare-Thee-Wells

5. Gifts

A Brief Prelude to the Songs

His friends called him "Bob Wade." My mother called him "Robert Jr." My sister and I called him "Daddy." He was born in Natchez, Mississippi, around 1912 in a sharecropping family that had no formulas for the conversion of arid Mississippi dust into fertile soil. From my mother, who told my father's story far better than he, wrapping every word with a love for him that never waned, I learned about the forces that shaped the man my father had become when they met: poverty, racial violence, and the death of his parents when he was but a young boy. "Your father," she would tell my sister and me, "had a hard life." After the death of his mother, whom he loved passionately, and a short time thereafter the death of his father, he and his three siblings moved to Memphis, Tennessee, to live with a paternal uncle, an exemplary surrogate father who must have been a descendant of the Watusi of West Africa, so tall, thin, dark, and angular he was. In the few father-stories that came from his lips, Daddy would praise this uncle—Luke he was called—and recall with gratitude the regular meals, the loving care, the sense of belonging that so transformed his world. When he and my mother created their family of two girls—the first child, a son, died in infancy—my father, I am certain, had all intentions of staying the course as Uncle Luke had and sending us forth into the world prepared to become as large as the dreams he had for us, if not larger. Unfortunately, the gates of hell were thrown open in Memphis, as elsewhere then and now, and the white demons who galloped past trampled freely on the lives of Black families. By the time I was about two, my father left

Memphis (around the same time that his contemporary Richard Wright left) and traveled north to freedom and manhood, north to Southside Chicago. My mother followed, bringing my sister and me, but soon we moved back south again without him. The rest is history—mine and that of many other Blacks of my generation. My sister and I were reared into adulthood in two different cities.

It was so logical, my mother's decision to leave Chicago. The fast northern pace was too fast for the rearing of two girls, and the world of concrete and closed-in city spaces seemed as arid as the dry soil of Mississippi. We returned South to home and sunshine and familiarity and extended families. Daddy was both miles away and close. He wired money. He called frequently, charming us through the wires with his warm and joyous personality as he did whenever we were with him. And we were with him frequently. Each year, at the end of school, the tickets would arrive, and we would begin preparing for a ride on the Illinois Central that would take us, jubilant and privileged, from the South of segregation to what, in our young minds and Daddy's fantasies, was the North of freedom.

In that world, he was a princely man, walking on gorgeous legs (which my sister inherited) into restaurants, apartments, and downtown department stores with his "girls," daring anyone to bar our entrance or to look at us with anything other than admiration, if not envy. We were princesses in his eyes, and he was a prince in ours. We knew he was when people would call his name—"Bob Wade! Bob Wade!"—from passing cars or when in the drugstore hangout on the corner of Calumet and Cottage Grove people would listen in rapt attention as he shared stories about his experiences as a Pullman porter on the Illinois Central, moving dramatically the soft hands that were never meant to plow the hard ground and never did. He would not linger over these stories, however, if we were visiting, for more important than his desire to entertain friends with the foolishness of white people who wanted service with a smile was his determination to inform his friends about his "girls," how smart we were and what ladies we were, compliments that bore Mama's name and justified our being in Memphis rather than in Chicago. We were going to be as large as his dreams for us, if not larger. What he couldn't give from hundreds of miles away and what the fast-paced world of Chicago wouldn't give, my father knew we would receive abundantly at home.

My mother never judged my father for staying up North. In part she didn't because she could have remained in Chicago, but mainly it was because she had touched those parts of him that defined and shaped him, those parts that had their roots somewhere in the Mississippi soil of his youth, those parts that breathed when he lay next to her, and she understood that he needed the freedom that Chicago's broad streets and the absence of "colored" signs provided him. She knew my father would have lost his mind in the racist world of Memphis, Tennessee. My mother was sure he would not have been the good father he was in Chicago had he remained in Memphis. Taking our mother's lead, my sister and I never judged our father and, really, we had no reason to do so, for though he lived in Chicago, an eight-hour train ride away, he was very much a part of our lives—adding weight to the anchor that kept us grounded in values that would help us realize those dreams he predicted. Editing this anthology reminds me of how well he managed to be away from us and closely with us at the same time. Therefore, on a high note, I sing with my brothers and sisters in this collection of father-songs.

The G-clef of truth calls for both sharps and flats, high notes and low notes; notes sung briefly and notes sustained; screeching notes and soothing notes; notes that, hearing once, we do not wish to hear again and notes we want to sing, and do, again and again. This is an anthology of "both/and" songs. Both distance and closeness, joy and sadness, pride and shame, bonding and alienation, lingering rage and healing reconnection. It includes the writings of both daughters and sons. Some of the daughters are "Daddy's Girl" while others are "daddyless." Some of the sons are loved and affirmed by their fathers while others are rejected and even scorned. Some of the fathers, regardless of the quality of their parenting, are biological while others are surrogate, but no less clear in their identity as father. There is no one way to sing our father songs, no one way to see his reflection in the mirror that shows us the contours of our own.

Why did I undertake the editing of this book? Some readers might answer that I yielded to the rancor of Black men over what they consider to be Black women writers' overemphasis on women—most especially on mothers—and turned my attention to the subject of fathers as a channel for positive images of Black men (and there are many in this anthology). If this is fact, it remains in my subconscious. The truth is— the truth that I can cognitively know—the influences were otherwise. The first is a combination of my age and my identity as the mother of a son and a daughter. As I become older and anticipate the joy of being a grandparent, I wish for a book that brings Black women and Black men together in a dialogue on Black fatherhood, a dialogue that comes not from sociological studies and statistics, but rather from memory. A how-to and a how-not-to book written by both Black women and Black men that I can give to both my son and my daughter. While they have positive models from their own experiences, I want them to have a book that they can open, again and again, dog-ear from frequent readings, color with the highlight of poignant quotes, and pass on, with their own father stories and father songs, to their children. If it is true, as I was taught early in life, that a book has the power to confirm and reaffirm truths we already know, then it is a given that our sons and our daughters need a book on our fathers written by Black women and Black men who dig deeper into the soil of memory, and truth. *Father Songs* answers that need. It is a first. I hope it will inspire many others. We need them all for our children, for ourselves.

The second influence, and perhaps the greater one, is the bleakness of the new century that is now so close we can feel its dry winds. We must begin now, right now, to seed the clouds so that with the wind comes rain, a steady, quiet rain that presses our soil back against the earth and bathes the bitter dust from our faces. Without the rain, our throats will be too parched to speak and our eyes so blinded that we will see our beauty even less clearly in the twenty-first century than we do today. I believe we can begin this urgent work by strengthening father-daughter and father-son relationships that are now strong and by transforming those that are now weak.

Quickly, let me explain that I am not urging a return to what conservatives call "family values," for such a turn backwards would mire all of us deeper in conflict and confusion. Those so-called family values represented power and control rather than happiness and love in family relationships. I am looking not to that past but rather to a new and different future in which fathers are whole enough to love their sons and their daughters, to anchor them in trust and security, and to affirm them in the dreams and identities they claim in the free space of independence and wholeness. Ushered forth from such relationships, Black women and Black men in the twenty-first century can confront the demons already dressing in armor on the near horizon and, in a battle that draws no blood, exorcise them—all of the demons—from our souls. This book was written in anticipation of both/and: both the victory and the celebration. It is a gift from Black women and Black men who want us now, right now, to hear their stories and filter their truths through the alembic of our understanding of our need for a new world.

I place my hands on the drum of gratitude to say thanks to: Haki Madhubuti, Jim Hunt, Fleda Jackson, Angela Getter, Audree Irons, Jana Novotna, Tamara Plummer, Candace Raven, and Helen Spencer for their invaluable support and encouragement.

The drumbeat becomes deeper and more marked when I call the names of Asha Almo and Tahra Edwards of Spelman College, who read all the manuscripts submitted, prepared all the files, and, through careful research, located epigraphs for the various chapters in the anthology; Deb Chasman and Tisha Hooks of Beacon Press who distilled my work through their editorial genius; and Lydia Howarth, a gifted writer in her own right, who touched the manuscript with her expertise as a talented and thorough copyeditor.

And when I remember how much I learned from my sister Faye about the uniqueness of our father, I beat the drum, I sing, and I dance.

I

Are You My Father?

A stocky man walked up to me and kissed me on the cheek and as he held me tight, smiling and looking into my face, I was terrified. I had no idea who he was, and all I kept thinking was that he smelled like cigarettes and coffee. There were no introductions. He just kept squeezing me. As soon as I could get free from him, I ran down the church steps to my mother.

"Who is that?" I asked, pointing up the stairs to the man who had frightened me.

She glanced up and then covered her eyes. "That's your daddy."

CHARMAGNE HELTON

Marcia Dyson

Is My Daddy Here?

Daddy strutted the streets as if he owned them, puffing on a big cigar, with his hands in his pockets. He was a gambler; without hesitation, he placed a wager on any "hot tip"—horses, dogs, boxing matches, anything that brought in the cash. Even policy, better known as running numbers.

Mama could explain the policy racket well. She worked for a big policy lord named Buddy. It was at Buddy's station, in 1948, that Mama and Daddy, who was ten years her senior, met. Daddy treated "Rose" with respect. He wined and dined her. She swallowed it all. He mesmerized her with his smooth coffee-brown skin, high cheek bones, beautiful glistening teeth, and bright eyes. He cradled her in his brawny arms, well developed by labor in the railroad yard. His smooth-talking ways reeled her into his life, hook, line, and sinker. It took two years before Mama felt like a fish out of water. She had given birth to two daughters: Beverly, the oldest, and Elaine, eleven months younger. Despite Mama's many requests, Daddy refused to marry her. A month after Elaine's birth, Mama put her foot down.

"Duke, you are going to have to make this union legal," Mama insisted.

Grudgingly, Daddy rode with Mama on the CTA bus downtown to the justice of the peace where Daddy made her an "honest woman." I was born thirteen months later, October 29, 1951, the baby of "Duke's girls."

In 1953, Daddy decided he couldn't take the babies crying, having to spend his money on milk, food, and diapers, having to give an account of where he had been all night, and not being able to come and go as he pleased. It took him less than ten steps down the front porch to exit our lives. Mama did not try to stop him.

Mama stood on the front porch and watched "Duke" fade down the street. When Daddy left Mama, he left me too.

"God don't like ugly," Mama constantly repeated to us. And Daddy acted ugly. He told Mama that he had moved to a nearby hotel. The truth is that Daddy moved in with his "woman," Amanda McWhorter (Mama Mack), down the street from us. It was only by accident that Mama discovered where he lived. Daddy had gone shopping at a local grocery store and requested that they deliver the two boxes of food to his home. Gene, the delivery man, didn't know Daddy had left us, so naturally he brought the groceries to us.

"Duke sent these," Gene told Mama as he dropped the boxes on the kitchen table. "He did?" Mama quizzed him as he left.

Minutes after Gene left, Daddy rushed into Mama's kitchen and a stormy argument ensued. Daddy was "madder than hell" at Gene for not taking the time to look at his new address. "God don't like ugly, Duke," Mama scolded him. Unrepentant, he picked up the groceries and left, without leaving us anything.

Daddy wiped us from his life for nearly a year. Then, like a rabbit pulled out of a hat, he magically appeared at our door. He finally found the time between gambling, womanizing, and playing poker, to visit us. He and Mama would mostly argue. I hated the noise. I would go on the back porch and play. On the nights Daddy visited, I would wet the bed. I was ashamed because my sisters teased me and it increased Mama's work load. It was a habit that took six years to break.

Daddy began to take us out during his sporadic visits, but he never took us to his house. One summer afternoon, he told Mama that he was going to take us to visit Aunt Dorothy. We got off the bus in front of a twelve-unit, brick apartment complex. Curtains floated out of the windows where curious mothers poked out their heads to check on their children. Winos were talking "trash" to women passing by. Young girls, in pedal-pusher pants and calico tops, jumped double Dutch before the entrance to the apartments. I grabbed Beverly's hand as we climbed three flights up a filthy staircase to reach "Aunt Dorothy's" apartment. The odor of urine and a baby's whining cry tainted the warm breeze flowing through the hallway window. The door to the common bathroom was ajar.

Daddy unlocked and opened the door. I could see roaches feasting off the greasy kitchen walls. Food crusted dishes, and glasses stinking of booze filled the kitchen sink. Paint was peeling from the ceiling, revealing its former beauty. Mama's cleanliness had caused me to dislike dirty houses, especially dirty kitchens and bathrooms.

"Aunt Dorothy" appeared from the tiny bedroom that was at the end of the dark hallway. She didn't say anything, she just looked at Daddy, and then at us. We looked back at her. Her full, dingy-white slip was peeping from her robe, which was tied with a robe belt. She ran her hands through her unkempt hair. She obviously was not expecting "Duke," and surely not us. Daddy gave her one of his wide grins and kissed her on the cheek. Then he sent us to play. "Play?" "Where?" Elaine, Beverly, and I looked at each other, puzzled. Beverly led us out of the kitchen window onto the fire escape landing. Mama would not have allowed this. We could see 39th Street Beach from the landing. Watching the Lake Michigan waves gently fall and roll up and down the beach was calming for a while, but soon dogs were barking in the alley below. Crash! "God damn it!" One of the winos had dropped his bottle. To kill time, we each chose a color and watched for approaching cars. The person with the most cars in their selected color group won. The time limit would depend on Daddy.

"I got to pee," I announced to my sisters. I climbed back into the apartment to use the bathroom. I did not see Daddy or Aunt Dorothy. I went out of the apartment and down the pissy corridor to use the toilet. By the time I got back to the apartment, Daddy was coming from the bedroom.

"It's time to go, babies," he said warmly.

We waited for the Cottage Grove bus to take us back home. I looked around the neighborhood again. I despised Daddy for bringing us here. I could not wait to tell on him to Mama. I told her that we had two Aunt Dorothys. I told her everything I saw and did. And everything Daddy did. Mama called Daddy's job and gave him a stern warning about taking us around his women. We never went to visit that Aunt Dorothy again. Good. Because I would get that Aunt Dorothy mixed up with the other Aunt Dorothy, whom Daddy called "sister girl."

The following fall I started kindergarten. I attended the afternoon session. Mama had become friends with one of the crossing guards and felt it was safe for me to trek the one-and-a-half blocks to school. Sometimes, the neighbor's older kids, Paul and Shirley, came home for lunch and walked back to school with me.

"Let's go to the candy store," Paul said. We took a detour from the usual route to school which led to the neighborhood store.

"That's where Mr. Duke lives," I heard Shirley say, pointing to a three-story frame house.

"Huh?" I thought. Beverly had confided to Shirley about where her Daddy lived. The blood rushed to my head. I etched the image of the house in my mind. Beverly had found out where Daddy lived and had not shared the information with Elaine or me.

Where you live, Daddy? I often asked.

Oh, here and there, he'd gamely reply.

Can I go home with you? I pleaded.

Not today baby, he'd gently refuse.

My head tried to think of all the excuses Daddy gave me as to why I could not go home with him. That was okay though. The next school day I would pay Daddy a visit.

I have always been, and probably will always be, secretive. I did not tell Beverly what I had found out, although she kept wondering why I was rolling my eyes at her. I didn't tell anyone what I was going to do. It was none of their business. I wet the bed that night. When morning came, I put my pee-soaked slip in the sink and washed it. I bathed myself, watched the *Howdy Doody Show*, and ate my lunch, as usual. I was not going to give myself away. When Mama gave the order, I dressed for school and darted out of the door. My heart was beating fast. As I approached 53rd and Princeton, I thought my heart was going to jump out of my chest. I withdrew the picture of Daddy's house from my memory bank. That's it. I saw the house. I stood back to see if any lights were on. They were not. I approached the house with teeny-tiny baby steps and sat on the steps of the porch for a half-hour. I tried several times to get up the nerve to ring the bell. What if Daddy doesn't really live here? Is he going to be mad at me? Finally, I got the courage to do it. I wiped my running nose on my gray-flannel poodle skirt and rang the doorbell.

"Who are you looking for?" asked the bewildered woman behind the closed screened door.

"Is my daddy here?" I asked her between sobs. The door opened and I stared into the woman's face. She was not pretty. Her leathery reddish-brown complexion reminded me of building bricks. Her goldish-brown hair was tied in a head rag and she wore a faded house dress.

"What is his name, baby?" she asked.

"Clarence Earl Dukes," I replied.

"Who?!" she spoke in disbelief.

"Clarence Earl Dukes!" I loudly repeated.

"What is your name?" she asked in an irritated voice.

"Marcia," I enunciated clearly.

"He is not here, but I will tell him you came by," she calmly stated as she shut the door in my face.

Dorothy Perry Thompson

Daddy, Saved in Snatches: The Quilting

I.

I am squatting, hacky-doodling with my fingers in the dirt of a front yard. Someone is squatting with me. Perhaps even a third child is there. Then, the car comes. A man smiles and coaxes me onto the car seat beside him. I feel happy.

I remember the bend of knees and the concentration of making continuous circles in the earth more than I remember the coaxing, the trip, or the car. It would take a quiet, right-lived-according-to-Mama adolescence, and a mind free enough of background noise to keep and piece together overheard family secrets before I understood that the smiling black face had belonged to my father, that he had come to kidnap me from my grandmother's yard, and had ushered me into a fugitive's life in Charlotte, North Carolina. That was 1950.

What I remember first of Charlotte is feeling like an ugly stepchild there: my piles of kinky hair pulled and hot-combed straight every single school morning by a teenage cousin who must have hated (envied?) the crowning glory she couldn't seem to grow on her own head. My fat ponytails were singed down to fuzzy little bunches of hair by the time I had finished half of first grade. I still don't know why Daddy didn't stop Cousin Janie from frying my hair every day. He was big enough to scare her out of the habit—over six feet. But "charming," Mama would explain—deep-set eyes and pearly white teeth. That's what took you in, she said: the spread of those lips in a broad smile, the very black-brown of his eyes. Maybe he was just too easy to want to fuss with anybody, even about the hair on the head of the little girl he called his "cold-nosed baby." Maybe his own background didn't give him any how-to's: how to

protect a child from the trivial jealousy of a female cousin; how to tell
the teacher that at music time it might be a good idea to spread the instruments around and not always leave the dumb little bells for the un-
fortunate children whose last names didn't start with an A or B; how to
be mother and father to a five-year-old who missed Mama's hugs and
biscuits and syrup for breakfast.

All I know of Daddy's immediate family is that his mother's name
was Marie and his grandmother was called Edna. They say Edna looked
"just like an Indian." Daddy didn't know his father.

What I know of my father comes back to me in snatches:

—the time I was about twelve and he came home from New York and
drove along the dirt road until he saw me playing in front of our house.
The woman with him was a redbone (Mama said he liked that kind) and
she chided him into giving me money to see a picture show.

—the time Ms. Lila Mae's Sylvia walked over to our house to tell me
my daddy wanted to see me but was afraid to darken Mama's door.
Mama had remarried and didn't think much of Daddy, so he thought it
would be better to wait at Ms. Lila Mae's.

—the time before he left us in the house on Wheeler Hill. Mama was
mad enough to throw canned goods out of the white metal kitchen cabinet through the back door and into the yard—yelling the whole time at
the tall, quiet black man behind her.

The can-throwing incident (one Mama says I was too little to remember, but I do) is the one I go back to when I need to establish some
sense of how it was—us, together in one place. In my adult-mode re-
flections, I've supposed that money must have been the issue, especially
since Mama said Daddy would rather have held his pants up with a rope
and a rusty nail than work to make the money to buy a belt. Was Mama
mad that Daddy felt too much satisfaction at providing only food for his
household? Did she throw out the food to show him that she didn't need
him? I don't know. I do know that she never threw out the pink ceramic
twins Daddy bought and placed on a table in the living room. I do know
that she once told me that I should never take any "mess" from any man
just because he gave me money. She said that her daddy told her that she
should never let herself be mistreated, that as long as she could rub two
nickels together, she should spend one on her children today, the other

on her children the next day, and the third day the Lord would provide. I would find out later that many times my mother's brothers, Uncle Booby, Uncle L.G., Uncle Reb, and Uncle Snuke, together with my Grandaddy Henderson (Mama's father) substituted when the Lord was busy tending other members of his flock who were worse off than we were. (Later, I vowed, with my new husband, never to fuss about money. If we had some, good; if we didn't, we just didn't. Perhaps the vow has worked because my husband always has.)

Other things come back:

—the summer Daddy suddenly emerged from the back of a car stopped out by my mailbox. Years had passed—perhaps fifteen—since I'd seen him. He calmly walked around the side of the house and into the backyard where he must have heard the noise from the beginnings of a family-and-friends barbecue. Watching from the kitchen window (I'd seen the car drive up), I saw him mop sweat from his brow with the whitest handkerchief I'd ever seen. He joined the bid whist game with my husband and friends as though he'd been among them forever. When I explained who he was, my children found some excuse to go into the house, stood in the den, and stared at their grandfather through the sliding glass doors.

I wondered, quite often, how he could show up like that, sporadically, over a period of about twenty-five years, wanting to see us, knowing how to find us. When he was dying, I began to piece the mystery together.

In the winter of 1983, Aunt Munch called from Elmira, New York, to say that Daddy had lung cancer and was not going to last much longer. Would I let my sister Edna know? I had vague memories of Aunt Munch, a big dark brown woman who had big dark brown twin sons and a couple of daughters. I would play with these children on the church grounds, especially on Big Meeting Sunday, the third Sunday in July when everybody's moved-away-to-the-north family came back for revival. But somehow, I had forgotten *how* Chester, Eugene, Diane, and June came to be my cousins. So, before Edna and I took the train from Columbia, South Carolina, to Elmira, I asked Mama a lot of questions. I was reminded that Aunt Munch was married to my father's uncle, a man whose name was Shoot Perry. (How could anybody forget a name like that? I hadn't; I just hadn't remembered the nature of the kinship.) Anyway, Mom filled us in, making me recall vague faces from the past. Edna couldn't remember anybody. I thought about the time that, out of the blue, Daddy had called my sister from the Jacksonville, Florida, bus station and simply stated (according to her), "Edna, this is your father. Can you come pick me up?" By that time my sister's last name was no longer Perry. She was married and had two sons, and had no earthly idea how Daddy had found her. It would be the only time she would see him before the long train ride to upstate New York to see a wizened, baldheaded man sitting on a couch coughing up his life.

Edna had not had her first birthday when Mama and Daddy broke up. Thus, she didn't know who to look for at the station that time in Jacksonville. Also, each time Daddy would come to Columbia and send a messenger to get us, Edna would refuse to go, saying, "He's not my father. I don't even remember him." But I did, and so I'd go. I remembered:

—rides on his hip, bouncing with his long stride to the corner store for licorice whips.

—his nervous pacing the day Edna was born. We lived in the Park Street house then, the one with the long stairs up to the front porch. Mama was giving birth inside, so all the ladies asked Daddy to take me outside to wait.

—the careful way he packed my schoolbooks in a little carry-on for the train ride from Charlotte back home to Mama. He must have decided he couldn't keep me after all—though he'd gone to the trouble of carrying out a kidnapping, finding relatives to help with my rearing, and risking the wrath of the entire Corbitt family (Mama had four brothers, a father who could scare you simply by pressing his lips together, and a mother who wielded a pretty good baseball bat). Daddy took out the books and encouraged me to read all the way to Columbia.

After Aunt Munch's call (winter, 1983), and a long, nervous ride, Edna and I found Daddy living in Elmira with his uncle Shoot. Before I could see his eyes, I couldn't believe that the little man sitting there was my father. His presence did not dominate the room. This was not Joe Roger Perry, same family genes that lately could boast: "Yes, we produced William 'the Refrigerator' Perry and Michael Dean, defensive tackles, NFL!" No, my father had to look the part of progenitor, grandfather to my own son, destined, in ten years, to become the 220-pound, six-foot-two-inch, sixteen-year-old first-stringer for his high school football state championship contender team. But the shriveled man on the couch said in my father's voice, "Hey, Dorothy Mae. So you did come to see your old daddy!" When he asked who was with me, I ushered Edna from behind me; she seemed to be trying to fade into the wallpaper. We sat beside Daddy and had a hard time with conversation until a young woman breezed in the front door, and, with a big hug around Daddy's neck, gushed, "Aw, Rainbow, why didn't you let me know you were sick?"

We felt displaced. Here was someone who knew Daddy—*really* knew him: that he was called Rainbow, that it was okay to enter without knocking, that she had the right to be teasingly indignant because she hadn't heard from him. He introduced us to the woman and she explained, surprised and embarrassed, that she didn't know who we were, that our father had been like a father to her. I noted her shiny hair, perfect rouge and lipstick, and wondered what Daddy thought of how Edna and I looked: my bushy curl-fro and boots, Edna's long thick locks and the serious eyes just like Mama's. I searched his eyes. I saw pain. Was it physical? Emotional? Finally I began to *feel* what I really wanted to see in those deep-set eyes. It became an almost palpable presence in the room: my father's love, reaching, touching us across the threads of the couch, across the years . . . *real.*

"Did you bring pictures of the children?" he wanted to know. We had, but they were in our suitcases back at Aunt Munch's. When we took them to him at the hospital the next day, he surprised us by knowing how many grandchildren he had, and the gender of each. It had been so long. He kept in touch, indirectly, he explained. I found out that he meant he always asked Aunt Munch to inquire of Cousin Cellestine where and how we were. (But that didn't explain how he ever found Edna in Jacksonville. She had a new last name and an unlisted number, and, besides, by that time Cousin Cellestine had gotten lost from us somewhere in Trenton, New Jersey.) Daddy stared and stared at my oldest son's graduation picture; then, about my daughter he said, "She looks just like your mama."

When I got back to South Carolina, I asked Mama to talk to me about my daddy. She replied, "I ain't lived with that man in over thirty years, so I don't know how you expect me to talk about him." After a few moments she added, "I'm sorry he's dying, baby, but that was so long ago."

Aunt Munch called again. She said we had to "gee or haw," as Daddy was really low. Then a second call came from the doctor at the hospital. Daddy was dead. He had lasted only two weeks after our visit. My sister had sprawled out on Aunt Munch's bed and cried before we left Elmira. She said she felt guilty because the experience seemed simply a matter of having taken a long trip to see a stranger, deciding to stick him in the hospital, and then leaving him in the hands of other strangers. She didn't remember Aunt Munch, the twins, or any of our other cousins.

When we returned to New York for the funeral, everybody seemed to have been waiting for Edna and me to come and take charge of Daddy's business—insurance, the apartment he left when he had to move in with Uncle Shoot, final funeral arrangements. We couldn't. I offered that since his friends and family there knew what he'd want, they should handle everything. I wanted only to have a minister who wouldn't rant and rave the way some Baptist ministers can at funerals and to plant a flowering shrub at Daddy's grave. I voiced the second wish but kept the first to myself just in case Daddy liked ranting and raving. Some city ordinance wouldn't permit me to plant the shrub, so Aunt Munch agreed to put it at her back doorstep in memory of Daddy. She and her family gave us pieces of the Joe Roger "Rainbow" Perry they had known:

—a brief explanation concerning the woman who came to the funeral with a tawny-colored boy. She had been Daddy's last sweetheart. When I asked if the boy was my brother, I got an emphatic *no*, but Daddy had loved the woman and her child like "nobody's business." He loved all children, they said. He had even reared one female child almost single-handedly. (I begged someone to point her out to me. When I saw her, later, at Aunt Munch's house, she was too distraught to speak. I envied her memories, but rationalized this surrogate fathering as my daddy's love for his own missing daughters.)

—news that Daddy had lived alone before he'd gotten too sick to take care of himself. They gave us the keys to his apartment. Edna took the matched set of blue clear glass cups and saucers from the kitchen. I preferred the gild-edged white bowl splattered with green flowers, the yellow ceramic rooster, an oriental fan, and a small skee ball trophy. The figure on the trophy wore bell bottoms, and since this was 1983, we figured the trophy was about ten years old, the date long ago faded from the base plate.

—pictures from Aunt Munch's family album. The one I like best is of Daddy smiling in a big Buick, a large two-story house behind him. His arm is dangling lazily out of the car window and his other hand is resting on the steering wheel. He is young; his arm, muscular. I do not like the picture of him in a red tie. He is frail and standing between two friends in Aunt Munch's dining room. The pained look is in his eyes and he seems to be propped up between the other two men. His head is cocked slightly to the side, the same way mine frequently is when I'm not paying attention.

II.

When I was choosing white eyelet for my daughter's room, I thought of the very white handkerchief next to my father's shiny black face, the way the sun and sweat made his forehead glisten that day in my backyard. I thought of the strength it must have taken for him to show up and face his grandchildren's stares and a son-in-law's drop-jawed face, the courage it took to answer "How long are you here for?" with an "Oh, just a day or so" and a calm trump of my husband's ace. His starched, laundry-pressed shirt wilted in the heat.

Once, passing through a country town on a long day trip, I saw a horse and wagon clopping down a wide side road. The sight of it took me back to Charlotte, when Daddy and another man would go possum hunting at night in a horse-drawn wagon. We lived in one of a long row of gray board houses and Daddy had friends up and down the street. One of them was a gay and pretty woman who always seemed glad to see me coming, jumping up her stairs to the front porch, then pressing my nose against her screen door to look inside. She always had something to give me because I was Joe's "cute little black-eyed baby."

I remember that I could stand on our porch and see the tall buildings of downtown Charlotte, but I have only one recollection of ever going into one of those buildings. It was the day Daddy took me to City Hall to get my vaccination so that I could go to school. The walk there took us up an embankment, across a railroad track, and eventually onto neat, concrete streets. We had a good time that day because Daddy let me take my time and he told me to watch out for potholes and stuff.

When the Daddy Grace parade came to Columbia during my teen years, I had a vague sense that I had seen the honest-to-God real man one time in Charlotte. But then I couldn't remember whether Daddy actually had taken me to see Daddy Grace or whether he had told me one of his fantastic stories about him. In any case, my mind always connects with Charlotte when I hear Daddy Grace's name, and I imagine a man with long gray hair and painted fingernails. I can even hear my daddy's voice describing those fingernails—long and curled, each one a different color. People are throwing money at him and women are bowing down at his feet. To this day, I don't know the truth about the origin of this image.

Sometimes, after a downpour, I imagine Daddy showing up, like a strange, quiet rainbow. He's smiling and mopping sweat under the fresh sun. At other times, I watch Michael Dean or The Fridge playing football and their shoulders become Daddy's shoulders, and I am hugging the breadth of them from his back, happy to be jostled to the store for sweet black candy.

When I tell my sons and daughter about their grandfather, I choose from among these snatches, but mostly I tell them about the thing that happened in Uncle Shoot's living room that day—the thing that melted the years between my father and me on the couch, the thing that made me know I can make of my father's love a blanket, and pull it around me anytime I want it or need it. The pieces I have of Daddy are enough for quilting and warming.

Lee May

In My Father's Garden

The narrow concrete walkway stretches barely twenty feet from the street to the porch, but this nervous-making visit made the distance seem more like a mile.

I had come to my father's home. Once, it was mine, too. On this scorching, Mississippi-dusty June day, the house on 30th Street seemed one of the few things in life that had not changed; it still was small. Two bedrooms, a kitchen, and living room, its shell sheathed in those white asbestos shingles. On the faded burgundy-painted concrete floor sat two green metal chairs, the kind that spring back and forth as you rock your body.

Getting out of my little rental car, I peered up the walk to see my father, sitting still in one of the chairs. He was wearing a tiny smile, a light-colored shirt and newish overalls that floated around his body. He seemed so old. And so thin. So changed.

No wonder, I told myself as I yelled, "Hey! How ya doin'?" and started the long walk toward the porch. No wonder. Now, June 20, 1989, it had been thirty-nine years since I was last at this house. And since I last saw my father, eighty years old by this time. I was forty-eight.

"I'm doing tolerable well. How you?" Ples Mae answered. During those decades in which I had not seen him, whenever I thought of him, I always wondered about his name. His first name is pronounced *Plez*, and his last name is spelled differently from mine. Someday, I would always think, I'll find out why.

But that could wait. It was time to walk that mile, a journey through almost four decades, through tons of events, memories, and lives. My father and my mother, Riller, split up in 1950, when I, their only child, was nine. They both remarried. He to Mary Sterdivant, she to Milton

Walker, the man I called Dad. The word stepfather would not have done him justice. My mother and dad and I moved from Meridian to East St. Louis, Illinois, in 1955, severing all contact with my father. Funny how seeing him after all these years recalled memories of my other two parents. Ironic that this was the eve of what would have been my mother's sixty-seventh birthday.

As I reached the porch, I did not know what to expect. Would we hug? We did not. My father did not rise. We shook hands. I sat. On one level this first meeting went as if we had seen each other just days before. There was no rush of questions about the past, no obvious look to gauge what the years had done. Weirdly, it was natural. How could we possibly catch the years we had lost? Better to go from now.

But Mary was much more demonstrative. She rushed through the door with a large grin and yelled, "Sonny! Sonny! I'm so glad you're here to see your Daddy! You don't know how many years I've prayed for this to happen." My father looked a little sheepish as Mary, a thinly built woman, hard of hearing but not hard to hear, darted back inside the house, talking over her shoulder: "Y'all talk. Go on and talk. I'm fixing dinner. Sonny, you got to eat something. We got butter beans outta the garden. Frozen fresh."

Just as I was unprepared for him to be so old, I also did not expect to see so much of myself in him. I noted that we were about the same height, six feet, and our facial structures, along with balding hair pattern, showed our connections.

Physical similarities aside, we had lived two disparate lives, worlds apart in many ways. Mine had been spread over many addresses, while most of my father's had unfolded right here. Sitting on the front porch, we made small talk to try bridging that time gap. I looked out onto 30th Avenue, then across the street, trying to recapture long-lost memories of my years in this neighborhood.

Searching for lost memories of my father, I felt a flush of discomfort and doubt. Was it really possible to make any meaning of a relationship that had not existed for forty years? Was coming here a bad idea after all?

"Been a hot one today," I said, wiping my forehead. "Hadn't been much rain."

"Yeah, I been having to water every day."

After about half an hour that felt like much longer, Mary appeared at
the front door, calling us in to a wonderfully intoxicating meal—gifts
from the garden. Around noonday, this meal was dinner to many southerners, while the meal I would eat later, around 7 P.M., was supper. As
Mary had advertised, there were butter beans mixed with peas, tomatoes, collards, okra, and corn bread, washed down with sodas.

Pretty soon, we took a stroll, to see what he was having to water. I was
amazed at how orderly was his garden, rows straight and clean as arrows.

"Those tomatoes oughta be ready to eat any day," I said.

"If the squirrels don't get 'em first," he replied.

That first walk in my father's garden was filled with so much of my
past. In that space, that deep, narrow lot, I could see the cages of rabbits
that had infatuated me as a child, revolted me when I realized we were
supposed to eat them. My dachshund, Pup Pup, had trotted from one
end of the lot to the other, under the cages, among the vegetables.

And just as it had done almost forty years earlier, the sun-drenched
garden grew just about everything a family might need. Collards, corn,
butter beans, peas, tomatoes, peppers, squash, watermelon, potatoes.
And, amazingly, peanuts, their vines twirling out of a network of old car
tires. Proudly, my father pointed out each crop, giving me a rundown on
its progress, how well he expected it to bear.

"Now, this okra gonna make more than we can eat," he said in a voice
that combined deep tones and heavy punctuations, one that must reflect
something from his western Alabama upbringing. "And we gonna
freeze these butter beans and peas, 'cause we get so many. Always do. We
eat 'em all year long."

From the peanuts in the front of the garden, near the house, to the
gnarled grapevine at the garden's end, near the spot where mosses and
ferns grow in the wet, we walked during that visit and each subsequent
one, looking, talking—a lot about gardening but also about my journalism career, neighbors long gone and half forgotten, politics, his health;
he had long suffered from high blood pressure, alerting me to a danger
I had feared for years, as mine had been borderline.

We must have been in the garden for about thirty minutes when he
introduced me to his garden shed. A small corrugated-tin structure
near the house, it contained the usual assortment of hoes, picks, shovels,

and trowels. All were clean and oiled. There also was a monstrous gasoline-powered plow that he was to later offer me—an offer I took as a huge measure of affection but had to decline as my space would not accommodate it.

Suddenly, my father grabbed a BB gun that was leaning against the shed's wall. Striding a few feet from the shed, he turned and fired, "Ping!" striking a tin can fifteen paces away. The proud father had shown off, just as his son might have forty years earlier. "You got to be able to shoot straight to get them rats," he said, all but blowing across the top of the gun barrel. I was impressed.

I was glad that I had come.

I had decided to reach out to my father when a writing assignment brought me from Washington, D.C., where I was living, to Meridian. The story centered on the twenty-fifth anniversary of the murders of three civil rights workers in nearby Philadelphia, Mississippi.

Also, I knew then that my wife, Lyn, and I would in a few weeks be moving from Washington to Atlanta, as I was being promoted from correspondent in the *Los Angeles Times* Washington bureau to chief of its southern bureau. This meant that my father and I would be only three hundred miles apart.

But such practical reasons were nothing compared to the emotional ones. I wanted some questions answered. Who is this man? Would seeing him show me what I might become? Could I learn what afflictions might strike me? Should I worry about my borderline high blood pressure, my over-two-hundred cholesterol?

As Mother and Dad both were dead, shouldn't I have some sort of relationship with my sole surviving parent?

I had looked up his telephone number and made the call, knowing that this could backfire, that I might be awakening a bad relationship. Through all the years, he never wrote, phoned, or tried to visit. And neither did I. Why is impossible to know. Fear of rejection? Pride? Anger? Fear of nothing to say? Fear of intrusion? When I got him on the phone, neither of us brought up the whys.

And we did not bring them up during the visit. Nor did we confront one another about the gulf that so long separated us.

I hoped that our meeting would represent a kind of closure, or at least the beginning of one, resolving questions about what kind of father and son we might have been.

We met much like two strangers, but strangers with a history. In a couple of hours, we touch on highlights of the previous thirty-some years. It seemed unrealistic to reach for more than highlights at that time.

Then, visit by visit, talk by talk, we found kinship in our love for growing plants, gradually expanding that to include other parts of our lives. This first meeting, tough as it started out to be, was the start of something tender.

Thaddeus Goodavage

"Are You My Father?"

"Fathering" has saved my life. Twice. The first time it was by getting a father, and the second time it was by becoming a father. For at both points in my life, fathering—that need and potential in my soul to father and be fathered, had to be nurtured and made real. Initially, I desperately needed a father-caretaker, and later I was so paralyzed with feelings of such a deep loneliness and worthlessness that I was unable to understand why I was a valuable person and why I should try to remain alive. Having kids is just one attempt at solidity during this type of moment. My children—all three of my young sons—affirmed and continue to affirm two fundamental yet competing and sometimes contradictory impulses: my lifelong desire to be parented properly and my need to know another person with whom I have a genetic link.

I was an adopted child. Twice. My first parents, who liberated me from state care when I was seven months old, died tragically a year later. My second parents, who liberated me from state care for the second time when I was two years old, remain my loving, sacrificing, beautiful Black parents. Their caretaking, though rich with practical support and ripe with an incredible caring love, did not leave space for sensitivity to the specific needs of an adopted child. I marched through life with them with just one discussion of the reality of our relationship: at seven years old a friend with whom I happened to be playing some funny hair-combing game, asked me, in the presence of my mother, why I did not look like or have hair like either of my parents. My mother, interrupting, suggested that I looked a whole lot like my father (which was somewhat true). After my friend's departure, she immediately pulled me into her room and told me that I was adopted and that I should never let anyone else know this fact because it would cause "embarrassment"

to our family. Thus began my history of harboring the secret of my beginnings, my family, and myself. . . .

Fathering a biological son provides a certain space to celebrate maleness intergenerationally and genetically. In the elite context of biological father-son relationships, maleness—that sacrosanct quality
grounded on falsely constructed notions of power—moves along un-
criticized, as a father essentially remakes himself in another who closely
resembles him.

Adoption means that this resemblance is not present. This father, no
matter how hard he tries, is confronted with the "other" as son. A certain kind of distance is, then, a built-in component of adoption. This
distance becomes a site of anxiety, and the father, who only wanted to
uncritically pass on his manhood to someone like himself, finds himself
facing a young male he does not know. Adoptive Father looks desperately for himself in his son, and he cannot find himself. Adoptee son
looks desperately for himself in his father, to no avail. Both, probably,
are tremendously lonely.

My dad was a boxer, a weight lifter, and an all-around tough guy during his youth. I was a skinny, sissy-like kid (which he constantly reminded me of), afraid of every insect, animal, and person I encountered.
After he concluded that I was lagging way behind in my physical development, he decided to help the developmental process along. He sen-
tenced me to twenty-five push-ups a night. Every day at ten o'clock I had
to go into the living room, where he would be alone watching television,
lie at the feet of his Laz-y Boy chair, and do the push-ups while he
watched for form and counted. I never could do more than four. He
would yell and moan about how weak I was and how I wasn't improving
until, after wobbly completing number five (I always cheated and used
my knees on this one) he would send me directly to bed and make me
turn the lights out. My constant feelings of being deeply alone height-
ened, I would get under my covers and read with a flashlight. Then I
would turn my transistor radio on softly and place it under my pillow. I
would click the light off, and the music would carry me to sleep. Sometimes I wish I still had that radio.

Adoption demands a profound reconstruction of the notions of father, son, parent, and family. This different type of psychic orientation
to fatherhood is, it seems to me, of some import, and, sadly, no one talks

about this. Families affected by adoption have gone through (even before the adoption occurs), critically or subconsciously, the process of
turning the traditional notions of family upside down. They have developed a way of gaining a new self-understanding in relation to these
terms, of redefining these traditional notions, and creating a structure
based on their newly arrived-at understanding of what constitutes a
family. It is important to recognize this deeply radical shift in consciousness that my parents, particularly my father (for the purposes of
this essay), had to contend with, for this helps me to lift the veils.

What really happens psychically to individuals in a culture that has
very fixed and unchanging notions of family, parenthood, etc., when
they realize they cannot/do not fit into these traditional conceptions?
How does one build a family when he begins from a different starting
point than most other families? How do Black people, already viewed as
not fully human in our culture, live with this fact and still work to construct a family, particularly when that family is one with adopted children? How does a Black woman, whose body and skin are despised and
devalued in our society, come to terms with the fact that she cannot do
the one thing that all women are supposed to do, which is to produce
offspring? How is her womanhood affected by this, and if she decides to
construct a family with adopted children, how are these issues going to
manifest in her mothering? How does a Black man, already disaffirmed
and demasculated by the wider society, affirm his own manhood when
he cannot create, produce, or sustain anything, even children? What
kind of father will he be? How will his legacy as a father affect a twice-
abandoned, twice-chosen child? Why have I always felt so alone? These
are just a few of the questions with which I grapple.

Some of these issues and their ramifications are clearer to me now
because I am older and because I know what having biological children,
sons, has meant for me. I feel sorry for my parents who could not—and I
feel guilty for being a daily reminder to them *that* they could not—have
biological children. The anxieties, fears, paranoias, strengths, and in-
sights that have resulted from my early trauma I think I can contend
with. Yet when I think of my mom and dad, I wonder how they deal with
these cruel, hard facts that none of us has ever talked about. They have
never tried to lift the veil. I can only surmise that their own deep self-
sacrifices have reaped only partial benefits in their soul. Yet I must ap-

preciate their sacrifices and try to imagine how important the fact that
fathering an adopted son is less a stroke of the ego than an exercise in
commitment and sacrifice. I deeply appreciate these sacrifices, and
given my own history around these issues, I marvel at my dad's constitution around them.

My father and mother, hardworking providers that they were, never
verbally articulated that they loved me; they expected that their sacrifices would say it for them (in many ways, they did). For Depression-era
Negroes who had undergone the migration northward, the movement
to integration, and so many watershed historical moments regarding
race, gender, economy, and technology that it is mind-boggling, this
type of emotional calm and understatement is understandable, maybe
even typical behavior. In addition, given each of my parents' family histories and issues and the fact that I was adopted, maybe this is quite acceptable behavior. But I still wonder, when I say "I love you" to my children and my partner (not their mother) every day (and quietly wait for
them to repeat it to me), what would have been different in my life, if
anything, had I gotten the opportunity to hear my parents tell me they
loved me with some regularity during my childhood and adolescent
years? Would I have felt so profoundly alone if they had verbally and
physically articulated an unconditional love more clearly? Or was I already destined to feel alone based on being adopted, my emotional
makeup, etc.? I wish I knew.

When I lift the veil of my family life I am faced with the fundamental
question: Why do I feel so lonely? Which, phrased in a more useful way,
would read: *am I loved, am I worthy of love, and will I be left alone in the
world without love?* These are the questions with which I struggle most
and which my existence seeks desperately to reconcile. . . .

Having a child conquered my sense of being entirely alone in the
world. Here was someone who was entirely dependent on me, who I had
unlimited access to, who could not leave me. My life had been saved. Finally, I had established a link, a bond, an unbreakable connection, with
someone else in the world. This worked incredibly well for a while, then
three things happened. The first had to do with my father. Having a
family, in some ways, made me feel more like him than I had ever imagined I would. Certainly, I had my own parenting style, but when I felt
like I began to act like him, I became afraid that I would become him

and I needed to change direction quickly. Second, I began to lift the very delicately laid veil around my biological parents and found out about my biological father. And third, because of the first two reasons, a new baby (and another on the way), and my wife's own history and issues, my home life became deeply disharmonious. I moved out—just far enough to escape the craziness, but not too far to be without my sons—up to this point the only source of genetic perpetuity and unconditional love that I had ever known. Let me return, however, to the second most impactful occurrence I mentioned above.

Part of the secret around being adopted I had actually never resisted. Until the time I was twenty-five I had told only three people about my status in the world. Ever. When my well-intended wife suggested I find my biological parents for medical reasons having to do with our child, it all came back in a rush. What I had been doing with my new baby son had not been done with, or for, me. I decided to find my biological parents. During adolescence I would frequently dream about a rich, glamorous biological heritage. I would imagine somehow bumping into people on the street who looked so much like me that I would immediately recognize them to be my real family. They would also recognize me and take me home with them to some amazing castle-like home and be the family I always imagined. Needless to say, this never happened.

Uncovering my biological roots was much easier and more difficult than I expected—it was a process that took many years. After numerous phone calls, letters, and discussions with family welfare workers to private investigators, I received a telephone call one day from someone claiming to be my biological brother. He was the second of six children to be born from the woman who had also borne me. His voice sounded a little bit like mine.

I talked to him for an hour. He knew about me. His mother had told him and all of his brothers and sisters that she had had me and had given me away and that I was, she hoped, safely placed somewhere in the universe. She told them how hard it was to have a child and not know him. Every year she and her children would celebrate my birthday. She told them that my father (they all had different fathers) was a kind man who had died some time ago.

I told him to tell his mother that I was not angry with her (the fear she had articulated to him as the reason she had not called me) and that

I would love to speak to her. But I was torn. Here I was betraying the sacred bond that my parents had worked so incredibly hard to establish with me. I did not want to betray this bond, yet I was intrinsically unhappy with my relationship with my parents, I was curious about my biological inheritance, and I was excited about the possibilities of meeting the source of my genetic makeup. She called the next day. . . .

Trains, planes, and a rental car finally brought me face to face with the woman whom I had grown inside of. When I saw her nose, her hair, her chin, her ears, her face, her shape, her walk, her laugh, I felt a different kind of link to the earth. I felt a different kind of link to myself. We communicated with the movements and gestures and feelings and hopes and sadnesses that only we knew. She knew me. This was quite a significant experience for me, and I felt as if my loneliness was fading. For a moment.

My biological father, I found out after this long journey to find my mother, was said not to be alive anymore. Yet in his day he'd had a reputation as being one of the most renowned small-time pimps, hustlers, and charmers in his community. My genetic roots are as follows: repeated sexual abuse by her parents motivated my biological mother to run away at the age of fourteen. Survival on the streets meant that she became a prostitute, a drug addict, and an alcoholic. My biological father was her thirty-three-year-old, thrice-married pimp who, according to her, also fell in love with her. She got pregnant with his child.

They tried to abort me. Twice. They agreed that she was too young to be a mother and that the circumstances would make it impossible for me to grow up healthy. The first time she took pills. Two weeks later, she tried a coat hanger. With nowhere to go, after her man went back to his wife, this fourteen-year-old girl and chaotic home of mine, dragged herself back to her parents. These cruel, sexually abusive parents of hers, who had driven all of their children to depression (my biological mother's brother killed himself at eighteen), refused to let her in. All alone, she went to her church. Those good Catholics helped her deliver me and immediately handed me over to the state during the first ten seconds of life. We both cried.

Racism has affected me more deeply than most. Twice. The first time (which I realized only much later) was when my biological mother's parents would not let her back in their house when she was pregnant. My biological mother is white. My biological father is Black. The second time was when I found this out.

Much like the children's story in which the baby bird falls out of its nest, begins a frantic search for his mother, and is finally saved by her (and fed by her) after confronting various other entities to ask them if they were his mother, I felt like I was rescued. I had found her. She was like me. But she was white. When I saw her skin, her hair, her lips, her nose—I studied them. I looked at her so closely, as if I had a microscope, and I saw her whiteness in a way that I had never seen whiteness before. I saw it in relation to me.

I had never imagined that I was not a Black person. That is to say, I never thought that I might have a white biological parent. For some strange reason, it actually never crossed my mind. Now I had to confront the fact that I was biracial, that I did not comfortably and easily fit into any race category, and that I had been living a lie. Or had I? What constitutes one's racial identity? Was I really Black or not, and how did it matter? I was still lonely. The truths I had been taught were now crumbling at my feet. Veils were being lifted. I was not feeling safe.

Moreover, the stories of my biological mother fed me were much more impactful than I thought, especially when she told me about my father. She told me how he talked, how he walked, what he thought about, how he engaged the world. I didn't tell her then, but much of what she said he said, I had said before. Much of what she said he thought, I had thought before. Much of what she said he did, I had done before. I found myself in my biological father—pimp, hustler, charmer, social activist, sensitive thinker, sometimes poet, incredible dresser, musician, neighborhood conversationalist, all around cool brother. My God. Who was I? How could I reconcile him with me? The recognition that one's genes are descended from a criminal father (and "crazy" mother—who was, and for a long while had been, a hooker), especially a father who you existentially resemble, is enough to confuse you about yourself.

I had nowhere to turn but inward. My two fathers pulled at my soul. Responsibility and commitment tugged me in one direction, and the smooth-operator mentality pulled me into the other. I got a divorce.

My past feelings of being alone, of being homeless, and of being abandoned were now at an all-time high. I felt that I had nowhere to turn and felt that nobody really loved me. Except for my children. I had so much to give them, I wanted to have them around me all of the time. Yet their mother would not allow that. The only link to the type of unconditional love I cherished was now being taken from me. I tried to get joint custody of my children. I lost.

Could I ever find and sustain the type of love that I felt I needed? I hoped so, but I decided to stop looking for it.

Love found me in the form of a realization. That realization was that I needed help. I needed to lift the veils to find the truth, to be open about myself, to grapple with the truth, use it as best I could to improve myself, to ultimately be happy with the person that I am. Love was to start the process of self-discovery that I am now beginning. Asking myself about my family life, asking myself about how I was fathered, forcing myself to remember my pain is about my beginning to heal. . . .

Every day I try to get under another veil, to get back to a truth, no matter how painful, and grapple with the me that I am. Doing this has shown me that both of my "fathers" have affected me in profoundly different ways. I blame neither of these noble men totally for my issues—circumstance has created me. Like everyone else, I have some wonderful qualities and some problems. I try to work on my problems so that I can be more loving, happier, and more able to give and provide for others.

Allowing myself to think openly and critically about my fathers brings me back to me. From this place I can do the liberating work of lifting the veils and uncovering the secrets that have caused me, and others, problems and pain. From this place I can discover myself in all of my richness—the good and the bad. From the truths of my fathers—and how I was fathered—I can understand myself better as father and convert my issues into assets to help me to be successful in my intimate life, my parental life, my life as a son, a friend, a writer—everywhere. Here I stand at the beginning of that process.

All parenting requires a certain degree of heroism. I struggle, and ask you to struggle, to be the superheroes we need to be.

Charlie R. Braxton

An Open Letter to My Dad

Sorry that I have to communicate with you in a public forum, particularly since this is a personal message, but the way I see it, I have no other real alternative. I haven't seen you on a regular basis since you walked out on me and my brother thirty years ago. It was a hot summer evening in 1964. I was three years old at the time. I remember you were supposed to have been baby-sitting me and my baby brother, but instead you decided to pack your bags and take everything in the house that wasn't nailed down. When I asked you what you were doing with all of our stuff, you told me that we were moving to a brand new home and that you would be right back to get us after you had put everything up. You and some guy left in a truck full of our furniture. It was three years before I saw you again. I was still waiting for you to come and take us all to our new home. It never happened.

For a long time, I was confused because you never explained to me why you left. It was always "a long story" that I was "too young to understand." As a result, I grew up thinking I was the real reason you left. I thought you were ashamed of me for being handicapped. You swore there was no harm intended when you named my half-brother Charlie Braxton, too, but the bottom line is that Charlie Braxton, Jr., *can* walk, I can't.

Divorces are never easy. I understand that. But yo, Pop, did you have to turn your back on Calvin and me? I thought you divorced Mom, not us.

It wasn't easy growing up Black, male, and handicapped in Mississippi during the sixties and seventies. There were a lot of obstacles and hurdles to overcome. I had to deal with two kinds of discrimination practically every day of my life. And, while it may appear to the world that I've made it through all right, I will be among the first to admit that I have some horrible scars. No, Pop, I'm not blaming you for any of the crap that the world threw at me during your painful absence. That's life. But I do believe that I would have been able to deal with things a lot easier if you had been there for me. But you weren't.

Pop, you don't know how many times I tried to hate you for what you did to me and my brother. Yet, try as I might, I still find hating you hard to do. You see, it's like my grandma says, some of us are "mother's child" and others are "father's child." Well, I'm a father's child with no father. You see, despite all, I still got love for you, Pops. But, I would be less than honest, if I didn't admit that loving you is hurting me in ways that I'm still struggling to understand. And as much as I would like to let you go, I can't. Thanks to my new set of circumstances, I need you now, more than I ever did when I was growing up.

You remember Kwame, don't you dad? He's your grandson—the one that looks just like us. Well he's four now and he's having a real tough time right now. You see, his mother and I have been divorced for about a year or so, and I am currently struggling to maintain our father/son relationship. It's not easy, especially when you don't have a hands-on role model to rely on. But I'll keep trying, because I love and need my son in my life. Something about him makes me feel connected to the magic rhythms of life.

Like I said before, divorces are never easy, and children are often the major casualty of this intense war between the sexes. But, thanks to my experiences with you, I am determined that Kwame's life won't be anything like mine. Divorce or not, I am still Kwame's father. I am still the central male figure in my son's life, regardless as to whether I or my ex-wife decides to marry again.

But, still, there's just one problem. Lately, Kwame's been asking me about you. He wants to know things like: who are you, where do you live, how do you look, and, most importantly, why don't you come and see him like Grandma does? Telling him that I don't know the answer to all of those questions is one of the most painful things I've ever had to do in my life. Writing this letter is another.

Pop, come on. Pick up the phone and give me a call. Let's start some kind of relationship between the three of us. I've reached the point in my life now, Dad, where I realize that good or bad, right or wrong, my son still needs to know you. And, that you deserve a place in his childhood memories. I know that there are still a lot of things that you can teach Kwame and me, and there are a lot of things that we can teach you. If you're willing to try, give us a call.

Katie Lee Crane

S.W.A.K.

> Some things take awhile to get used to. Finding out
> that you're an Alien—well, half Alien—when you've
> spent your entire life thinking you're an Earthling is
> one of them. BRUCE COVILLE,
>
> *I LEFT MY SNEAKERS IN DIMENSION X*

S.W.A.K. Sealed With A Kiss.

It was scrawled as an afterthought on the back of the envelope. The shaky hand suggested age (not fear) and signaled an older, more unsteady person than the strong, hearty voice I'd heard for the first time on the telephone five days earlier. But there it was. *His* hand. And an endearment he'd probably used for years—probably used with *her*. This was going to take awhile to get used to.

And why not? The whole process had taken awhile—almost five years, in fact. Five years of sifting through shreds of information, tiny clues that would lead me to my birth family. Sometimes one fact—like a date or something someone *thought* she remembered—would lead to months of searching. So many roadblocks. So many dead ends. All I wanted to know was who conceived and bore me. Was that a crime? (Well yes it was, actually, in most states).

Some people were compassionate; a few stretched the rules to help. But most just told me to mind my own business—*don't go where you're not wanted*—told me not to make trouble. A few, though, a few courageous people spread out across five states, were working for me, working *with* me.

Along the way, I gathered facts. She was a nurse. She was from Ohio, born in 1921. She was twenty-six when I was born. He was tall. He had dark hair. Dark eyes. He was thirty-five. Discovering that took seven-teen months.

Four months later I confirmed her name: Lois James. And then it took only a month to find out her birth date. It should have been easy with that much information, but it wasn't.

I chased two Loises for more than a year.

"Why are you so sure that the Lois James on Olive Street is the right one?" I asked one of the volunteers helping me.

"Because the other one is Black," she said matter-of-factly, knowing my fair skin scalds and bubbles in the first strong sun, she *knew* the Black Lois could not be my birth mother. Someone else was not so sure.

"How do you know this Black woman isn't your mother?" he asked.

"You haven't seen me," I insisted. "My skin is practically transparent it's so white. I don't think my mother could be Black."

But it was the Black Lois we found first, living in a nursing home. It took three conversations with the social worker, checking facts and hoping for a match, before I thought to ask: "Is the Lois who is a resident there a Black woman or a white woman?"

She was annoyed that I had not asked this question earlier.

"Black," she said. "She is Black."

Shaken, I continued searching for the Lois on Olive Street. I talked to neighbors. I hired a private investigator. I met a friend who knew a social worker who was willing to make some calls.

Weeks later, someone found the white Lois in a different nursing home, living not far from the other Lois, the other nurse, the other woman from Ohio who was born in 1921. But after a few intense con-versations back and forth with social workers and family members we confirmed my worst fear. She, too, was the wrong Lois James. Four years of searching down the tubes. Back to square one.

After the second false find (that's what they call it in the searching business), I found the clue we had all overlooked. It was on a computer printout called the "Nationwide Death Index": *Lois Smith. Born No-vember 18, 1921. Died 1968.* Her social security number had an Ohio prefix.

I remembered chasing that lead. Could Lois Smith be the Lois I was

seeking, the Lois who gave birth to me in 1947? I remembered discovering the names of her three children: Sandra, Dale, and Barbara.

Now I was a woman obsessed. I set out for the city where this Lois
had died. As soon as I arrived, I searched newspaper obituaries and
phone books. I called every male in the city phone directory with the
same name as her son (I assumed the daughters had married and
changed their names): eight Dale Smiths. In a matter of a few hours, I
talked with seven of them. They wished me luck, but no, they weren't
the Dale Smith I was looking for. In one case, maybe the third or fourth
call, I reached an answering machine. The voice sounded like that of a
Black man; I ruled him out.

How, I wondered now as I held the precious envelope, how did I do
all that? How did I dare to make those calls? How did I keep moving toward this moment and a letter from this man who was her husband.

"You look good, girl!" he'd said in our first phone conversation.

"Sandy say you got your Mama's hair," referring to the photo I'd sent
with the letter.

*Dear Mr. Smith. . . . I hope what I have to say will not shock or offend
you. . . . I want nothing from you except information.*

"Yessir," he continued, "you do me proud! Just a while back I saw this
Oprah show, y'know, and they brought someone together that was way
up in age, a brother and sister, I think. Got me to puzzlin' if they could
do that, look like I could be brought together, too."

Proud. He said he was proud. He said the heavens were smiling on us.
He said he always knew, *everybody* knew. He said they wondered what
kind of home I got into, even thought about trying to find out, but
thought it might cause problems.

*You worry, ya know. I mean I wondered what kind of peoples you was with.
You think maybe they started out with good intent but went bad. Makes you feel
like shit thinkin' about it. When I found out you come up in a good home and
got a good education, I praised God. That's all I wanted to know. I never wanted
to interfere or take any respect from them—just to know.*

"She name you *Lee.* That's all she told me: 'I didn't give the baby a
name, all I did was call it Lee.' *Lee* is my middle name you know."

"So I'm named for you?"

"Yup. John Lee's my name," he confirmed and then he was off again, telling me more facts than I could handle in one telephone conversation. "I met your mother at the hospital where we was both working in 1946. . . ."

I'd known she named me Lee. That fact slipped through on some forms that came from the foundling home. And I knew it was his name, too. His full name was on her death certificate.

When I finally fond her—I found her first—I was at a counter in City Hall. Ten dollars bought a certified copy of a death certificate for Lois Smith born November 18, 1921, died October 19, 1968. Forty-six. Pulmonary embolus. The clerk asked me what I wanted, went to get it, and handed me the paper. I couldn't believe it. Surely if she knew she would have given me a hard time, or the wait would have been hours, or the photocopier broken. But, no, it was so simple, even legal, to request and receive that document. I knew instantly I had the right Lois. The facts I knew matched: Female. White. Father: Gordon. Mother: Ruth. And new facts surfaced: John Lee Smith. 3393 E. 143rd Street. Evergreen Cemetery. All the pieces of the puzzle fit into place.

I couldn't believe I'd spent four years looking for a Mrs. John Smith! Nor that I could open the three-inch-thick city phone directory and find a listing for John L. Smith at 3393 E. 143rd Street. Could it be that after twenty-five years he still lived in the same house?

That was enough for one day. I couldn't call right away.

But the next day, I went to the cemetery and ate lunch at the hospital where she had died. The next day I had the nerve to call.

"Hello . . ."

"Hello, my name is Katie. I'm studying to be a minister and I'm doing some genealogical research on the James family. I'm looking for a John Smith who married Lois James . . ."

"He ain't here."

"When might he be available?"

"Who are you? You be from the insurance company?"

"No, I'm not from the insurance company. I'm just seeking some information about Lois James Smith."

"Well he ain't home now."

I was at a pay phone in the corridor outside the hospital cafeteria. My knees were buckling, my whole body coursing with adrenaline.

"Thank you, I'll try again later," I said.

She sounded . . . well, she sounded different. She sounded Black, or maybe illiterate, or maybe poor. She also sounded suspicious and protective. I wondered if he was really out.

I had directions to 143rd Street. Someone where I was staying knew the area. He said it was a Black neighborhood now (*it's pretty rough, be careful*), though it had once been a blue-collar, immigrant neighborhood. That would fit; Lois was of German descent. I imagined postwar frame houses, each a carbon copy of the other, now past their prime.

I imagined wrong. It *was* a tough area. Burned-out houses. Boarded-up houses. Poverty evident everywhere.

So this is it, I thought to myself as I drove slowly along 143rd Street looking for number 3393. This is what I've been looking for. But there was no 3393. It ended in the 900s and no matter how much I looked for a continuation, it just wasn't there. I couldn't believe it. Another dead end.

"Oh, I'm sorry," said my host. "I forgot. The highway divides that street. The part you're looking for is here (pointing to my now well-worn city map). It's not that far away from here, see?"

"That's interesting," he continued.

"What's interesting?" I asked.

"Well," he continued slowly, choosing his words carefully, "that part of town is a solidly Black neighborhood."

"Had it been something else earlier?" I wondered aloud.

"No," he said matter-of-factly, "it's always been a Black neighborhood for as long as I've lived here, fifty years at least."

That day's developments did point to a new possibility, one I had never considered: the man Lois married may be Black.

I didn't find out right away.

I remembered the woman who was "different" at his house and the "Black-sounding" voice on the machine of the one Dale Smith I hadn't reached. Maybe it was worth another call.

"Hello, you've reached Dale at . . ."

Forget it. I didn't leave a message. What would I say? "Hi, I think I might be your sister!"

The next day, on my way out of town, I did drive by 3393 E. 143rd Street. It was the neighborhood I'd imagined. Postwar row houses.

Once a proud neighborhood. Now a little run down. Number 3393 was a white frame, two-story house with green shutters. I didn't have the nerve to knock. I just drove by two or three times.

I stopped at the McDonald's on the corner near his house and bought a cup of coffee. It was the first time in my life I was the only white person in a room. I sipped the coffee whose only virtue was that it was hot and what I was learning began to sink in. Lois was dead. Dead at forty-six. She married a man named John who might be Black. There were three children. Two sisters and a brother. They grew up here. She died here. I might have lived here.

That was April. I didn't have the guts to call or write. I sent for the birth certificates of the three children. That confirmed it. *Father: John Lee Smith. Negro.*

In August I wrote him a letter; in September, I sent it. I told him what I knew. I knew a lot about Lois, but virtually nothing about my birth father. I knew John Smith was Black and his children biracial. I asked him to tell me about her and, if he knew, about the man who is my biological father. I sent my picture, too. I hoped I would look enough like Lois that he could not deny I was her daughter.

He called within two hours of receiving it.

I came home to a message on my machine: ". . . I been readin' your letter. I'm the one that was married to Lois James back in . . ." And then his voice cracked. And then he left his number—a new, unpublished number—and then he said, "I'm glad to hear from you. Lois always said she'd like to try to find out where you were. The heavens are smilin' on us, I guess."

His voice was strong yet he sounded vulnerable and warm. Yes, he also sounded Black. (I was embarrassed to say that, even to myself, but I knew no other way to describe what I was hearing.) He sounded articulate. And nervous. Genuine. He sounded genuine.

We spoke for the first time the next day.

That's when he told me he is my father.

The possibility had crossed my mind when I learned his middle name, but instead I had constructed a fantasy based on earlier evidence. Lois had a one-night stand, got pregnant, and left town to have her baby. After I was born, she gave me up for adoption and returned home to marry the man she loved. They had three children. She died when they were seventeen, eleven, and ten, respectively.

But that's not exactly how it happened. In that first telephone conversation, John L. told his version. ("Don't call me John Smith," he'd said, "it sounds like an anonymous person!")

"You supposed to be my kid," he explained, "according to Lois and according to me now, you're mine." Then he unraveled this story:

We started goin' around together in 1946. In 1947 she got pregnant. I guess because of the nature of her and I—she was concerned about her family— she went away to give birth. She was torn, I know she was torn. She came back and we spent some time together then she went back. A lot of times you make up your mind and they take the baby point blank after childbirth. But they didn't in this case. She got a chance to handle you. And she called you Lee.

We didn't get married. She put you up for adoption and then in 1949, she got pregnant again. She did everything to get rid of that child. Said she couldn't go through it again what she went through with you. She went to one doctor for an abortion, but he was afraid to touch her. He thought she was a plant, 'cause she was a nurse. Then her being white, too, it was like she was double scarred. We knew he did those kind of things, but she come back out and said: 'He won't do it, Johnny.'

When she couldn't get rid of it, she said, "Well, we put one kid up for adoption, let's go on and get married."

They married in July. And a boy was born five months later.

That one died though. We didn't bother namin' him. 'Cause they showed him to me and he was just there, poor thing. All deformed and . . . He had a real fair complexion like you. But the kid didn't have a chance. She'd taken some real strong stuff to do away with that child. He just didn't have a chance. Boyohboy-ohboyohboy. She sure would have loved to see you, girl! She cried somethin' awful when we got home. Just kept sayin' over and over: "I wish we had Lee. I wish we had Lee."

So he was Black. And he was my father. I couldn't take in much more after that. I would look at my skin, light, freckled, blue veins bulging beneath it and stare disbelieving. I would stare at my nose, my lips. No one would ever mistake me for a high yella sistah! No one would ever call me cinnamon sugar! Honey, maybe, but never honey pecan. There was no evidence to suggest that I am biracial.

I wanted it to be true. I wanted this warm, loving man to be my father. I wanted the man who loved her so, who stayed with her, who loves her still to be my father. I wanted it but I couldn't believe it.

Others couldn't either.

"The way you tell," someone said, "is the fingernails. No matter how light their skin, Black people have a dark line around the perimeter of their fingernails."

I had no dark line.

"You don't look Black," people said routinely as I spread this new information among my friends. "Not with *that* nose," they would say.

I began to wonder what Black looked like. Maybe Black looked like me and I was too "white" to know.

Too many people had a voyeuristic curiosity as if I—or he—were a freak in a side show. A few of my friends wanted him desperately to be my father. They fell in love with him—with the idea of him—almost immediately. They would say things like, "How's your father doing?"

He wasn't my father, really. My father died in 1988. Semantics were important to me. Lois was my *birth* mother. John Lee was my *birth* father—or so he said—but I couldn't call her *my mother* or him *my father*. It seemed to rob my adoptive parents of the title they'd earned sitting up nights when I had earaches, buying shoes and skates and books, scraping funds together for tuition and a down-payment for my first house. No, I couldn't call him *my father*; I called him John L. or Big John.

Sometimes I called him Papa John.

Sometimes.

Then again, I didn't spend five years, and a thousand dollars, and more than a few sleepless nights to come to an ambiguous conclusion. I wanted to know.

His story didn't fit the facts so exactly as Lois's had. In the birth records, Lois had described him as thirty-five, 6′3″ tall, dark hair, dark eyes. That matched. She also said that her child's father was a manager at General Motors. That didn't match. John L. claims they first met when she was a nursing supervisor and he was a hospital orderly at the state psychiatric hospital. It wasn't until years later that, at the peak of his career, he was elected president of the International Chemical Workers Local 10.

Lois listed the father as being of French and English descent. Lois told the social worker that she had been drinking, that she and this man had intercourse, and that, because they had no prior relationship, marriage was out of the question. Big John says they'd been together nearly a year. He'd dared her to kiss him in the utility room at the hospital. She did—and "it was a real kiss," he remembers—but when he kissed her again she pulled away. "You're not blonde enough for me, Slim," she'd said.

I try to imagine how she felt at that moment. This incredibly handsome man. The scent of his strong, lean body. The power of that first kiss. There must have been something in that kiss that was stronger than her fear because, according to John L., "we started goin' around together after that."

He claimed she said that marriage was out of the question because she feared her family would disown her if she married a Negro. In fact, they did not, which he said was a source of great joy and great sadness to her. Great joy because she was so delighted that they would welcome her husband and, later, their children into their homes and lives; great sadness because she wished she'd married sooner and never given away her baby girl, Lee.

So was he or wasn't he my birth father?

"You could have a DNA test," several people ventured. How could I ask this man who loved me so much and so long—loved me immediately and without condition—how could I challenge his paternity? Would I ask a white man who claimed to be my father to have a DNA test? And what would it prove?

If the test showed that he is not my father, what would that do to his untarnished image of Lois? And where would it get me? After all, if she had changed her mind and brought me home, it would have been to his home, their home. *He* would have been my father. Just as the man who raised me was my father.

Maybe Lois lied to the social worker, hoping her light-skinned baby girl would have a better chance in a white, middle-class world. Maybe she lied to her beloved Johnny, hoping he would believe that the girl child she conceived in a moment of passion (or whatever it was) was his baby. Maybe she really didn't know. Maybe she named the baby *Lee* because she wanted him to be my father as much as I want him to be.

I wish I didn't care about these details. I wish I could let it go. I wish

I could love him and forget my doubts, but I can't. I've tried. I've really tried, but I can't.

I want to know. I want to know at least as much as the records show. Lois gave a name. It was not *John Lee Smith*. I know that now because I've called the social worker at Catholic Charities where the records of my adoption are stored. The records list another name. The social worker will confirm that it is not John Lee Smith, but it is illegal for her to say what it is. A stranger—ten strangers, one hundred strangers— can see this information; I cannot.

And then I hear his voice. His warm, wonderful voice. The voice that calls me and sings to me, invents verse for me. And I remember what that hug feels like. That strong, unconditional hug that transmits a life- time of love. And I hear him say, "Your mama and I . . ."

Or I finger the now worn envelope. *I thank God I have found you. I pray every night that you'll never be ashamed to be part of this family.*

I *am* ashamed, but not for the reasons he worries about. I am ashamed because I remember what it was like to ride in my father's truck (my *other* father, the father who reared me) on Saturday mornings when he took me with him to the shop. He repaired cash registers. He worked half days on Saturdays. He sometimes took me along to give my mother a break.

When I was with him, he always drove the long way around so he could avoid "nigger town," the Black neighborhood that abutted the building where he worked. I am ashamed when I remember the remarks in my home—*It's raining pitchforks and nigger babies*—when I remember their words, their attitudes, their fears. I also remember how much I loved them and how I understand now that they learned those words and attitudes and fears from the parents and grandparents they loved, the family *I* loved. And I remember times when my father took food from our freezer or money from our savings account to help "some poor nigger." I remember the year he gave away our Thanksgiving turkey and my mother refused to cook!

I am ashamed when I realize that my sisters and brother grew up in a neighborhood my family would have called "nigger town." I am ashamed when I remember that Sandy and Dale and Barb were among the first youth in their city to be bussed. While my father delivered me to the door of my school, Sandy and Barb got up hours early to make the trip across town to the school where each in turn took the swim team to the state championships. My family thought bussing was "shit for the birds."

I am ashamed to be white in this new family of mine. And regardless of my genetic composition, I *am* white. I was reared in a white world. Granted white privilege. Taught the white rules.

John Lee worried I'd be ashamed. My worst nightmare was that he would say: "We didn't want you then and we don't want you now!" I wasn't prepared at all for a warm, gracious, and loving response. I wasn't prepared for the impact of that first phone conversation. I call it "dial-a-family": *Come on down, Katie, you have another father and two sisters and a brother and six nieces and nephews and countless aunts and uncles and cousins and . . .* I wasn't prepared for that first photo, that first hug, that first family gathering.

I'm not sure how to be his daughter. I don't know how to be a sister. It isn't easy to integrate(!) the mother and father I know with a father and mother I never knew.

I don't know what to do next.

Some things take awhile to get used to.

Rebecca Carroll

May the Circle Be Unbroken

I imagined that he would look like Easy Reader from *Electric Company*, the children's show that came on after *Sesame Street* on Public Television when I was a kid. Long before Superfly shaped our young Black views of ultra chic and unearthly hip in the early seventies, Easy Reader was The Man.

Easy Reader had a glide to his stride that was all his own. It got him where he was going, plan or no plan. His long, lanky legs were half-bent to cushion the weight of his six-foot frame as his feet touched the ground with each rhythmic step. He seemed to be always in motion, smooth like butter, or at least heavy cream. He was quiet, but all about words. "Easy Reader, that's my name," he would gently chant as his face held a wide, satisfied, and knowing smile, and his body rolled like mercury across the screen.

Having been adopted into a white family at birth and growing up in a small, rural New Hampshire town, I did not have Black culture in my life, around me, incarnate, until I was about fourteen years old. I didn't know it then, but I know it now like the air I breathe that I hoarded those few moments I spent with Easy Reader every afternoon and kept them with me for years. I couldn't have afforded not to.

Naturally, when I heard of these "birth-parents" that existed for me, and that the birth-mother was white and the birth-father Black, I matched the Black birth-father with the likes of Easy Reader. How else could I have possibly envisioned him? Although our subsequent re-union was not what either of us had hoped for, I was lucky to have at least had a positive Black male image to go on. Were I growing up today, or even had I grown up in a more urban environment, invariably I would have been given an image of *all* Black men as absent fathers, drug dealers, and gangster leaders. Easy Reader saved me from a tainted, racist view of what my birth-father could have been and allowed me to hold faith in a day I would look forward to for twenty-five years.

As I got older and more inquisitive, nobody had kind things to say about my birth-father. When I was reunited with my birth-mother at age eleven, even she responded to my question of, "What was my father like?" with, "Basically, he was a dog." I didn't have to understand what being a dog meant in adult terms to know that she did not look favorably upon my birth-father, and wasn't all that interested in discussing it any further.

When I was a teenager I spent summers with my birth-mother who lived in a small city. It was no booming metropolis, but there were Black people there. Wednesday and Sunday were "under-twenty" nights at the local speakeasy. It was the early eighties and breakdancing had just come on the scene. I thought I had died and gone to heaven. Back home and at school, I was viewed as everybody's friend and fun to have around, but *definitely* not a girlfriend prospect. The attention I got from young Black boys at the speakeasy was exciting and fortifying. When the then hip, but now old-school, rap music would come on, a few of the boys would converge onto the center of the dance floor and do an impromptu performance; bodies popping, gyrating, flipping. And when a slow song would come on, every single girl there was hoping that one of those lean, agile, young breakdancers would choose her as his homegirl. I was lucky to get asked almost every time. He would pull me close, leaving a hot whisper of space between our bodies. Blue and red strobe lights shooting through our bones. His breath on the back of my neck like honey slowly pouring out of a jar. I hoarded those moments. I couldn't have afforded not to.

By the time I got to college thoughts about my birth-father had become omnipresent. And *he* had become omnipresent. I felt like he was always there, always around me; watching over me, protecting me. In spite of the bad things I had heard about him, I continued to believe that he had to be a good person at heart. Having learned that he had no surviving family and had grown up in foster homes, government institutions, and on the street, I thought for sure that once we met and he saw that he had a strong, healthy daughter, he would immediately redeem himself, and we would instinctively connect. For if he had no surviving family, I had no surviving family; he and I were each other's sole-surviving Black relative.

I began telling friends and family, both birth and adoptive, that I thought I was ready to seek out my birth-father. After I graduated from college I moved to Boston, where he had last been seen by my birth-mother's brother a few years before. I tried to make eye contact with nearly every Black man I passed on the street to see if I could find my eyes in his. I made several trips to the Berklee School of Music, where he was said to have frequently hung out, asking students, administrators, and teachers if they had heard of a man by the name of Joseph Bankes. Nobody had. One time I was in a shop on Newbury Street and began talking with a woman who turned out to be a Berklee School alum. I asked her if she had known anyone named Joseph Bankes while she was there. She paused for a few minutes. "Yeah," she said. "I think I did." I told her that I was a distant relative, and that it was important he not know I was looking for him.

"Okay, I think I can help you," she said. We exchanged phone numbers and I left. I never heard from her again.

One day about a year later, I got a phone call from my birth-mother. "Guess who Gary (her brother) saw coming out of the Cambridge Public Library yesterday?" she said, reluctantly. I didn't have to guess. I knew. Suddenly, all of the arrangements were made without me. Both my birth-mother and her brother thought it was best for my safety if I was not involved with the initial exchange of information. I was not to go alone. My birth-uncle, Gary, would go with me. It was he who had driven my birth-mother to my house in New Hamsphire for our reunion fourteen years ago. He knew the way.

I agreed that he would accompany me to meet Joseph Bankes.

Gary and I walked through a crowded Harvard Square in the center of Cambridge to get to the designated meeting point, his left arm on my shoulder, his right guiding the path. It was like being inside of a life-giving arc.

We waited for twenty minutes. Gary tried to call from a pay phone. "He must have gotten the time mixed up," he said, trying to sound hopeful.

First I felt myself regress back to the traumatized infant who my mother tells me was inconsolable for the first year after the adoption. And then I felt Black life slipping from my grasp. While I was growing up, I had been able to find ways in which I could moderate the basic and primal sense of rejection that came from being given up by my birth-mother. What I had not been able to overcome was the deprivation of Black cultural support. Meeting my Black birth-father was meant to lend necessary blood to my veins. I needed to stand next to his dark skin. I wanted to take his hand and bring him to the Black kids from college who had taken me to task for the authenticity of my Blackness: "What kind of Black girl are you anyway?" "Why do you talk like that?" "How come you don't know what 'fly' means?" Even my white friends at school had said things to me, thinking that they were being kind and ac-cepting, like "We don't even think of you as Black." God forbid.

A second meeting was arranged. We were to meet at the same place as before, in front of a small café. I was emotionally guarded this time as Gary stood in front of me, my body rigid, trying to harness the pending teardrops of disillusion. Just as I was about to say we should go, that he wasn't coming, I saw Gary look beyond my shoulder. I turned around and saw a round, nocturnal-colored face, wet with perspiration. After a brief and awkward pause, we embraced. Gary left us alone, and my fa-ther and I went to sit down at a table inside the café.

He was shorter than I had imagined he would be. Aside from my loy-alty to the Easy Reader prototype, my birth-mother had mentioned that when she knew him, Joe had been tremendously vain, working out with weights, staying in good shape, and wearing fine and expensive clothing. He wore a tattered, red nylon gym suit—the elastic waist pull-ing up over a round pot belly—a bicycle helmet, and eyeglasses with candy-apple red, plastic frames that matched his gym suit. He wouldn't take his helmet or his glasses off until I had asked him twice, and even then, he wouldn't keep them off. Underneath the helmet his coarse, greyish-black hair was neatly cornrowed to his head: "A woman at the shelter did it for me." He fidgeted as he sat across from me, but seemed somehow rested.

He didn't want to know anything about my adoptive family: "It's no different from slavery the way they took you from me." He held all white people in contempt, yet claimed to have been and still was, completely in love with my birth-mother (who is white), and by the way, where was she? And did I have any pictures of her? He insisted that I call him "Pops" ten minutes after we met. He didn't ask me any questions about my job, my personal life, what I liked or didn't like. He just looked at me as if I were his prize after all these years of hard living: "Now I understand why God put me on this earth—I look at you and feel good about at least one thing I did in life!" That *he* did? What did he do? He was looking at a full grown, self-contained woman! I reserved judgment during and after our first meeting. I was determined to give this reunion a chance.

The next time we met was for dinner at another Cambridge café. It was close to Christmas time and Joe had come with presents that I knew he could not afford. When I saw the joy in his face as he gave them to me, I quietly accepted them.

The next time we visited, we met for brunch at another restaurant. This time Joe brought me a book about all the white men in history who were really Black, and he also brought a document verifying the fact that he was filing a civil suit against the city of Boston for unlawful punitive damage. He spoke almost incessantly about the "Underground Organizations" that were after him, and assured me that it had been men from those organizations who had stolen his 1968 Mazarati car. When he wasn't talking about that, he would speak in a slur about my looks, telling me how beautiful I was, how soft my skin was, and how sparkling my eyes were. I started to feel uncomfortable.

A few months later, on the morning of Father's Day, I was at a restaurant with a friend whose former girlfriend unexpectedly came into the restaurant with their baby boy. She stopped to speak and my friend took his son in his arms.

When I saw the connection being made between my friend and his barely two-month-old son—so simple and graceful, my soul shifted and I burst into tears. The experience wasn't as kind as an epiphany; it was, rather, an emotional revolution, and the concept of choice suddenly crystallized for me. The first choice I made was to allow Joe to be who he was, independent of his blood relation to me. I have continued to call him Joe since our reunion, although my recent move to another city, and the difficulty in getting word through to him by phone or by mail has left us at somewhat of an impasse. I suspect we will see each other again. The second choice I made was to respect, love, and claim the self-invented self who I have become; both birth and adoptive, Black and white. I think that's what Easy Reader was trying to tell me all those years ago: "Speak your name, be who you are, and glide along."

2

Pain and Healing

"Hi, dear," the postcard read. "I'm sitting by the pool here in Nassau having a wonderful time. I wish you all were here. Love, your daddy." Who? A thin, tanned white woman lounged on coffee-with-cream-colored sand, her arched feet crossing the line where the brown sand met the sapphire waters. Behind her were coconut trees with leaves so flaxen they reflected the sun. Across the top of the card was written, "Nothing can be better than the Bahamas." It was a paper missile launched by a man I did not know or love. A man who did not love me more than the Bahamas.   TAHRA EDWARDS

My father was . . . belligerent toward all of the children, except me. The older ones he would beat almost savagely if they broke any of his rules—and he had so many rules it was hard to know them all.

MALCOLM X

Handsome, proud, and in-grown, "like a toe-nail," somebody had said. But he looked to me, as I grew older, like pictures I had seen of African tribal chieftains: he really should have been naked, with war-paint on and barbaric mementos, standing among spears. He could be chilling in the pulpit and indescribably cruel in his personal life and he was certainly the most bitter man I have ever met; yet it must be said that there was something else in him, buried in him, which lent him his tremendous power and, even, a rather crushing charm. It had something to do with his blackness, I think—he was very black—with his blackness and his beauty, and with the fact that he knew that he was black but did not know that he was beautiful. . . .

. . . When he was dead I realized that I had hardly spoken to him. When he had been dead a long time I began to wish I had.

JAMES BALDWIN

The relationship between African-American fathers and their sons is, in a very special sense, beyond politics. It runs to the bone of what we are afraid to say: that we need our fathers desperately, and frequently, we feel we are not men because we have not been so in our fathers' hearts.

SCOTT MINERBROOK

A MOTHERFUCKER, AIN'T IT. THIS DADDY SEARCH. Looking for a father under every brick or rock or coal pile and me signifying such a search is the very brick-and-rock foundation of various political philosophies, survival strategies from integration to separation to burn-baby-burn to self-annihilation and starting all over again. Maybe the search for fathers is finally only a trope, a ropa-dope trope containing enough rope to hang you up terminally, you black bastard.

JOHN WIDEMAN

Cornelius Eady

A Little Bit of Soap

One of the things my father never liked about me was my dark skin. *You used to be so pretty* was the way he'd put it, and it was true, there is proof, a baby picture of a curly-haired, just a hair's breadth away from fair-skinned child, me, my small fingers balled up into fists.

And then, as if some God shrugged and suddenly turned away its gaze, something caved in, and I was dark, dark, and all that it implied.

So what happened? My father always seemed to want me to explain, what did this desertion mean? This skin that seemed born to give up, this hair that crinkled to knots, this fairy tale–like transformation?

You used to look real good, my father, a man of slightly lighter hue, would say to me, his son, his changeling. *Maybe you ought to wash more.*

Toi Derricotte

Poem for My Father

You closed the door.
I was on the other side,
screaming.

It was black in your mind.
Blacker than burned-out fire.
Blacker than poison.

Outside everything looked the same.
You looked the same.
You walked in your body like a living man.
But you were not.

would you not speak to me for weeks
would you hang your coat in the closet without saying hello
would you find a shoe out of place and beat me
would you come home late
would i lose the key
would you find my glasses in the garbage
would you put me on your knee
would you read the bible to me in your smoking jacket after
         your mother died
would you come home drunk and snore
would you beat me on the legs
would you carry me up the stairs by my hair so that my feet
         never touch bottom
would you make everything worse
to make everything better

I believe in god, the father almighty,
the maker of heaven, the maker
of my heaven and my hell.

would you beat my mother
would you beat her till she cries like a rabbit
would you beat her in a corner of the kitchen
while i am in the bathroom trying to bury my head underwater
would you carry her to the bed
would you put cotton and alcohol on her swollen head
would you make love to her hair
would you caress her hair
would you rub her breasts with ben gay until she stinks
would you sleep in the other room in the bed next to me while
        she sleeps on the pull-out cot
would you come on the sheet while i am sleeping. later i look
        for the spot
would you go to embalming school with the last of my
        mother's money
would i see your picture in the book with all the other
        black boys you were the handsomest
would you make the dead look beautiful
would the men at the elks club
would the rich ladies at funerals
would the ugly drunk winos on the street
know ben
pretty ben
regular ben

would your father leave you when you were three with a mother
        who threw butcher knives at you
would he leave you with her screaming red hair
would he leave you to be smothered by a pillow she put
        over your head
would he send for you during the summer like a rich uncle
would you come in pretty corduroys until you were nine and
        never heard from him again

would you hate him
would you hate him every time you dragged hundred pound
      cartons of soap down the stairs into white ladies'
      basements
would you hate him for fucking the women who gave birth
      to you
hate him flying by her house in the red truck
      so that the other father threw down his hat in the street
      and stomped on it angry like we never saw him
(bye bye
to the will of grandpa
bye bye to the family fortune
bye bye when he stomped that hat,
to the gold watch,
embalmer's palace,
grandbaby's college)
mother crying silently, making floating island
sending it up to the old man's ulcer
would grandmother's diamonds
close their heartsparks
in the corner of the closet
yellow like the eyes of cockroaches?

Old man whose sperm swims in my veins,

come back in love, come back in pain.

Langston Hughes

The Big Sea

Hurry up! My father had tremendous energy. He always walked fast and rode hard. He was small and tough, like a jockey. He got up at five in the morning and worked at his accounts or his mail or his law books until time to go to the office. Then until ten or eleven o'clock at night he would be busy at various tasks, stopping only to eat. Then, on the days he made the long trek to the ranch, he rose at three-thirty or four, in order to get out there early and see what his workers were doing. Everyone else worked too slowly for him, so it was always, "Hurry up!"

As the weeks went by, I could think of less and less to say to my father. His whole way of living was so different from mine, his attitude toward life and people so amazing, that I fell silent and couldn't open my mouth when he was in the house. Not even when he barked: "Hurry up!"

I hadn't heard from my mother, even by July. I knew she was angry with me because I had gone to Mexico. I understood then, though, why she had been unable to live with my father, and I didn't blame her. But why had she married him in the first place, I wondered. And why had they had me? Now, at seventeen, I began to be very sorry for myself, in a strange land in a mountain town, where there wasn't a person who spoke English. It was very cold at night and quiet, and I had no money to get away, and I was lonesome. I began to wish I had never been born—not under such circumstances.

I took long rides on a black horse named Tito to little villages of adobe huts, nestled in green fields of corn and alfalfa, little villages, each with a big church with a beautiful tower built a hundred years ago, a white Spanish tower with great bells swinging in the turret.

I began to learn to read Spanish. I struggled with bookkeeping. I took one of the old pistols from my father's desk and fired away in the afternoon at a target Maximiliano had put up in the corral. But most of the time I was depressed and unhappy and bored. One day, when there was no one in the house but me, I put the pistol to my head and held it there, loaded, a long time, and wondered if I would be any happier if I were to pull the trigger. But then, I began to think, if I do, I might miss something. I haven't been to the ranch yet, nor to the top of the volcano, nor to the bullfights in Mexico, nor graduated from high school, nor got married. So I put the pistol down and went back to my bookkeeping.

My father was very seldom at home, but when he was, he must have noticed my silence and my gloomy face, because if I looked the way I felt, I looked woebegone, indeed. One day in August, he told me he was going to Mexico City for a week, and would take me with him for the trip. He said I could see the summer bullfights and Xochimilco. The trip was ten days off, but I began to dream about it, and to press my clothes and get ready.

It seemed that my father couldn't resist saying, "Hurry up," more and more during those ten days, and giving me harder and harder book-keeping problems to have worked out by the time he got home from the office. Besides, he was teaching me to typewrite, and gave me several exercises to master each evening. "Hurry up and type that a hundred times before you go to bed. Hurry up and get that page of figures done so I can check on it. Hurry up and learn the verb, *estar*."

Hurry up . . . hurry up . . . hurry up . . . hurry up, began to ring in my ears like an obsession.

The morning came for us to go to Mexico City. The train left at seven, but unless you reserved parlor-car seats, you had to be in line at the station before dawn to be sure of getting on the train, for the coaches were crowded to capacity. My father did not wish to spend the extra money for parlor-car seats, so he woke me up at four-thirty. It was still dark.

"Hurry up and get dressed," he said through the dark.

At that hour of the morning it is bitter cold in Toluca's high mountain valley. From the well Maximiliano brought us water for washing that was like ice. The cook began to prepare breakfast. We sat down to eat. At the table my father gulped his food quickly, looked across at me, and barked for no reason at all: "Hurry up!"

Suddenly my stomach began to turn over and over. And I could not swallow another mouthful. Waves of heat engulfed me. My eyes burned. My body shook. I wanted more than anything on earth to hit my father, but instead I got up from the table and went back to bed. The bed went round and round and the room turned dark. Anger clotted in every vein, and my tongue tasted like dry blood.

My father stuck his head in the bedroom door and asked me what was the matter.

I said: "Nothing."

He said: "Don't you want to go to Mexico City?"

I said: "No, I don't want to go."

I don't know what else he said, but after a while I heard him telling Maximiliano in Spanish to hurry up with his bags. Then the outside door closed, and he was gone to the train.

The housekeeper came in and asked me what I wanted.

I said: "Nothing."

Maximiliano came back from the station and sat down silently on the tile floor just inside my door, his blanket about him. At noon the cook brought me a big bowl of warm soup, but I couldn't drink it. My stomach kept turning round and round inside me. And when I thought of my father, I got sicker and sicker. I hated my father.

They sent for the doctor. He came and gave me a prescription. The housekeeper took it herself and had it filled, not trusting the *mozo*. But when my father came back after four days in the city, I still hadn't eaten anything. I had a high fever. He sent for the doctor again, and the doctor said I'd better go to the hospital.

This time my father engaged seats in the parlor car and took me to the American Hospital in Mexico City. There, after numberless examinations, they decided I had better remain several weeks, since they thought I had a stomach infection.

The three middle-aged Mexican sisters came to see me and brought a gift of guava jelly. They asked what on earth could have happened to make me so ill. I must have had a great shock, they said, because my eyes were a deep yellow. But I never told them or the doctors that I was sick because I hated my father.

Elaine Brown

A Taste of Power

Ultimately, I decided I did not want to meet my father. I decided I would meet him only to tell him everything I thought. If he was so ashamed of his bastard daughter he had invented another one, I wished he were dead. If his wealthy, Negro, Washington, D.C.–based family, about which there were various notations in certain Negro history books, did not want to acknowledge his bastard child, I wished they, too, were all dead. No, I thought, I did not ever want to meet my father.

I was finally on my mother's side. She was right. *We* were nothing! I had no business worrying about my color. It was nothing compared to being nothing at all. I had to work, to fight, to become something other than nothing. I had finally learned that, firsthand. . . .

. . .He was running for Congress on the Republican ticket. Waiting for my bus to go to school, I had caught glimpses of his enlarged poster face, distorted by North Philly dirt and graffiti, and by PUSSY and FUCK YOU scrawled across his nose and chin. He was handsome, I saw, without giving thought to him at all. I was passingly sorry when he lost the election, though it, and surely he, meant nothing to me at all, I maintained.

His face in person, on the other hand, was different. It was my face, my eyes, my lips, my nose, the face of my father. I did not know what to call him when he touched me from arm's length for the first time I knew about. He and my mother had arranged it. It was in the beginning of my tenth-grade year at Girls High. He was proud of me, proud of my grades, proud of everything I had become, my mother told me. He wanted to develop a relationship with me, she said.

I had to meet him at his office, a neat, brownstone, two-story structure in a clean pocket of North Philadelphia. No patients were there when I opened the double door, the top half of which was made of stained glass. He opened the door of his inner office as I was about to sit down in the outer one. He was not much taller than I. His brown skin and mine matched. He had some freckles and wavy hair. He was indeed very handsome, I felt, as he finally embraced me.

"Your mother has been telling me everything about you over the years, you know," he said, studying me.

I was speechless, trying to figure out whether I looked like the most beautiful girl in the world to him. Was my tailored clothing proper? I wondered. Could he see that I really did look like him?

"You've grown into quite a young lady," he continued in a rather formal way, showing me to an office chair across from his desk, on which he sat. His suit was brown, accented by his highly polished, expensive-looking brown shoes and stark-white shirt, the cuffs of which bore his initials.

He told me about "our" family, most of which my mother had, of course, already told me. He emphasized how special our bloodline was, pointing out specifically that I was the image of his sister Clarissa, who had been perhaps the very first colored woman to graduate from Wellesley College. I decided that was where I would go to college; it was, after all, among the preferred colleges for Girls High girls. He asked me about my grades, my life in school, my friends. He said other things to which I paid little attention, I was so dazzled by his handsome face and beautiful eyes and smart appearance. Before I left, after about an hour, I let him know that I accepted the secrecy of our meeting, and he let me know we could continue to see each other in this way.

I did not want to return to my mother. I did not want to return to our latest apartment in another part of Tioga, or to our room. I wanted to start over, to start life over with that fine, refined colored man who was my real and only father, who wanted me in his life. I was noncommunicative with my mother that afternoon. I told her nothing about it, not even my impressions. She was incapable of understanding, I felt. She did not really know him, or me. We, my father and I, were alike, I concluded that day. We were one—not my mother and I—but *he* and I.

As I walked from the bus stop to his office for my next visit, about a week later, I determined to convince him to take me into his life on a full-time basis. The details were unclear to me. I imagined we could stay

together in a small apartment, probably in Germantown, where I could
take care of myself, or something, while he maintained his other life
with his wife and adopted daughter on Lincoln Drive. I did not think of
my mother at all. . . .

"I see she hasn't told you. Of course not. You see, we've always
wanted you in our family, but she wouldn't have it."

I remained blank, not comprehending.

"I mean," he continued, "you are, after all, the only child any of us,
my brother and sisters, has ever had; and we wanted you to live with
your aunt in Chicago, a fine woman, whose husband is a prominent attorney there . . ."

"As my mother and father?"

"Well, yes. But your mother has always stood in the way," he said
with little-subdued acrimony. "Now, of course, I'm not sure what we
can do. So I just want to see you whenever possible."

"I guess I'd like that, too," I said rather idiotically, wrestling with the
shock of everything he had just calmly told me, at once ashamed of my
designs to leave my mother and angry with my mother for concealing
so much from me.

As he continued speaking, mostly about how much like his family I
was, I began to wonder why he had waited so long to see me, to tell me.
Then I wondered what he wanted me to do. Then I tried to imagine life
with *his* family. Then I wondered what he thought my mother should
have done, or been, to me. Then I remembered what my mother had
asked me to do.

We had no food and no money, because my mother's payday was on
Monday and it was the weekend. She had instructed me, more times
than I had listened, to try to get ten dollars from him.

Nearly an hour had passed. It seemed time to leave.

"By the way," I asked him casually, and somewhat embarrassed,
"could you let me have ten dollars for some school books." My mother
had told me to make it seem as if the request was for me personally. I
smiled at him flirtatiously.

"Is that what your mother told you to ask me?" he said, suddenly
very cold.

"Uh n-no," I stuttered.

"You tell your mother if she wants money from me to take me to court like she does every month. Has the gall to try to get a bench warrant for my arrest. Every damn month! Tell her don't *ever* again send you to get money out of me!"

Tears filled my eyes as they widened with shock and shame.

"But it's only ten dollars, and we need the money for food!" I cried out, surprising myself.

"That's what *she* says," he responded passionlessly. "She's got a job. She can handle everything. You just tell her what I said. And tell her not to try to play games with me anymore!"

I checked my tears and transformed myself. I became a Girls High girl, or maybe a North Philly girl. "As far as I'm concerned, *you* are the one playing games," I stated firmly, looking directly into his dark brown eyes. "But don't worry about me asking you for a cent again," I said in my most arrogant tone. "You don't have to worry about me again!"

I was holding the outer office door open, and he was looking at me in disbelief.

"As a matter of fact, I don't want to see you again!" I screamed. "I'd rather see you dead. And when you die, I'll spit on your grave!" I bellowed, borrowing language from some old movie, it seemed. I slammed the Dutch door, cracking the stained-glass mosaic.

It was the last door I would have to close, I thought, as I walked back to the bus stop, less damaged than determined. My mother and I, alone, would survive in his world, in "their" world, whoever they were, and without their help. That weekend, we ate eggs and hoe cakes with dry eyes and knowing expressions that we needed no one at all anymore.

Brent Staple

Parallel Time

My father had become a series of sounds in the dark: the jingle of keys in the door lock; the *clump clump clump* of motorcycle boots up the stairs and down the hall to their bedroom; more jingling of keys and pocket change as he slipped out of his pants, the groan of the bedsprings as he lay down. There was one night when we were guaranteed a face-to-face encounter. That was report card night. My brothers and I went to bed early to be out of his way, hopeful that he'd let us sleep. Instead he hauled us from bed, sometimes at ungodly hours, and harangued us about our grades.

He was always drunk at the time. We stood in our underwear in the blinding light of the living room, asleep on our feet, as he thundered questions at us. "What about this 'C' in arithmetic!" Then there was the teacher's written assessment, the dreaded, "not working up to potential," which they seemed to write on everybody's card, and against which there was no defense, even when you were awake. "What have I told you about all this!" He slapped and shook us, trying to wake us up. But the fog of sleep kept us from answering. By the time we woke up, we were back in bed.

It did no good to ask my father for money directly; he would only slink off to bed saying he'd think about it. The next morning was a grotesque version of Christmas: We woke up at dawn to listen to him leaving for work. Then we ran downstairs to see if our requests had been granted. There was no way of predicting. The money for the class trip or for the new pair of shoes was either there or it wasn't. When he came through, it was to the nickel and not a penny more. When he came through, the dollars and coins lay in the appointed spot (which changed with every house we lived in). When he didn't come through, the spot was heartbreakingly empty. The strategy then was to catch him in front of one of his brothers and shame him into it. "Go ahead, Melvin, give the boy the money," one of the uncles would say. And he would.

The surest way to get money was to steal it. This I began to do with regularity. My father, when we asked him for something, would say, "Christ, you all think I'm made of money!" In fact he was. His pockets bulged with the quarters he needed for tolls. He cultivated this stash of quarters, breaking bills whenever he could to get more of them. This habit got out of hand on Friday nights, when he got the drunkest. He came through the front door clinking and jinking like a sack of gold in a pirate movie.

I stole on Saturday mornings, when the drinking he had done would keep him sleeping soundly through the burglary, when the quarters that he had so manically collected were too sweet to resist. I crept into the bedroom, careful of the creaking floorboards, and went to the chair where his clothes lay in a heap. The pants could have fallen into the chair in any number of positions: bottom first; top first; heavy pockets perched on the edge of the cushion, ready to drop to the floor. I passed up the bills; they were too hard to get at. The chain on the wallet was noisy; the wallet itself was fastened with snaps that would make even more noise. Anyway, going after the bills would be stepping up from petty theft to grand larceny. That required more courage than I could muster.

I got down on my knees and snaked my hand into the pocket and down to where the quarters were. I stacked as many as I could between my thumb, middle, and index fingers, then I drew the stack out slowly, carefully, applying just enough pressure to keep the quarters from slipping out of line. I transferred the stack to my other hand, and went in for seconds. Half-dollars could be used only at the base of the stack. If you inserted them into the middle, the stack could slip out of balance, even disintegrate, and fall noisily back into the cache. I sweated through this. Quarters hitting the floor would mean curtains for sure.

I left the room with the same caution that had brought me in: I stepped around the same creaking boards and hoped none of the little kids got up and bounded down the hall to jump into bed with my parents. Four or five dollars at a haul was common. My mother was a light sleeper, but I counted on her not to give me up. Though I was never caught, I suspected that, at least some of the time, my father lay there wide-awake, watching me steal from him. I especially thought this when he stopped snoring in the middle of my heist.

Then there was the way he brought up theft and lying out of the blue. "A thief and a liar are the two worst things in the world. Yes, sir, the first one is the thief, the second one is a liar. I can't stand either one of them." He said this as he leaned red-eyed into my face, reeking of booze. It was a mantra with him; I mouthed the words mentally as he spoke them. I couldn't tell if he knew I was stealing or if he was just playing a hunch. This didn't stop me. If he wanted to nab me, he'd have to wake up and catch me in the act.

I was a successful thief at school, too. My sixth-grade teacher volunteered me to sell milk and potato chips during the morning and afternoon breaks. The profits went toward our class trip, which that year was to New York City. When making change, I palmed a quarter at a time and slipped it deftly into my pocket. At first I stole just enough to pay for the milk and potato chips that I had no money to buy. Then I stole more, but just enough so that the shortfalls would look like honest mistakes. If caught, I was prepared to lie and cast suspicion on my fellow salesman. I enjoyed stealing for its solitary nature and because it was one of the few things I was good at. I was terrible at baseball, football, and gymnastics, but a regular whiz at pilfering.

My thefts left me flush at midweek, by which time my mother was broke. When she questioned me about my Coca-Colas and candy bars, I told her that I'd won the money on sporting bets at school. What a ludicrous lie. I knew nothing at all about sports. I had thus become the two things my father despised most: a thief and a liar.

John Wideman

Fatheralong

I think I'm beginning to discover as I shuffle through childhood memories of my father, not so much recollecting as reexperiencing them, something of a paradox. I was of his flesh, fashioned in his image. Everybody said I looked just like him, but it was my body, the mirror of him, estranging me most from him. The ways I learned my body. The secret, inner life growing as my body grew.

For a long time, from birth and before, my body belonged to the women in my family. It was the sum of the intimacies they lavished on me. Hugged and bathed and tucked in a warm bed, rocked on a knee, pressed to a bosom, snuggled in a lap. They cared for me; I was totally comfortable only with them. They taught me my body's alphabet, taught it to speak and listen. Often my body would merge with my mother's or with one of her sisters who lived with us in my grandmother's house. Cuddled up for a nap or occasionally sleeping all night beside a woman sleeping, the intimacy of merging was also an exploration of difference. Learning boundaries, places I could touch and not touch, places where the women's bodies changed, attracting me, scaring me, where they became so unlike me I could not decipher the mystery of difference solely with my senses. I needed more than the creature-to-creature rubbing and sniffing and listening intimacies a child was permitted. If my eyes, ears, nose, fingertips, and toes couldn't explain difference, perhaps daydreaming would. I believe it's at this juncture my father materialized. As soon as I began to stand apart, ponder, and worry the power of women's bodies, he stepped into the room. Not in the flesh, the flesh we shared, but as an absence, someone like me who would know exactly what I was up to, peeking, sneaking around. Wasn't I on my way to being him?

In the room full of women's secrets I birthed him; the idea of him, a man, a father, allowed me to be in the room but also elsewhere, thinking about the room, perhaps visualizing it as he might. Didn't I need a father to explain my bewilderment, my desire, the hidden part of me that spied and calculated, the predatory part I hadn't been aware of until differences between the women's bodies and mine created space, curiosity, the compulsion to verify and simultaneously remove what separated me from them?

I learned the differences between women's bodies and mine couldn't be willed away, even with a father's help. Difference created guilt, pleasure, and pain. If my father knew my secrets, if we shared them, would he punish me? Or understand and welcome me. Did my ambivalence about what I was doing, what I was becoming, anger me as I grew away from the women? Did I blame my father? His presence, his absence. Wanting him gone, missing him so much, I imagined him as a kind of deity, all power in his hands, confused him with God because he bore God's names, because God was up in the sky, far away, invisible, and didn't the women, my mother and her sisters, love him?

One evening, during one of those rare dinnertimes my father wasn't working and the family could sit down together for a meal, my mother told some tale on me and my father laughed and called me a knucklehead or one of his other words for little-black-sambo dumbness. I was feeling feisty, reading lots of Edgar Rice Burroughs's Tarzan books, picking up a vocabulary of hunting, tracking terms, lore about jungle flora and fauna, a casebook of examples illustrating how the superior intelligence, courage, and civilization of a lone white man enabled and entitled him to achieve dominion over all God's creatures, including the savage, ignorant, black natives he found himself stranded among in Africa, natives beneath my contempt as I turned pages and swung with Tarzan through the treetops. So I didn't appreciate that knucklehead-sambo shit and snapped back at my father.

Well, you're a spoor.

What did you call me?

Spoor.

Pow. He smacked me across my face. My father's hands boxer quick. I never saw the blow coming. Heard it before I felt it. A red blur, one whole side of my face on fire. Burning from shame as much as pain. The crimson color inside my skin suddenly exploding outside, turning the world blood red as I squinted through hot mist. My cheek stung but the smack hadn't been intended to hurt as much as humiliate. The loud, openhanded, sudden impact of a cherry bomb booming in the middle of this quiet family dinner of meatloaf, peas, mashed potatoes, and gravy. I was the eldest. The younger kids seldom saw me punished. If they ever did and I caught them looking, they knew they'd catch double or quadruple what I'd caught. But here we sat around the kitchen table and our father had smacked me in the face and no way I could perpetrate on them the shock of what they'd witnessed happening to me.

With everyone's eyes and ears focused on me I couldn't cry. If he'd knocked me down or out, it would have been better. Out cold on the floor I wouldn't be burdened with inventing a response and everybody would have taken my side. The younger kids would be bawling, my mother rushing to rescue me. Oh my God. Have you gone insane? Are you hurt, baby?

I'm sure I raised my hand to my blazing cheek, probably both hands up to hide my face, give myself time to compose a mask. *Why, why, why* ringing in my ears.

The outraged innocence and indignation of those whys disintegrated as quickly as the ringing from the blow. Behind the screen I instantly began to plot my revenge. There couldn't be a reason why. My father was bigger, stronger, and bullies don't need reasons for bullying. *Spoor.* He probably doesn't know what the word means. He's mad cause he doesn't know cause spoor is worse than knucklehead cause I'm smarter already and he knows it. I beat him and that's why. I scored on him and all a bully can do is retaliate like a bully, reach across the dinner table and *pow*, knock me upside the head.

Who do you think you're talking to, boy?

I hoarded the glare that was a perfect answer to his question behind my hands. When I raised my head, the expression on my face told everybody I was a stranger just passing through the neighborhood and didn't have a clue about what might be transpiring in this obscure kitchen. Dry-eyed I stared blankly at a spot midway between the ceiling and the top of the head of the tallest person sitting at the table.

Look at me when I speak to you.

You shouldn't hit him like that, Edgar.

You heard his smart mouth. You heard what he called me.

What did you call your father?

Spoor.

Spoor. Where'd you hear a word like that? What kind of word is that?

It's the trail they follow when they hunt some elephant or something.

The pee and poop, and I better not hear it in your mouth again or next time I'll give you more than a love tap. Now finish your dinner.

Nothing but the sound of chewing, of forks cutting meatloaf, the quietest dinnertime in America that evening, none of us kids even breathing till we heard the signal to leave the table. My visceral anger, my sense of being publicly humiliated, the sting of the blow reminding me to "honor thy father" were easily forgiven, if not so easily forgotten. My father seldom hit me once I'd outgrown short pants, and I wasn't stupid enough to challenge him once I'd started wearing long pants, so the few times I did get popped are checkpoints that help me reconstruct the hazy outline of adolescence.

Less easy to forgive is what my father did with my word gleaned from the Tarzan books. How he changed its meaning, used it against me. I hadn't intended to call him a piece of shit or a piss puddle. Hadn't even considered *spoor* as a thing. Spoor to me meant something vaporous, like a cooking odor or the cloud a woman wearing too much perfume leaves behind in a room. Airy like that. An unpleasant smell, armpit, toejam, funky, yes, but nothing as concrete as an actual turd in the bushes you could step on, smear all over your jungle boots. Calling my father a stinky smell was about equal plus a little bit extra to him calling me a knucklehead or whatever comic-strip word he'd used to characterize the dumb thing I'd done in my mother's tale. His translation of *spoor* removed play from the word, put it in a context I hadn't intended, put other words in my mouth, nasty words he felt obligated to punish me for saying and dare me to repeat. What bothered me not a little was the suspicion he might be correct. The incident might have revealed he knew something about spoor I didn't. And what you didn't know, could hurt you. And what you thought you did know, could hurt you too. The trickiness of words, the ownership of words was tied up with this confusion and menace. Part and parcel, root and branch.

Whether or not such a textbook-clear lesson registered for me that night at the dinner table is questionable. Stories are onions. You peel one skin and another grins up at you. And peeling onions can make grown men cry. Which raises other questions. Why does one transparent skin on top of another transparent skin, layer after layer you can see through if each is held up to the light, why are they opaque when bound one on top of the other to form an onion or story? Like a sentence with seven clear, simple words and you understand each word but the meaning of the sentence totally eludes you. You might suggest there is no light source at the core of the onion, nothing similar to a lamp that can be switched on so you can see from outside in. Or you might say an onion is the light and the truth, or at least as much truth and light as you're ever going to receive on this earth, source and finished product all rounded into one and that's the beauty of solid objects you can hold in your hand. Peeling away layers turns them into something less, something other, always. Each skin, each layer a different story, connected to the particular, actual onion you once held whole in your hand as the onion is connected to stars, dinosaurs, bicycles, a loon's cry, to the seed it sprouted from, the earth where the seed rotted and died and slept until it began dreaming of being an onion again,

dreamed the steps it would have to climb, the skins it would have to shed and grow to let its light shine again in the world.

Patrice Gaines

EXCERPT FROM

Laughing in the Dark

My father came home to live with us, but he was a stranger to me. By the time he returned from the Marines and moved in, I had found my own man to fill the wound in me that longed for affection and love from a male person. All children who miss their fathers find a replacement. Some lavish their affection and adoration on uncles and grandfathers, or on the good friends of their mothers. If this affection is returned in a healthy way, it nourishes the child's self-worth and neutralizes the effect of the absent father. But this doesn't work all the time—and not for all children.

Fathers are just as important to girls as to boys. As an adult, I have seen young Black boys who miss their fathers turn angry at the world, their rage festering into violence against women, whites, and even their own Black brothers and sisters. As a reporter, I have seen young men turn a drug dealer into a father, a drug crew into a family. At the same time, I have seen girls who miss their fathers try loving their way into a man's heart. These young women are usually considered promiscuous, but I recognize them for what they are: lonely and fatherless.

Some fathers, like mine, are absent even when they are physically present. By the time my father came home to live with us, his time unbroken by assignments abroad, I was a stranger to him. He didn't like the way I walked or talked, the way I had grown into womanish ways while he was away. He didn't know it was all a fake, that I was really a little girl in a big girl's body, that what I wanted and needed most was a father to call me "princess" or to treat me like a queen. My deepest self knew that before I went out into the world and found a man to love I needed to be loved by the first man in my life. I needed a rich and basic love by which to judge the love of all other men.

Maybe I made it difficult for my father, too, because he could probably tell I didn't like him. He still barked orders in Marine Corps lingo,
expecting us to rise before the sun to start our chores. "Get up and swab
the deck!" he'd say, meaning "scrub the basement floor." When his children answered him, it was always with a "Yes, sir" or "No, sir." Stiff, formal words that wedged between us, pushing us further apart.

He went to work immediately, finding a job cleaning government office buildings at night. Within a year, he was working as a grave digger
at Arlington National Cemetery. In a way his coming home was worse
than his being away. When he was home, I could see and feel what he
didn't do. No kisses. No hugs. No "I love you." My mother, who is very
affectionate, taught us to always say good night to each other, to kiss
good-bye, to never go to sleep angry. This had been ingrained in me already before Daddy came home, so I kissed and hugged him and hoped
he would do the same.

I wanted to hear my father say, "I love you." And he never did, not to
me, not once in his life.

Mary Helen Washington

Neither Forgiving nor Distant

My father died in 1965 from a series of tiny strokes that happened over three years from 1962 to 1965. In those years, I graduated from college, began teaching eleventh and twelfth grade English at Glenville High School in Cleveland, took my first real trip—to New York City—began reading about Black Power, let my hair go natural and finally got the courage to leave home. He was dying just as I began to grow up. Preoccupied with my own dreams and desperate to experience such signs of adulthood as my own car, my own apartment, my first job, my first charge account, the facts of his dying were barely a footnote in my life.

Most of what I know about his dying I learned from phone calls from my mother since I was then in Detroit working on a master's degree in American literature at the University of Detroit. Each stroke would paralyze another part of his body and his mind until he grew quite senile, lost control of his bodily functions, and grew more and more like a lost child, calling my mother "Mama," wandering around the house, dragging one leg and trying to find the Lucky Strikes that he was no longer allowed to smoke. On the phone my mother told me about his last trip to the hospital. He didn't want her to leave him. After all the years of bullying her, he was now clinging to her, begging her to stay with him, a pathetic little figure, searching for cigarette butts in ash trays, staring at walls, dribbling food down his chin.

It was a shock to hear that my father no longer existed, and I was surprised to feel—not exactly sorrow—I was surprised to feel anything, but I felt sorry that he had died. One father is all you get, no matter how he turns out. When I try to imagine him now, I always see him in the same scene, walking from the garage down the driveway, home from work in his Cleveland Trust Bank uniform, a chauffeur-like black suit with crisp starched white shirt, black tie, black airplane-pilot cap, looking like a police sergeant. I realize only now that he looked African—dark, polished skin, large, rather kingly features, ramrod straight, stiff-legged walk, somber. He speaks to no one but walks around to the front door, surveying his property, looking for the least thing out of place. I remember one afternoon when he came home early and confronted my mother with a crushed flower, demanding to know which of the eight of us or of the twenty or thirty neighborhood children had stepped on his plants. He was so menacing a figure that all of the neighborhood children, as well as his own, scattered and hid as soon as we spotted his black Ford Fairlane turning onto Grantwood Avenue. His name was David, and he wore a hearing aid that buzzed, so the kids on the street named him "Shortwave Dave," a cute nickname, but still, they, like us, were terrified of him. This is my first attempt to write about him, to weigh and measure the facts. It's not easy to write about a parent you once hated and feared. Now after thirty years, I don't know what I feel.

He was born in Forsythe, Georgia (near Macon) in 1899, the second youngest of nine children (Frank, Carrie, Ella, George, Harry, Dolly, Lizzie, David and Lenora) born to Carrie and Green Washington. He ran away from home when he was about sixteen and went to Cleveland, like most migrants, following his sisters and brothers who had settled there looking for work and relief from the hardscrabble existence of sharecroppers and farmers. I know almost nothing about his life between 1899 and 1939, when he and my mother married, except what she told me, though, in the process of writing this memoir, I have found out more than I wanted to know. The stories he told my mother when they were courting were of violent beatings and hard times. I know that he did well in school but finished only the eighth grade. As far as I know, after he left home, he never saw his parents again. I never heard him say anything about them—no grandparents stories, no "when I was a boy" tales, no recipes from down home, no calls from Grandpa and Grandma on Christmas. Though he never wanted to return to the South, he never stopped dreaming of a house in the suburbs (his urbanized idea of how to re-create country life) where he would have land, flowers, grass, and privacy. My mother said she would never go to the country. She wanted neighbors, handy stores, her sisters and brothers, and protection from my father's moods. When I was in my thirties I came across a picture of

Carrie and Green for the first time and was surprised to see a soft-faced, reddish-colored woman who looked like an Indian, wavy hair in a bun on top of her head and a ruggedly handsome man, graying at the temples, with my father's exact face and build, arms hanging at his side, staring into the camera as if to kill it or whoever is in his way. It is not hard to imagine the belt or strap in his hands and the look of rage as he brings it down across my father's back.

When Richard Wright returns to Mississippi after twenty-five years and sees his father for the first time since he was eight, he sees—not the menacing figure that tortured his childhood—but a toothless old sharecropper, a burnt-out old man in ragged overalls, a stranger who looks like him. In his autobiography, *Black Boy*, he says he understands that his father was simply "a black peasant whose life had been hopelessly snarled in the city," and who in turn had deserted his wife and children. But Wright's forgiveness is undercut by the crude portrait he paints of his father in his autobiography as a primitive old man, "chained to the animalistic impulses of his withering body," a man who could never understand the educated writer son. I suppose my status as a university professor would allow me the same distance from my father with his eighth-grade education and country ways, but I cannot dismiss him as an unlearned man who lost his way in the city. I feel neither forgiving nor distant. Nor do I have the sense of compassion James Baldwin expresses for his father in his memoir, *Notes of a Native Son*, in which Baldwin struggles to recall memories of a once-loving and proud father. In his preacherly voice Baldwin speaks to all of the mourners at his father's funeral warning them—and us—not to judge a man whose burdens may have been impossible ones. Baldwin's response to his father is so balanced and restrained as he weighs his father's cruelty against the violations his father endured that it makes me feel petty and mean by comparison, for I feel none of this compassion for my father—even after thirty years. He was smart enough to figure out a lot of things. In 1939 he bought our house on Grantwood Avenue for $4,800, and when he met my mother at the Cleveland Trust Bank where they both worked, he proposed to her in six months, knowing that this lovely, clean-living, talcum-powdered, smiling, thirty-five-year-old-almost-spinster woman would cherish his two daughters and build him a home. He organized his entire adult life around his needs. He treated the six

children from his second marriage like stepchildren, as though we were
an evil visited upon him. I have no recollection of his ever touching me
or even speaking kindly to me. I find it almost impossible to think of being fair to him as I write this. I want justice. I want the record set
straight. I feel like Lucille Clifton as she shouts at her father in her
poem, "today is payday, payday old man." I want to disturb my father in
his grave and make sure he has not one peaceful moment until he
hears me.

But what's on the other side of anger? What would it cost me to try
to understand what turned him into such a cruel and hateful man? I suppose I could rely on the facts, but the facts I have about my father's life
before 1939 are embarrassingly meager, as though he were a boarder in
our house. I know that he and his first wife, Ernestine Robinson, were
married in 1925 when he was twenty-nine and she, sixteen. For thirteen
years they had no children, so, according to Ernestine's sister, Ann, they
put all of their energies into making a beautiful home. Ann, now
seventy-five, tells me tactfully and reluctantly over the phone that Ernestine was not happy in the marriage. I ask if he treated her badly, and
again the answer is evasive, "Well, she was much younger and very sub-
missive to him. He was kind of stingy and close with his money. Once
she took his Halle's charge and bought a coat she had wanted. He raised
a lot of hell, but she had worn it by then. My sister had the best of everything, a beautiful home on 130th with everything in it. She didn't want
for anything, but, as far as a lot of affection [this said slowly and regret-
fully], she did not have that." Everything Ann tells me sounds vaguely
familiar as though my father's first marriage was a trial run, getting
ready for the championship bout with my mother.

I discover through my conversations with Ann that Ernestine and
David, still childless after many years of marriage, took a four-month-
old foster child named Nancy to whom they became very attached.
When she was five or six, the county took her back and placed her with
her family. They were devastated, especially Ernestine. Is this one of the
many injuries that turned my father into himself? Then in her late
twenties Ernestine developed breast cancer and had a mastectomy,
which in those days meant radical surgery, leaving her with a horrible
scar that she was bitter and secretive about. Apparently none of her doctors warned her that a pregnancy might activate the cancer. A year after

the surgery she was pregnant with her first child, Beverly, born in July of 1935. My father was awestruck by his first daughter. He told my mother that when he looked at Beverly for the first time, his whole life changed. For the rest of his life he was as devoted to Beverly as he was hateful to the rest of us. A year later Myrna was born and, with another pregnancy, the cancer spread throughout Ernestine's body. She died on November 6, 1938, when her two girls were three and two years old. At her funeral her grandmother was inconsolable and angry: "Dr. Baumgartener knew she had cancer. He could have stopped her from having children." Women asked fewer questions and made fewer demands in 1938.

I suppose it looked as if my father's life was shipwrecked. A forty-year-old widower exhausted from the years of dealing with his young wife's illness, beloved wife in an early grave, two young daughters to care for. His hearing problem growing worse under all the stress. Was it Providence that sent my mother? What seems more likely is that my father set out to put his life back on course, and there was my mother working at the same bank, working, in fact, in the Bank's cafeteria making eleven dollars a week, serving meals to bank officials and terrified that she was going to end up an old maid. She wanted a future and there was none in the dead-end bank job, or in the claustrophobic cottage where she lived with her widowed mother; none in the long solitary walks on Sunday afternoon, nor in the occasional trip when she was invited by friends—as the spinster lady—to help with the children. In the letter she wrote in 1939 to her best friend, Evelyn, announcing her upcoming wedding, she is beside herself with excitement, but I read all the signs of misgivings and doubts. She's heard the rumors that my father mistreated his first wife. Her family's approval is guarded. My mother's hesitancy is written all over this letter. "Perhaps," she writes, "we are in love with each other. . . . I know the Dear Lord is tired of me worrying him about my affairs."

In June of 1994 I send away for Ernestine's death certificate and see for the first time that there are only ten months between her death and my father's second marriage. Can you meet, court, fall in love, plan a wedding, and mourn your first wife in ten months? I discovered in the process of writing this memoir that my father did not tell my mother he was married when they started courting. Ann tells me after many phone calls that my mother found out about my father's first marriage on the day of Ernestine's funeral when a neighbor let the cat out of the bag. By then she and my father had been seeing each other for several months, their courtship taking place as Ernestine was dying. After such a deception, how could my mother have been persuaded to marry him? What did he tell her? That since his wife was dying, he might as well get on with his life? She must have been devastated by this breach of faith. He must have had a good story. Was she in too deep to back out? Did she tell herself he lied so that he wouldn't lose her? Was she that desperate to marry? I don't suppose I can rail too much at the process by which I came into the world, but it does seem abundantly clear to me that in a world where "powerful and creative acts were hard for women to come by," my mother struck the only bargain she could: herself in exchange for a future. For my father, this picture was perfect. He had a wife; someone to take care of him, *his* two daughters, and *his* house, someone to cook, clean, and wait on him, to do his bidding. Had he been kind, my mother would have thought herself fortunate.

When they married in September, 1939, they were a family of four. If my father had expected another pliant younger wife—he was forty and my mother, thirty-five when they married, he had failed to reckon with my mother's staunch and steadfast Catholicism. While he dreamed dreams of a small family, a large bank account, and a suburban dream house, my mother—using the church-approved rhythm method of birth control—produced six children in seven years. Between Pearl Harbor and V-J Day, their family doubled—from four to eight. World War II was the perfect metaphor for the first years of their marriage except that there was no armistice. By the end of the war they were barely speaking. When the last child, Bernadette, was born in 1948 there were ten of us in the house on Grantwood. To punish her, he refused in many ways to acknowledge the children he didn't want. Birthdays, First Communions, graduations—he ignored. I felt as though every celebration in my life was an affront to him, and I tried to make myself as inconspicuous as possible on those days so as not to anger him. By the time I was ten, he was distant, hateful, unknowable, and unpredictable—a man who felt that the existence of most of his children had permanently shortchanged his life. Imagine this: on the third Sunday in May of 1948 I made my First Communion at St. Thomas Aquinas Church. All week-

end I have been at Aunt Bessie's being transformed. Hair in Shirley
Temple Curls, fitted for the white silk dress made by my godmother, the
whole family, minus my father of course, watch me walk to the altar.
Later there is a huge family dinner at Aunt Bessie's. That night as my
uncle drives us home we get more and more uneasy as we approach the
house. My mother has Bernadette, age two months, in her arms. Beverly
has Betty Ann, age two, by the hand. The three boys, David, six, Byron,
four, Tommy, three, are together. Myrna is safe—she's from the first
marriage. I am afraid to go in, to pass him. In my white dress and veil, I
feel like a target. He looks at us without speaking, a silence that is fright-
ening and menacing. I go into my bedroom and pray that nothing happens. Nothing does—that time.

As I look back at the choice they made to marry, it is easy for me to
see what they could not have seen. After all, I am in possession of the
facts—or rather I should say I have the luxury of being able to reconstruct the facts, to look at the cards they were dealt, knowing the out-
come or, more accurately, deciding the meanings for myself. My mother
and father could not have been more different. My mother, a lifelong
Catholic (a cradle Catholic, as she liked to call herself), the baby in a
family of nine, born when her parents were in their forties, was, in a
word, cherished. The last act of her mother's life, as she lay dying, was
to pick up her youngest daughter's hand and kiss it. She was the apple of
her father's eye. Her brothers and sisters from her mother's first marriage were old enough to be out working and to send presents home for
their baby sister. She seems to have spent a good part of her early childhood opening gift boxes and getting her hair curled. "I could have been
a fool," she told me, laughing. But her father's illness ended all that. She
left school at sixteen and went to work with my grandmother cleaning
Union Station in Indianapolis at night. Nonetheless, my mother's family was genteel poor, and in this marriage she was clearly the classy one. I
have never considered this before, but he must have been dazzled by her.
After all *she* had gone to high school. *She* had studied classical piano under Miss Lily Lamond in Indianapolis and at the music settlement in
Cleveland. *She* had traveled to New York and Chicago and Rochester,
using her father's railroad pass. She looked like a white woman. Everyone I ever met who knew my mother as a young woman spoke of her in
soft hushed tones as though her shy beauty and softness and gentleness

had touched them deeply. In black Catholic circles in Cleveland she was known as the innocent and lovely Mary Catherine—a rose, they called her. She was also a staunch, uncompromising Catholic. Somehow, between the time of their engagement and their marriage, my mother engineered a triple baptism—both my father and his two daughters were Catholic by the time they married. It is clear to me now that, in 1939, my mother had the upper hand—though not for long.

It would not have been easy for my father to be a part of my mother's family. No matter how nice they were to him, they thought my mother had married beneath her. Descended from white grandfathers on both their mother and father's side, my mother and her sisters and brothers were strongly in favor of keeping light skin and straight hair in the family. They watched closely after each baby was born to see if skin or hair would revert, which of us would get my mother's skin and hair and which (unfortunately, in their view) would take after my father. I am sure they thought he could contribute nothing of worth to their family gene pool. I got to know my father's family only after he died. Ella, George, Frank, and Dolly lived together on 99th Street with Aunt Ella's son, his wife and three children and Ella's two foster sons. They were southern country folk who went to church for hours on Sunday, came home to a big Sunday supper of fried chicken and deep-dish peach cobbler, then slept for the rest of the afternoon. My mother was as northern and citified as they were southern and country. She served Sunday dinner in the dining room on the best dishes: roast lamb, scalloped potatoes, French green beans, and lemon meringue pie. She never napped during the day. She liked to be "up and doing," as she put it. There was no deliberate haughtiness in this, just that she and her sisters had worked for years "in private family" and had seen up close how the wealthy lived. Her sister Cora from Indianapolis ordered two huge Oriental rugs for my parent's wedding present, and while my mother and father were on their Detroit honeymoon, my mother's five sisters—Bessie, Cora, Sarah, Elsie, and Helen—almost completely furnished the house on Grantwood: Oriental rugs downstairs, starched curtains, floors polished, all their wedding gifts put away neatly in drawers and cabinets lined with good paper. The newlyweds walked into a picture-perfect house, and my father was angry at what he saw as her meddling relatives. I want to recreate this scene of their return, but I have only the one statement my mother made: "The house looked so pretty, but Dave felt that we should have done the work ourselves. It was our business." Years later my mother found out that Aunt Cora had come upon those Oriental rugs through the black market operated through her husband's liquor joint on Indiana Avenue and, had they not been threadbare from years of wear, she would have packed them up and sent them back, I'm sure. My father probably sniffed out these signs of the feebleness of my mother's class superiority, he may have had some idea of the wild and reckless years in my aunts' backgrounds, which made them, in his weird way of estimating things, more on his level, but my mother was no dissembler; she was just what she seemed to be—an aristocrat—a woman who lived by her principles, could set a table properly, never swore. She was like one of the early Christian martyrs—unassailable, good, honorable. A David against Goliath. All eight of us, "her" children, were always on her side. Against Him.

Still, as I try to put together the fragments of memories of my childhood, I can remember—faintly—the times he seemed almost like a normal father. "He's in a good mood," we tell Ma, as soon as we notice the slightest change in his behavior. Then he might walk down to the end of the street to the playground with us and read the paper while we swung and slid and jumped. Other nights, he might let us take off our shoes and run under the hose as he sprinkled. At these times he might call us "Duv," a strange nickname that meant he was feeling mellow and easygoing. Occasionally, he'd load us up in the car and drive out to the country (now the suburbs) to get some awful tasting water he called spring water that only he would drink. A drive to the country with Daddy. It sounds like an image from Dick and Jane, though we'd all try to get in the back seat because no one wanted to be up front with Him. For me this was the definition of a normal homelife: my father driving us somewhere, the kids in the back seat and my mother riding beside him in the front. At most, it happened two or three times. Even at these times, however, we were tentative and on guard against his moods. One time we came back from such an outing and on the way into the tight garage he scraped the side of his new Ford. We hear the scrape. Immediately we fall silent. He's not a man to laugh things off or take them lightly. The mood heats up. Before we can slink off out of his way, he explodes, "Now you see what you've done." The mood will linger for the rest of the week, and we will all live with the threat of his wrath. Maybe this is the week he'll pick a fight with my mother, maybe this is the week he hit her, leaving a black and blue bruise on her upper arm. Maybe one of us gets punished for no reason. The only peace is when he's asleep, and, fortunately, he sleeps a lot. Saturdays and Sundays were the worst days because he was home all day. When I went to kindergarten in 1946 I knew I would love it because it was a place I could be safe from him. To avoid saying the truth about him, my aunts said to us, "You have to pray for your father." I prayed for him to die.

He was a man who lived by ritual and routine, as predictable as the seasons. Up at six and out the door for work by seven. In the thirty some years he worked at the bank he was never late and never absent. Three meals a day and one nighttime snack, a bowl of cold cereal. He never gained or lost a pound, still in his sixties a trim 160 pounds at five feet, nine inches. He smoked on schedule—never in the morning; always after dinner, never in bed, a pack of Luckies a day. Every night before bed he got down on his knees, folded his hands, and said his nightly prayers. And every other Saturday morning he waited for my mother to come into his bedroom and ask for the food money—forty dollars every other week. Each Saturday morning he initiated a complicated and diabolical ritual making her ask for the money, he refusing until she had been sufficiently punished, then reluctantly parting with what he considered rightfully his since he worked for it: "What did you do with the money I gave you last week? Can't you ever stop begging? I don't know if I should give you any. What do you want it for?" We'd be in our bedrooms, trying not to hear, cringing in fear that there would be some kind of blowup and he'd hurt my mother, or, as he sometimes did, refuse to give her any money that Saturday. Forty dollars. Ten people to feed. Forty-two meals. When he died he had saved ten thousand dollars which he willed to my two oldest sisters. He left my mother and the six of us nothing. Perhaps because his deafness had already so completely enclosed him, isolating him from normal contact, he chose to shut himself up in his own world, hearing aid turned off, responding only to the simplest physical pleasures and his own needs: a two-hour bath on Saturday night (pity, if you had a date); bit Sunday dinners (cooking and cleaning done by others); his first new car—a 1956 black Ford Fairlane (which my mother was not allowed to ride in); a double-header on Sunday afternoon turned up as loud as possible (no matter what anyone else wanted to hear or watch).

A careful reader might observe how neatly I've enclosed in parentheses that phrase, "(which my mother was not allowed to ride in)." I see myself carefully tucking that fact away, normalizing—almost—my father's craziest behavior. How can I explain that my mother did the grocery shopping for our family on the bus, that she got eight children ready for church on Sunday by herself and rode with us on the bus while he drove alone in a new car to his church, passing us on his way to worship God? Why should anyone be shocked by this? My father was not that different from other fathers of the 1940s and 1950s. Some drank. Some beat their wives and/or their children. Some had other women. Some were simply moody and distant and unknowable. I was always surprised when one of my friends turned out not to be afraid of her father. Marriage in those years (and now) was designed to accommodate crazy and mean fathers, and every family I knew screened off enough of their family life to hide their craziness. Even now in 1966, I see women (I include myself) accommodating, making room for men's crazy behavior, for their moods, their silences, their rages. Last year I spent the weekend visiting a friend, a white woman raised in North Dakota, and when her husband went into one of his silent moods over some trivial inconvenience, we looked at each other knowingly and together did the female dance of pretending everything was normal. In 1996.

People had glimpses of my father's meanness, but no one outside of our family really knew what took place behind our screen. It was secret and shameful, like wetting the bed. No one told. Twice my mother took my father to court. I was old enough to remember the second time because I heard the results. The judge told my father to give my mother sixty dollars instead of forty and threatened to garnishee his wages if he kept the food money again. A small victory. For a while there was relative calm and my father seemed cowed by these larger institutional forces. Calm for us meant the period before another eruption. The last time he tried to hit her, my brother David, who was about thirteen, jumped in between them and threatened to fight him. There was a long silence, all of us tensed for what might happen. He glared and said something like, "You better get out of my face, boy," but he backed down and walked away. A tyrant *and* a coward.

My father died in the spring of 1965. He was sixty-six years old. I came home from Detroit for the funeral which scandalized our neighbors and friends. They said it was like a party, that they'd never seen such a dry-eyed funeral. I felt like Janie in *Their Eyes Were Watching God* who loved the freedom she felt after her husband died: "mourning oughtn't tuh last no longer'n grief." Who could possibly have grieved over such a father? And why this desire and need to cover over the truth? Even now friends wonder why I am willing to write these things about my father, why I don't forgive him. And I wonder why this coercion into silence. Another locked-up story. These things happened to me, to my brothers and sisters, to my mother. I want them in the record.

When I returned home after graduate school four months after my father's death, there was a lightness in the house on Grantwood as though someone had put a giant suction machine over the house and sucked out the evil. We spent a few days packing up my father's clothes and taking them to the Goodwill. We put his old wooden desk on the third floor, gave his guns to my brothers, and my mother moved into his spacious bedroom. My sisters and brothers and I (with a new job teaching downtown at St. John College) spent several weeks orchestrating a scheme to remodel the bedroom and surprise my mother. I bought a new bedroom set at Sterling Lindner Davis—a kind of blonde French Provincial. We arranged to have it delivered on Friday while my mother was at work. As soon as she left that morning we started into overdrive. We redid the floors, put down new carpeting, painted the walls robin's egg blue, bought and hung white organdy curtains, put on a new white chenille bedspread with matching pillow shams. The room was transformed. When my mother came in that night we waited downstairs for her reaction. She was so shocked that, with eyes wide with wonder, all she could say was, "It looks different." I had directed all this remodeling with deliberate intent. I wanted to erase him, and, in three or four months, it did seem as though he had never existed, no trace of him anywhere, except that, as I was to discover over and over in my futile attempts to evict him—in the jokes about "Shortwave Dave," the discarded photographs, the many afternoons in Dr. Carlson's office at Lafayette Clinic—he is a permanent fixture in the house I've made for myself in my head.

"Nothing," Baldwin preaches in the essay on his father, "is ever escaped." But I didn't want to end with that image of chains and confinement. Of the eight children David Washington fathered, not one of us is abusive or cruel or violent. One beautiful Sunday last summer when I was in Cleveland, we all gathered at Our Lady of Fatima/St. Agnes for mass, and as I saw us all in various pews, looking to hug one another at the Kiss of Peace, taking pictures after mass, making plans for brunch together with Sister Mary Frances, I thought how much we are like my mother. She lived twenty-five more years after his death, and in the final analysis, her goodness and love were more powerful than his destructiveness. I look at the calendar above my desk. For some unknown reason I've chosen today to revise and complete this essay. Today is December 2nd, my father's birthday. Payday. I will never have to write about him again. This is for the record.

Itabari Njeri

EXCERPT FROM

Every Good-bye Ain't Gone

I must have desperately wanted somebody to know how miserable I was living with my father. But since she had chosen to live with him, I saw no point in telling my mother. Bush-league pyromania having failed, I got ill—all the time. But since I was a sickly kid, no one saw that as a cry for help, either. Rheumatic fever, for instance, is a real, clinical disease. I went into the hospital for a tonsillectomy when I was nine and came out unable to walk. My father never visited me in the hospital. When I came home, I was on crutches.

"Go in the kitchen and get me the hot sauce," he told me the night I returned. I picked up my crutches and hobbled to the kitchen to get it. A few minutes later, he told me to get up and get him a glass of water. I started to get up again. My mother, clenching her jaw and wincing, said, "Sit there. I'll get it." Why she didn't tell the bastard to get up and get it himself instead of sitting there, boorishly chewing his food with eyes closed, as was his custom, was what I wanted to know. But I knew not to make waves. My mother would suffer for it if I did.

As I got older, I turned inward, escaping most afternoons to the co-coon of my blue room and music.

We had brought my piano from St. James Place. But my father had one, too. A beaten, black upright, in the parlor, badly out of tune. But its bench held a treasure of ancient sheet music: Vincent Youmans's "Through the Years" with a picture of Gladys Swarthout on the frayed cover. How I loved the chord changes to "Spring Is Here." And thanks to my father's musical cache, I was the rare eight-year-old who knew the opening verse of "My Funny Valentine": *"Behold the way my fine-feathered friend, his virtue doth parade. Thou knowest not my dim-witted friend, the picture thou hast made . . ."*

I had decided long ago to become a singer and had made a deal with my mother: I'd take boring piano lessons as long as she'd allow me to take singing lessons when I was old enough. But as I got older, music became less a destined vocation and more an obsession. And in a home where Mommy was a lapsed Catholic and Daddy an atheist, it became God.

But no one close to music is ever far from God. Daddy sat one day in an unaccustomed spot: on the couch, hypnotized by the image and sound emanating from the TV. He still wore only his boxer shorts. I peered around the French doors in his bedroom where I'd been dusting and watched his back as his bare shoulders suddenly heaved. I had to pass him in the parlor to reach the kitchen. As I did, I had to stop. His face was red and wet. Mahalia Jackson was singing "The Lord's Prayer." Oblivious to me, he got up, walked to his bedroom and pulled a clean white hanky out of his dresser drawer and blew his nose. He blew it hard so it honked, and then lay back on his bed and looked at the ceiling.

I put away the dust rag, then walked back to my blue-walled room. There I began years of wondering why an atheist would weep when he heard Mahalia sing.

I ventured from the sanctuary of my blue room one afternoon, walked down the long hallway toward the kitchen, then stopped abruptly at a right angle, the place where the wall turned sharply toward the bathroom. I heard my father in the kitchen several feet away. He was making an ice cream soda, something as forbidden to him as alcohol since he was a diabetic. I heard the clink of the metal spoon against a glass as he sang, ". . . for I lately took a notion for to cross the briny ocean, and I'm off to Philadelphia in the morning." It was an Irish folk song made famous by John McCormack. I backed up. Too late. He danced across the kitchen threshold in his boxer shorts, stopped when he spotted me in the shadows, then shook his head. He smiled, lifted one leg and both arms in a Jackie Gleason "and away we go" motion, then slid off.

Minutes later he called me. "Jill the Pill, you know this song?" I knew all the songs and wrote down the words to "Moon River" for him. Then he asked me to sing it. I was always ready to sing, even for my father.

He sat on the edge of his bed with the lyrics in his hand as I sang. When I finished the final phrase—"We're after the same rainbow's end, *waitin' round the bend, my Huckleberry friend . . ."*—my daddy looked at me and said what others would tell me years later, but with far less poetry, "My girl, you have the celestial vibration." And then he asked me to sing it again . . . told me it was "wonderful . . ." Then I left him.

For days, maybe weeks, a tense calm would reign in the apartment. Then without warning the hall was filled with harsh voices; he stood in the narrow, shadowy space hitting my mother. "Put it down," he yelled. "Put it down or I'll . . ."

My mother had picked up a lamp in a lame effort to ward off his blows. His shouting had awakened me. I'd been sick in bed with the flu and a high fever. When he saw me open my bedroom door he yelled, "Get back in your room." I did, my body overtaken by tremors and the image of my mother branded on my eyeballs. I swore that I would never let anyone do that to me or anyone else I had the power to help. I had no power to help my mother. And it was an oath with terrible consequences, one I'd have to struggle twenty years to disavow, so that I could permit myself the vulnerability of being human.

I know my father's fury was fueled by his sense of insignificance. He felt himself to be an intellectual giant boxed in by mental midgets. He could be found, Ralph Ellison once told me, pontificating in Harlem barbershops, elucidating the dialogues of Plato to a captive audience of draped men, held prone, a straight-edge razor pressed against their cheeks.

Unlike Ellison, Paul Robeson, or Richard Wright, all acquaintances and contemporaries of my father, he was never acknowledged by the dominant culture whose cachet he sought. Whether he deserved it or not, only a few are ever anointed in an era.

His unreconciled identities—the classic schizophrenia of being Black and an American, of which Du Bois wrote, the contradictions of internalizing whole the cultural values of a society that sees you, when it sees you at all, as life in one of its lower forms—stoked his alcoholism.

I know why my father, the Marxist, cried when he heard Mahalia. His rational mind would not accept God, but the spirit of Goodness— for what else is the notion of God?—in her voice could not be denied. Her sound, its cultural resonance, was a reminder of the traditions, the myths that have sustained Black people, but from which he was culturally alienated.

And since my father at once critiqued the society that denied him and longed for its approbation, he lived with the pain-filled consciousness of one who knows he is a joke. I think, sometimes, he laughed hardest, so often did I stumble upon him alone, chuckling into his balled fist at some silent, invisible comedian.

When his drunken rages ended, he slept for days, spread out on the bed wearing only his boxer shorts. I watched him on these days, too, daring to come closer, safe in the knowledge Morpheus held him. I examined his face, wondering who he was and why he was. As I watched, he'd lift his head off the pillow, then fall back muttering: "Truth and justice will prevail."

Theodore Jennings

Estranged

"Stay with God, Son. Stay with God," my father said . . .

The rule in my father's house was early-to-bed on Saturday so that we could be wide awake for Sunday morning worship. Tommy and I had been away for more than two hours, it was getting close to eight o'clock, and I asked him to take me home. When the car pulled into the driveway, I knew something was wrong because the porch light wasn't on. Within seconds, my father stormed out of the house and charged in anger toward the car. I could see his hands. They were calloused. Powerful. With his right hand, he reached for the shiny handle on the gold Monte Carlo door and with his left for the back of my neck. He yanked me out of the car, yelled at Tommy, slammed the door, and dragged me into the house. My father, my daddy, my friend, a righteous God-fearing man, had never ever lifted a hand to me, but on that night he hit me.

"This isn't happening," I thought to myself. "This isn't my house. This isn't my father. This isn't happening." My father hit me again. He continued to hit me until the blood from my nose and my mouth covered his hand. With each blow, he preached the sermon I had heard many times. Homosexuals were the "worst" of sinners. Hadn't he taught me about "those people"? Hadn't he taught me that they were filled with an "evil" spirit and that they would burn in hell's fire? In my father's eyes, I was guilty by association. Tommy was gay.

I cannot describe the emptiness and the fear I experienced. If I were guilty by association, all hope of my salvation was gone. God didn't love gay people. I had looked at men in an erotic way, but did this mean I was gay? If it did, why wasn't it evident in my childhood and why did I enjoy being "with" the opposite sex? Why should I have to choose between God and my sexual feelings? Who created the feelings? Was my father correct in thinking that I was gay? I prayed to God to take the "sin" from me and, having been taught that God answers prayers, I believed "salvation" would be mine. It did not come.

I started questioning my faith, reading and re-reading the Bible, and growing outside the four walls of my fundamentalist church. At seventeen, I knew I had to tough it out by myself. I understood how other people felt when their beliefs differed from those of the church. They stood alone. When I came out, my grandmother told me she and my grandfather had sensed something special about me when I was seven years old. My parents, on the other hand, have still not accepted this special part of me. They love me because I am their son, but in their spiritual judgment, they believe I am damned to hell.

My father hit me because he was afraid. Afraid of the prospect of his oldest son being gay. Afraid that I might have a "broken" wrist. Afraid that I might speak with a lisp. Afraid that I might wear fishnet stockings. Afraid that I might die alone with AIDS. Afraid of other tragedies, or deserved punishments, meted out—by God—to gays, lesbians, bisexuals, and other "deviants."

I have forgiven my father for what he did to me. I love him too much not to do otherwise. He knows this. And he loves me too much to "kick me to the curb." We are trying to rebuild our relationship and end the estrangement. It is much too painful to live without him. We need each other. After all, I am his number-one son. He told me so himself.

Opal Palmer Adisa

Father, No Longer Daddy?

"Daddy! Daddy!" I would shout, running to my father.

He would catch me, raise me high up above his head, bring me close to his face for a kiss before setting me down on the ground.

"How is my little Mus-Mus?" he would ask, using his nickname for me. Then Daddy and I, holding hands, would enter the house together. That was the evening ritual when my daddy came home from work.

Daddy had a swagger in his gait and a smile so warm and dazzling it was contagious. I remember him walking without any shirt around the yard as he gardened. He loved growing things, and as he bent to the soil, pruning, planting, admiring his vegetables, perspiration laced the matted hair on his chest. An emerging potbelly hung over his shorts. I would follow at his heels, playing in the dirt with my stick shovel.

These are the memories of my father that live sweet inside me: images indelibly inscribed on the memory of a four-year-old girl.

If there were angry words or screams, I don't remember them. What I remember is the stone silence that I did not understand. I remember terror, the day my mother left us without a word. No one spoke of her absence; everyone acted as if she had never been there.

Then three months later my mother returned as silently as she had gone. She hurriedly packed clothes for my sister and me, issued urgent orders to load this or that piece of furniture onto the truck parked in our driveway. My sister and I were soon dressed, complete with ribbons in our hair. We got settled in the truck.

"Isn't Daddy coming?" I asked.

"No," was my mother's flat reply.

Daddy stood on the veranda of our house, his face a frightened mask. I waved to him; he did not wave back. My mother went to say something to him. She returned shortly, took her seat, and pulled me onto her lap. The truck pulled off. I waved to Daddy even after the truck had turned onto the main road. My arm soon felt weightless, so I draped it around my mother's neck. I was excited to be going on a trip and glad for my mother's return . . . but anxious. I noticed tears trickling down my mother's face.

"Why are you crying, Ma'am? You miss your husband?" the truck driver asked my mother.

"No, he slapped my face," my mother said, drying her tears.

The little four-and-a-half-year-old girl, who is me, remembers that day, when my mother, my sister, and I left my father.

"Daddy come to get us!" my sister shouted, jumping up and down.

"Ah can't let you take them without their mother's permission, sar," the maid said, standing her ground, going to the telephone to call my mother at work. My sister ran into Daddy's arms. I stood back, playing with my skirt. Daddy opened his arms and called me. I moved toward him. He ordered the maid to pack our clothes while he sat on the veranda, the two of us jumping in his lap. I heard the maid inside the house, making noises and mumbling to herself. Daddy gave us candy from his pocket and tickled us. My sister and I tickled Daddy.

Suddenly my mother rushed through the gate with a policeman. She ordered us to our room. We walked away, pausing at the living-room door.

"You will get them over my dead body!" My mother, forgetting us, said in no uncertain terms.

"They are my children too!" my father shouted.

Their voices were loud and clamorous like glasses breaking on tile. Frightened, my sister and I tearfully hugged each other. Finally I heard the policeman telling Daddy that he had to leave, that if he wished he could go to court. I heard the gate open and close. The policeman told my mother to call if she had any more trouble. My sister and I came back into the room. My mother's entire body trembled as she took us into her arms.

"Daddy please leave and not make a fuss," I prayed silently. Time had passed. I don't remember whether it was my sister's birthday or my own, but like always, my mother had thrown a big party with lots of children and grown-ups. Daddy had come late, his hands empty. Now everyone was gone, darkness was secured, crickets sang, and mosquitoes were frantic in their search for blood. Yet Daddy still sat on the veranda, having drunk too much, insisting, "You're still my wife." Mother alternately pleaded with him and ordered him to leave. "This is my house," she told him. "You don't pay rent here."

Daddy growled, "You can't make me leave."

For two weeks during the late summer, when the days were particularly long and hot, my sister and I used to spend time at Daddy's house with Miss May and her daughter. (I was grown before I learned that Miss May had been the cause of my parents' divorce and that I had another sister, Miss May's daughter, two years my junior.)

During those two weeks at Daddy's new home, being left pretty much to ourselves, my sister and I played outside most of the day. But when Daddy came home from work in the evenings, when food was on the table and we sat to eat, Daddy would scold us constantly about our table manners: Use your knife and fork. Get your elbows off the table. Don't touch that juice until your plate is clean. Daddy's voice, the relentless buzzing of a wasp.

On Saturday afternoons he took my sister and me for drives. And very early Sunday mornings, when the air was still cool, he took us swimming at Gunboat's Beach. The beach would be closed that early in the morning, but we would crawl through the barbed wire fence. Even before my sister and I went into the water our teeth chattered. We'd wrap ourselves in large towels and refuse to swim, but Daddy would grab us one at a time and take us on his back so far out into the sea that we could not see the shore. I would squeal, cling to his back and tightly squeeze his neck. That far out, the water was soothing and warm. Still, I longed for dry land and prayed I wouldn't slip from his back and sink into the ocean. Daddy was a marvel in the water, swift and slippery as an eel. The sun would be out by the time we went home; the gate would be open and people would be coming in droves for their ritual Sunday at the beach. Once I asked Daddy why we went so early, before anyone else got there. Smiling, he said, "The water is best when there is still a chill to it."

When my father's father died, he left behind a wife who was younger than my mother and a son five years younger than I. I was eight years old at the time. My mother, my sister, and I arrived late the night after he died. Relatives greeted, hugged, inspected, and passed us from hand to hand. My grandmother, Daddy's mother and Grandpa's first wife, took charge of us. She said even though she was still angry with Grandpa, he was dead and gone so she came to bury him; and with the rest of us, she stayed in what had once been her house. Grandma and Daddy took my sister and me into the room where my grandfather's body lay covered with ice. It was customary in some parts of rural Jamaica, and probably still is, to keep the dead at home until burial. I asked Daddy why Grandpa was covered with ice. Daddy replied, "To keep him from rotting."

My grandfather had been a big man in the little village. His house and adjacent shop, the only store in the village, were the only place other than the church that had electricity. For four days we waited for the arrival of relatives and friends from around the island and abroad. I saw little of Daddy during this time. But on the day Grandpa was to be buried, Daddy came and snatched us from the yard where we were playing with the many cousins we had recently discovered. And he ordered us to be quiet as he led us into the small, dimly lit room where Grandpa was being prepared for burial. It smelled like dirty damp clothes in a bin. My mother was already there with some men I did not know. Grandpa lay there, bloated and ashy. Daddy washed my face and hands in a basin of water on the table next to Grandpa; then he washed my sister's. He told us that Grandpa would protect us. Next, he lifted me up and passed me over our Grandpa's body, handed me to one of the men on the other side. As he did so he asked my grandpa to always protect and walk with me. He did the same with my sister. Mother took us from the room then, and we waited for what seemed like an eternity in the dark, still hallway. Daddy came at last and took us back into the room, where we could see that in our absence Grandpa's body had been dressed in a suit. And Daddy helped first me, then my sister, to put on one of Grandpa's socks. My sister and I held Daddy's hands as we walked the hundred yards to the church. When it was over, we stood in the churchyard and watched dirt fill in the hole with Grandpa's coffin.

The night we left I didn't get to kiss Daddy good-bye.

Daddy disappeared from my life when I was ten. No more telephone calls. No letters. No birthday cards. No presents. Nothing. Mother said she didn't know where he was, but that she'd heard he had moved to America. Grandma claimed she didn't know where he was, but Mother didn't believe her.

Seven years later my mother took us to New York to enter college. Grandma would only say that Daddy was somewhere in New York, but refused to give us his address or phone number. Daddy did not seek us out or contact us. Four years rolled by.

A few months before I graduated from college—I was then twenty—my sister and I received a letter from Daddy. It was a casual "dear daughters" letter, written as though there had been no break in our relationship. I was angry and dismissed the letter, but my sister could not contain her happiness. She had to call him, but I refused. My father invited us to visit him. Mother encouraged me to go with my sister. Reluctantly, I agreed. During the train ride I remember being unsure about how I would greet the man who was my father, but who had chosen to absent himself from my life for more than ten years, then reenter it without any explanation. The train stopped at the White Plains station. As we walked down the stairs, I saw Daddy standing near the entrance to the station, looking older and shorter than I remembered him, but he still had that infectious smile. I would have recognized him anywhere. I realized that part of myself had been locked away from me and that I had only just found the key to unlock it.

Four years later I moved to California. After putting an abrupt end to several fairly good relationships for reasons that I did not understand, I decided to seek therapy. During one session, I recalled that last visit with my father. When my sister and I emerged from the train station on that Sunday afternoon four years earlier, Daddy embraced and kissed us and called me by my pet-name, "Mus-Mus." Immediately, I was a little girl again, longing for my daddy. I said none of the things I had rehearsed in my head. I had no accusations for him, nor did I ask him to explain why he had left us without telling us, or whether he had missed us or ever thought about us. We all acted as if there had never been a separation, never a rupture. Yet I do remember feeling cheated when Daddy expressed pride in my sister and me for having finished college.

I thought, "Convenient of you to surface now, when we no longer need anything from you."

My therapist suggested that my penchant for ending relationships might have stemmed from an impulse to leave men before they abandoned me, as I believed my father had done.

A few months after my therapy began I wrote to my father, addressing him by his first name and asking all those questions I had wanted to ask four years before. He replied, but ignored all my questions, the whole substance of my correspondence, choosing instead to focus on the manner in which I had addressed him. He admonished me never again to address him by his first name, but to call him "Daddy," or he would refrain from communicating with me. This response sent me into a rage. Had he been standing close to me, I could have ripped his heart out. I swore at him and promised myself I would never write to him again.

In a few years I relented. I wrote again and again, but he never answered my questions. Shortly before my first child was conceived, I wrote yet again—one last letter—determined to work through my ambivalence about him. I tried to explain that when I called him "Daddy" I felt too much like the little girl he had abandoned, that I no longer felt I knew him. I tried to convey my intense desire to know him.

To this day, my father has not answered the questions concerning our father-daughter relationship—questions that matter to me. Having children of my own now has helped me to find a comfortable space for the old hurts and to make space for love and sharing. Life with a sensitive husband has helped me to grow beyond my fears and to stop torturing myself about the things I cannot change. But even more than all that, the wonderful open, adult relationship I enjoy with Vinnie, my husband's father, has contributed to the healing of the old wounds. Vinnie, who is my father's age, treats me as an adult. We talk and share private feelings. I have learned that I cannot seek answers and love in places where none are to be found any more than I can demand that my father act in a certain way.

Four years ago my husband, our two older children, and I went to White Plains to meet my father. Seeing him again after so many years made me realize that my father is an old man, still set in his ways. Five years ago he was diagnosed with glaucoma and has since lost the sight in one eye. I thought then, uncharitably, "Justice for your neglect, old man. Maybe now, like Oedipus, you will be able to see the errors of your ways." But my father is not a tragic hero. He remains obdurate. In many ways he is a stranger. I no longer seek his love. I have both fond and painful memories of him. I no longer look to him for the answers to my questions. I have forgiven him his absence in my life. I send him pictures of my children.

And since I no longer wish him dead, I send him birthday cards.

Noliwe Rooks

My Father's Whistle

When I was a little girl, my father would whistle for me. Just two short, quick notes, the last a little longer than the first and ever so slightly higher. That was our code. No matter where I was—at the park, the beach, school, or home—I knew that within seconds he would be by my side and that we would do some fun thing together. The whistle belonged to my innocence, to the time before I learned to distrust him, to the time before he and my mother divorced, to the time before I learned my father was an alcoholic.

As a young girl, I found him more interesting, attentive, and accessible when he was drinking. He would wake me on a "whim" before day to go fishing or take me horseback riding into trails that were all the more fascinating because I was exploring them with him. When he was drinking, he seemed to care about what I thought and asked my opinions on everything from the presidential election to the state of Clearwater's Black community to appropriate gifts for my grandmother's birthday. I lived so completely for those fun times that I "forgot" about being left for hours in a hot parking lot at a dog track while my father gambled away his money and our time together. "Forgot" the hours when he either passed out or was sullen, depressed, and uncommunicative. "Forgot" that more often than not I did not believe he was going to do anything he promised. The memories we think we have forgotten never really go away. They are always with us and in us, waiting to be remembered.

Memories of the impact of my father's drinking on my life came rushing back when my grandmother had a stroke and my father wanted to be solely responsible for her care. There was nothing in our history—in my memories—that would have prepared me for this desire, this insistence on responsibility. I had heard that my father was very involved in rearing me when I was a "knee baby," but that had been a long time before I had learned a list of "don'ts" and their consequences.

Don't wake him when he's sleeping. He wakes up swinging.

Don't ever tell him he's wrong. He'll disappear for days, weeks, months.

Don't tell him he's lost, 'cause you'll just end up driving around for hours and how long can a child keep her legs squeezed together before the dam breaks and, of course, peeing in his car was an unforgivable sin.

Don't show too much affection or tell him you love him 'cause you won't get nothing back from it, except the sound of your own expectations hanging in the air and maybe, if he acted like he heard you, a very puzzled look.

So what was I supposed to do with his desire to care for my grandmother? Half of the family thought I should threaten legal action to keep him away from her. The other half thought that maybe this was what he needed to "get himself together" once and for all. I decided to ask my grandmother what *she* wanted. We were in her hospital room, just the two of us. My grandmother responded with the certainty of a mother's love: "I need him and he needs you. We are family." My father moved into my grandmother's house the day she was released from the hospital, and it was he who had made everything ready for her. During the last six years of her life, he cooked most of her meals, changed the sheets on her bed, combed her hair, took her through her physical therapy exercises, changed his schedule to accommodate care of her, and loved her better and in more ways than I ever knew he possibly could. He was sober most of the time during those years and for the past three years has not had a drink of any kind. He tells me, with pride and with relief, that this is the first time since he was seventeen that he has been able to make such a claim.

After my grandmother's death, my father and I began spending quiet days together, during which he talked to me about his life. He put names with the faces we found together in mountains of photographs my grandmother had kept and gave me a history and a connection I never knew I needed. I talk about my father all the time now and for some reason I usually start with his whistle.

The last time I heard that whistle—two short, quick notes, the last a little longer than the first and ever so slightly higher—was on Thanksgiving of 1994, when my son Jelani and I flew to Florida to visit my father. When we got off the airplane and looked around, I didn't see my father. Then I heard his whistle. My heart started moving toward him before my legs remembered what was expected of them. Jelani was way ahead of me, up in the air, arms around my father's neck, a smile plastered on his five-year-old face. I walked over to them and said, "I thought you had forgotten about us." Before my father could answer, Jelani said, "But, Mommie, he didn't forget. He was right here. Didn't you hear him whistle?"

Houston A. Baker, Jr.

On the Distinction of "Jr."

I am eleven years old, giddy with the joy of fire and awed by the seeming invulnerability of my father. He is removing dead coals from the glowing bed of the furnace. He is risking the peril of flames. We are sharing, I think, the heroism of taking care of the family. We are together. He is intense, sweating slightly across the brow. He still wears the shirt and tie from another long day's work. For some reason I am prompted to move with the pure spirit of being. I begin dancing around the furnace room with light abandon. My voice slides up the scale to a high falsetto. I am possessed by some primitive god of fire; I feel joyful and secure. I am supremely happy, high-voiced, fluid.

Then I am suddenly flattened against a limestone wall, bolts of lightning and bright stars flashing in my head. I have been hard and viciously slapped in the mouth as a thunderous voice shouts, "Damnit! Houston, Jr.! Stop acting like a sissy!" (sissy, *n.* 1. an effeminate boy or man; a milksop 2. a timid or cowardly person 3 [informal]. sister). Having heard my falsetto chant, my father had turned from the furnace with the quick instinct of an exorcist. He had hit me with the fury of a man seeing a ghost. The smell of woodsmoke is what I recall as I ran up the basement stairs and out into the Louisville night, astonished at how much I had angered my sacred and invulnerable father, whose moods of manhood were as predictable as the San Andreas Fault.

My name contains the sign of ownership and descent appropriate to the bourgeoisie. I am not a "second" or "II." I am a "junior" (junior, *adj.* 1. younger: used to distinguish the son from the father of the same name, and written, *Jr.* after the full name). The inheritance that passes to me from "Sr."—the man at the furnace—remains a mystery seasoned by small details.

He was born in Louisville, Kentucky, to a mother whose entire life was spent as a domestic for white families. His great-grandmother had escaped, or so the story was told, from a Mississippi slaveholder. She made her way to Kentucky with her owner in hot pursuit. His father, my paternal grandfather, was so light-complexioned that he might easily have been mistaken for the white slaveholder from whom my great-great-grandmother escaped. Harry was my paternal grandfather's name, and his greatest talent, or so I was led to believe, was fishing.

The cryptic unreadability of my father's life appears before me with the strange attraction and repulsion of a keloid (keloid, *n.* a mass of hyperplastic, fibrous connective tissue, usually at the site of a scar). I want to turn away from his wounds, the scars, the disorder that I believe ripped his consciousness and shredded his boyhood days. But I cannot turn away. With each new revelation or addition detail supplied by my mother, who is in her mid-eighties, or by my older brother, in his mid-fifties, my attention is more firmly riveted. My head and gaze are fixed like Winston's in Orwell's *1984.* I see the pain coming, but am never certain where it will fall.

Prostitutes were a successful and shame-free business for my father's grandmother. From my father's boyhood perspective, his grandmother's "girls" must have seemed like uncanny citizens of a bizarre extended family. I vaguely remember his telling me one day, in a faraway voice, that his first sexual encounter was with one of his grandmother's girls, who in effect "raped" him.

So much is difficult to turn away from in what I perceive to be the scarring of my father's life. There is his mother urging him to stay forever her own "good Negro Christian boy," yet regaling, tempting, titillating him with tales of the glory of white success. Tales of the spartanly clean windows, shining cars, and infinite spaces of white opportunity in America. His boozy father, hunkered down in an old leather chair with the radio playing schmaltzy popular songs, dozing in the middle of some urgent question his son was trying to ask. Reverend Shepherd, a white Anglo-Saxon messiah of a boxing coach, urging those black Presbyterian boys of Grace Church to self-extermination for the glory of God and the good health of a "Negro race" that white American insurance companies would not even consider as clients.

Houston, Sr.'s, answer to the aching incoherence of his boyhood was summed up in an exhortation that he barked at my brothers and me whenever we came close to tears or were on the brink of a child's response to pain. This exhortation—an admonishment that was his Rosetta stone for surviving chaos—was "Be a man!" There was nothing, mind you, ethnic or racial in this injunction. Just "Be a man!"

Since I remember no stories from my father's lips about being comforted by the arms of his mother or told fuzzy bedtime stories by Harry, I have to assume Houston, Sr., was like the children of the Dickens character Mrs. Jelleby, who just "tumbled up." This process translates in Afro-American terms as "jes' grew."

Houston, Sr., was left on his own to formulate commandments for his life. There were no tender revelations from his parents or burning-bush epiphanies from the mountaintop. "Be a man!" was therefore his resonant admission that only the most tightly self-controlled and unbelievably balanced postures could ensure a journey from *can't* to *can* in America. There was no time or space for sentimentality, tears, flabby biceps, fear, or illness in the stark image of American conquest my father set before himself. His notion of success was as deadpan and puritanical as the resolutions scripted by F. Scott Fitzgerald's Great Gatsby. Houston, Sr.'s, manhood code was every bit as full as Gatsby's of cowboy morality, gutsy goodwill, and trembling guilt about treating one's parents better. Mental control was like sexual control in my father's vision; it was a kind of *coitus interruptus* expressed in maxims like "illness and pain are all in the mind," "a woman should never make a man lose control," "race has nothing to do with merit in the United States," "the successful man keeps himself mentally, physically, and spiritually fit." Manhood was a fearless, controlled, purposeful, responsible achievement. And its stoutest testimony was a redoubtably athletic body combined with a basso profundo for speaking one's name—especially to white folks. "Hello," he would growl in his deepest bass, "my name is Baker—Houston A. Baker!" I often step back and watch, and hear myself in the presence of whites—especially those who overpopulate the American academy—growling like my father: "Hello, I'm Houston A. Baker, Jr.!"

If Houston, Sr., had a notion of heaven, I suspect he saw it as a brightly modern building where his own well-lit and comfortably furnished office was situated right next to the executive suite of Booker T. Washington. Washington's manly singleness of purpose and institutional achievements were taught to my father. He absorbed them into his very bones while putting himself through West Virginia State College under the mentorship of the great John W. Davis. Houston, Sr., and Booker T., building a world of American manhood, service, progress, and control; Houston, Sr., and Booker T., in their lives of service becoming swarthy replicas of ideal white businessmen like Carnegie or Vanderbilt the Elder.

And, like Booker T.'s paradise at Tuskegee, Houston, Sr.'s, ideal heaven would surely have housed wives tending children who if they were male would be vigorously instructed to "Be a man!" When not tending children, these wives would be satellites of manly Negro enterprise, raising funds and devoting themselves to the institutional growth of a world designed by and pleasing principally to men. In my father's heaven there would certainly be no confusion between love and sex, race and achievement, adults and children, men and not-men.

With the household furnace billowing smoke and ash on that evening long ago, my father must have suffered the fright of his life when he heard my falsetto and turned to see my lithe dance, accentuated by the whitewashed walls and the glow of the fire. Houston, Sr., could only, I think, have grasped this scene as a perverse return of his arduously repressed boyhood. His boyhood had been marked by a Louisville East End of commercial sexuality and muscular Christianity. The West End had been colored by a mother's ambivalent love for her light-skinned prodigy. He struck out in a flash against what he must have heard and seen as my demonic possession by the haunting fiends of unmanliness. What, after all, could God be thinking if he had somehow bequeathed to Houston, Sr., a sissy instead of a son? And so he hit me very hard. Walking in the woodsmoke air that autumn evening (actually just around the block and through the back alley, since I didn't dare stay out too long), I could not get a handle on what precisely I had done to make Houston, Sr., so angry.

Many years after the event, I learned the term "homophobia" and labelled my father's actions accordingly. As I think now about that moment long ago, I realize that my father was indeed afraid, yet his fear was not nearly so simple or clearly defined as an aversion to physical, emotional, intense and romantic love between men. There is a strong part of me that knows my father was fascinated by and even attracted at a level of deep admiration to what he believed, with great earnestness, to be the intellectual superiority and discipline of what he called the homosexual lifestyle. I think what terrified him on that evening years ago was not homosexuality as he ideally conceived it. Rather, he was afraid on that autumn evening that I was fast approaching adolescence and had not found what he deemed to be the controlling voice of American manhood. Clearly, then, it was time for Houston, Sr.—he knew this with both fierce dismay and instinctive terror—to busy himself with the disciplining of Jr.

The tragic emotional shortcoming of that evening was that my father did not realize that the letters at the end of my name were not meant to confirm his ownership or responsibility with respect to my name. "Jr."—as its formal definition makes abundantly clear—is meant to distinguish a younger self from the woundings of "Sr." It is sad that my father failed to realize that it was precisely those feelings of assurance, security, and protection which he had bestowed on me that overwhelmed me, that made me want somehow to dance for him.

It has required many hours of painful thought since that violent moment in which my father branded me a sissy to extract and shape for myself a reasonable definition of my life in relation to my father's. For decades I have sought patterns to fulfill a Jr.'s life. Mercifully, I have found some. They include much that my father was forced to ignore, deny, reject, or misunderstand. He could never, for example, have given approving voice to the informal definition of "sissy" that is sisterhood. Tragically, he never envisioned a successful man's life as one measured and defined by its intimate, if always incomplete, understanding and sharing of a woman's joys, dangers, voice, and solacing touch—shaped definitively, that is to say, by sisterhood.

Unlike the "Sr." produced by ordeals I have yet fully to comprehend, it is impossible for me to imagine "Jr." without a strong woman's touch. I am now the middle-aged father of a quite remarkable son. And at this moment I imagine that with God's grace I shall be able to live up to the standard of distinction the concluding marks of my name are meant to signify. If I do achieve such distinction, perhaps in some far-off fall twilight my son will dance for me. Speaking through rhythmic motion and with the very voice of possession, he will pronounce his own name in the world.

Jake Lamar

Bourgeois Blues

The summer after sixth grade, my first year in private school, Dad hired tutors for me in Spanish and math so I would have an edge over other students when junior high began in the fall. Working with the tutors, I found my nervousness around adults evaporating. It was 1973 and, much to my father's chagrin, I was developing a decidedly left-of-center political consciousness. When my father said something I found politically objectionable, I'd throw up my hands and say, "Aw, come on, Dad." When he launched into one of his adamant defenses of Richard Nixon, I didn't hesitate to criticize the president for Watergate and the bombing of Cambodia. I told Dad he had been rooting for the wrong side in the cowboy-and-Indian movies he loved so much. I could detect my father's irritation at being contradicted but, somehow, I didn't worry about it. As I saw it, my father and I were just having lively debates.

There was nothing—no toy, no treat, no childhood privilege—that I had ever wanted as much as I wanted to grow an Afro. Watching the Jackson Five on TV, Bert and I were mesmerized by Michael's enormous, fluffy helmet of hair bouncing as he bopped. We seethed with envy at the sight of schoolmates sporting 'fros the size of suburban hedges. For years, we'd begged Mom to beg Dad to please let us grow our hair long. Dad had always refused: "My sons aren't gonna look like stupid, raggedy-ass niggers." Every few weeks, Dad took Bert and me to the barber shop to have our hair cut to resemble his own: short, neat, carefully groomed with a pocket comb and Vitalis. Finally, Mom and Felicia persuaded Dad to let us grow our hair just long enough so that we could use Afro picks. My father bought a home barber's kit and Lish began cutting our hair, trimming off a little less each time.

One Saturday afternoon, our eleven-year-old cousin Asa came over to hang out with Bert and me. We went to the candy store, bought a bunch of comic books, and read them at the counter while drinking perfect Bronx egg creams. Leaving the store, Asa stopped to tie his sneakers. Bert and I turned the corner and hid behind a newsstand. As my cousin passed the newsstand looking bewildered, I called out, "Bye, Asa" in a goofy voice. Asa tilted his head in our direction—clearly, he'd heard me—but he didn't turn completely around. I could see him, in profile, smirking. He kept on walking. Bert and I stayed crouched behind the newsstand for a couple more minutes before we got bored. Walking the five blocks back to our house, we kept expecting Asa to jump out from behind a corner or a parked car to try to scare us. That's the way the game usually went. We arrived at the courtyard of our building; still no sign of Asa. Figuring he'd returned to the apartment, we headed upstairs.

"Where the fuck have you been!" my father screams as we walk in the door. Behind him, I see Mom and Asa sitting in the kitchen.

"We were at the candy store," I say, terrified and confused. "What's the matter?"

"What the fuck were you doin' leaving that boy alone!"

"We were just fooling around." I still don't understand what Dad is so mad about.

"Fooling around! You don't leave that boy alone by himself out in the street! What the fuck's the matter with you!"

Asa stands in the kitchen doorway, looking completely unharmed, but as stunned by my father's rage as I am.

"But Asa's fine," I say, unable to keep my voice from trembling. "He knows the way to our house."

"Don't you talk back to me!" Dad grabs me by the arm. "Anything coulda happened to that boy!"

"But he's okay!" I cry.

"Don't you talk back to me!" My father takes Bert by the arm and starts dragging both of us down the hall. "You wanna be a little smartass! I'll teach you a lesson! I'll teach you a lesson!"

Bert and I are both screaming and crying, squirming to get out of my father's grip. "We were just playing, I'm sorry, we were just playing!"

Bert begs: "Please, Daddy, no, please, Daddy!"

My father shoves us through the doorway of our bedroom. He slaps my face. I collapse on the bed, the whole left side of my head burning. "You wanna be a little smartass! Wanna be like your little smartass friends at school! I'll teach you a lesson!"

Sobbing convulsively, my stomach contracting, I fear I may vomit. Suddenly, I feel the crack of my father's belt on my thigh. The strap is slapping me everywhere: my back, my arms, my chest, my legs. Dad keeps screaming that he's going to teach me a lesson. I still cannot understand why he's so mad. His anger seems so out of proportion to the sin.

"Why are you hitting me?" I cry.

My father stops, holding the belt aloft, frozen in midstrike. "Why am I hitting you?" he yells, as if this were the most absurd question he'd ever heard. "Why am I hitting you?" He spits the words back at me. He gives me several more lashes, then goes to the other side of the room to whip Bert. He leaves, slamming the door behind him.

Just as Bert and I stop crying, my mother comes in. "Your daddy wants to see you in the kitchen."

My father waits for us with a chair placed in the center of the kitchen. The electric clippers, scissors, and combs of his barber's kit have been neatly laid out on the table. "Sit down," he says to me calmly. My father shears me so closely that I will be left practically bald, unable even to run a comb through the thin layer of hair that remains. Bert weeps as he watches the buzzing clipper slice through my Afro, knowing he's next.

And it occurs to me that this punishment has nothing to do with Asa at all. It is, I realize, about more things than I can comprehend; but the one thing I know it is about is power. My father is letting me know that he has all of it, and I, at twelve, have none. Dad's authority will not be challenged. And the only thing I can do to strike back is not to cry, not to let Dad feel even stronger at the sight of my crying. So I fight back my tears, as I watch tufts of hair tumble softly off the apron tied around my neck, forming a downy black pile on the kitchen floor.

Addison Gayle

Wayward Child

The contempt was evidenced when I visited him two weeks after he had been released from the hospital and one week after I had given him the novel I had completed. Handing him the manuscript to read, I recalled the night of its completion, remembered slumping across the kitchen table as I imagined Richard Wright might do, then, rising, holding my hands over my head, wanting to shout to the entire neighborhood that I had written a novel. I had tossed and turned on my couch all night, unable to sleep, already imagining myself a recognized writer, seeing the people who condescended toward me—who respected me. I remembered showing it to my mother in the morning, the next-door neighbor, my teachers, to whom I promised a copy (a promise I never fulfilled); I told my fellow students about it, told Red Drag and Tillie, called Alice for the first time in four months, told her, hoping that she would tell her father. I wanted to call every teacher at Huntington and tell them. Having given the manuscript to my father to read—my only, badly typed copy—I was unable to reread it at night, and forced to reconstruct the plot sequence in my mind, often falling asleep while doing so.

Over three hundred pages long, the book was entitled *Fear Not, Young Blood.* The major characters were Larry (white, handsome, bluish-black hair, blue eyes) and Joy (mulatto, pretty, creamy-white skin, blue eyes). The plot centered around Joy. Born in the slums, she was a child prodigy, able to read and write at the age of five, capable of doing college work at the age of fifteen. She completed medical school at the age of twenty-one, and soon became renowned as a surgeon, respected and admired throughout the world. Larry is also a famous surgeon, and the two meet and fall in love. Soon afterward, Joy contracts an eye disease, is blinded. She does not want to give up her profession, hoping to continue her role as a surgeon. She is rebuffed by the medical association when she pleads to be allowed to continue performing operations. After many such pleas, the association decrees that if she can prove her surgical competence, her appeal will be approved. Joy needs a guinea pig, someone who will entrust his life to a blind surgeon. In the final pages of the novel, Larry plunges a knife into his abdomen, providing his love with a patient. The novel ends with Joy about to perform the operation.

Expecting my father to be as enthusiastic about the book as I was, expecting praise, I was therefore surprised when, almost immediately after I had greeted him, having returned one week after giving him the manuscript, he calmly asked, "Why do you want to be white?"

I raised my hands, as if warding off some unforeseen blow, dropped the smile from my face, walked over to the little alcove which served him as a kitchen, and said, with obvious hostility, "Why do you think I want to be white?"

He had underlined parts of the novel and he now read them to me, concluding, "The only Blacks in this book are the servants of Larry and Joy. Joy has no parents; she is brought up in a white orphanage; so is Larry. No, there are no Black people."

I sat, looking about the room, letting the silence descend around us. He was wrong, I knew, but I could not then explain to him how wrong he was. Not in his descriptions, no, for in this book, black skin was at a minimum, thick lips and kinky hair nonexistent. But this was not, I knew, because I wanted to be white. I knew no white people beyond those I had done some work for, or those whom I had read about. No, he was wrong on that score, and I have often wondered if during those years before his death, he had ever calculated how wrong he was, if he ever, like me, came to realize that my desire was not to be white, but to be mulatto. But how could he have then known what I only surmised— that Larry was modeled upon Alice's father and me, that Joy was modeled upon the women who most attracted me?

His implication was that I was attempting to lose my identity, to deny my heritage. But of the reality of my identity, I knew little, having so often imagined myself, out of shame, to be other than I was. As for my heritage, whatever that was had been determined by mulattoes, who had made the great contributions—Booker T. Washington, Frederick

Douglass, George Washington Carver. Even Richard Wright was not
Black like me. How could I have known then, that almost on the eve of
my graduation from high school, I had come close to resolving the conflict within my own breast? Reason, thinking, knowledge were not ends
in themselves, ends which would leave me, like my father, defeated,
poverty-stricken, dreamless, but means toward another end: power, respect, admiration. Having not been born mulatto, I could only approach these ends through the route he had so often prescribed, but I
could only avenge myself upon others by attaining the other ends.

Leaving him later that night, when conversation between us, due to
my undisguised hostility, became impossible, I was broken, defeated.
This was not because of the charges that he had made, but because he in-
timated that the book was not a good one, telling me that I should write
about the things that I knew, adding that I could ask Saunders Redding,
a writer on the staff of Hampton Institute, to read it for me, get another
opinion. I went home, took my typewriter from the closet, covered it,
put it away in my mother's room, sealed the manuscript in an envelope
to put it out of sight, and tried not to fantasize about becoming famous
any longer, tried instead to think of my coming graduation, now only
two months away.

I was somewhat relieved three weeks later, though, when Saunders
Redding, who had agreed to read my manuscript, wrote, "You have
something to say, and one day you will say it. As for now, you must read
as much as you can and experience as much as you can." My depression
was not much eased. The vehicle that I had thought would raise me
above my condition, enable me to wreak vengeance upon my enemies,
pointing out to them that I was not a failure, had not worked. And perhaps, I thought, they were right. I was a failure, and no matter the effort,
would always be one. Writing and publishing a novel would have been
the quickest and most dramatic way of arousing them, of having them
sit up and take notice of me, and this I was unable to accomplish. Once
again, I felt rage, but felt also unable to expend it, to find a suitable target
for it. Due, perhaps, to these dual, conflicting feelings, I was not alto-
gether unhappy when, a few days after receiving Redding's note, I tried
to kill Walter.

Walter was as close to being white as one could come, without being
so. He was an albino, yet the other mulattoes treated him with disdain,

as somewhat of a freak. Everything about him was white—his hair, his face, legs, even the hair on his arms. Until he had been disowned by the mulattoes, I had treated him with a measure of condescension, but seeing that he was not considered among the elite of the Newport News mulatto class, I had started ignoring him. On those few occasions when I would go to the recreation center—a center established for Black youth, not far from my home—I would encounter Walter, sometimes argue with him.

Arguments among teenagers at the recreation center took the form of "rags," where one made insulting, derogatory remarks about one's opponent, hoping to draw laughter from the audience. Because of my vocabulary and my quickness with words, I was good at "ragging," and Walter was among my favorite targets. Comments by me, which were frequently directed toward his weird appearance, his slowness in school, his inability to find and hold a girlfriend, usually drew continuous laughter from others, and forced him to retreat in humiliation. Whatever our fight was about on that night, I do not now know, but my constant ragging him, I am sure, had something to do with it.

Yet, when he put his arms around me after I had walked into the center that night, and guided me outside, I had no idea that a fight would ensue. Not overly surprised at his behavior, I assumed he was attempting to ingratiate himself with me. Once outside, however, when we had moved a few feet from the center, he struck me upon the head, momentarily dazing me, the blow forcing me to my knees, where I tried to fight off the bright flashes of light and an interminable period of darkness.

I recovered from the darkness, groped, made my way toward a construction site nearby and armed myself with the heaviest bricks I could find. I cursed and cried each step of the way; the bricks felt gritty beneath my arms, in my hands. I entered the center. When I saw Walter glancing apprehensively at the door, I heaved a brick with all my strength and caught him in the stomach. He doubled over. I cursed loudly; the tears and mucus tasted salty in my mouth. I released another brick, aiming this time for his forehead. The brick found its mark and brought forth a long stream of blood. He fell to the floor, prostrate. I advanced upon him, raised a brick over the top of my head, coiled my arms, was poised for the kill, moved closer, closer . . .

I wanted to move close enough to feel his hurt, taste it, revel in it; I wanted to see him suffer. Out of the darkness of the rage of yesterday and today, there was seemingly a voice shouting, "Kill him, kill him!" and I realized that I wanted not only to kill him, but to destroy him, to obliterate him. I kicked him hard in the face. Reflexively, he rolled over upon his back. I raised the brick above my head again, felt a sense of delirium engulfing my body, began laughing, became happy, wanted to kill him, needed perhaps to kill him . . . the tears continued to roll down the sides of my face, and I continued to laugh, to cry, to scream . . .

I was crying and screaming still when someone grabbed my arm in midair, wrestling me to the floor—two, three, how many? I was crying and screaming too when the ambulance came for Walter, crying and screaming still when my mother, lecturing me all the way, led me from the police station. I did not stop until sometime the next morning, when, exhausted, I fell asleep.

But the next day, when my mother told me that Walter would not die, I began to cry again. She believed, I think, that these were tears of remorse, of repentance. I managed a smile, thought of how little this woman knew about her son, wanted to take her face in my hands, look into her tired eyes, move my lips close to her ears, say, "Momma, I'm crying because he didn't die. I wish I had killed him. I'm sorry that I did not." But I said nothing, dressed, took my notebook, and went to the garden, sat and wrote and fantasized. Because my book had not been a success, I thought, did not mean that I had to stop writing; indeed, I knew that I could not. I knew, deep down, beyond the anger and rage, that Walter was not the real enemy, only the symbol, and that the weapons I had used against him I could not use against them. But I could use those weapons I had polished and garnished, largely because of my father, to right all the wrongs done to me, to avenge myself, in isolation, in seclusion, could use them also to rewrite the past, to make it less fuzzy and more visible.

No, I would never have the powerful voice of my father, never be able to use words the way he did; but I could use them in another way, in a way that he could not. Perhaps, in so doing, I could end the hostility between us, the antagonism, tell him that I knew why this is so, that I am older now, that I meant nothing by the words I uttered when I was not so old, that I did not mean them.

The things that I realize now, from a distance of so many years, I am certain that I knew then. At least I knew my own feelings, if not those of others—though I could speculate about others—and during the course of the past, I am not so sure that I was not right in my speculation concerning my father. I remember a time when he would hold me, pull me toward him, bouncing me up and down on his knee. I was not frightened of him then, because he seemed affectionate, warm. I remember too when he seemed to stop being all those things, when he seemed to change abruptly, almost overnight, to becoming cold, distant, calculating.

He had finished a lecture, on the makeshift stand in the vacant lot of the poolroom. Accepting the applause, he hoisted me atop his shoulder, and announced to the crowd: "This is my boy, here, Addison, Jr. My boy." The crowd had responded again with applause and cheers. Bewildered and bashful, I had leaned my face close to his, feeling the hairs on the side of his face, asked, "Daddy, why you tellin them people I'm your boy?" He had held me back from him at arm's length, his eyes no longer on the people now beginning to disperse, and said, hurt and anger in his eyes, "What's the matter? Don't you want people to know you my son?"

I knew that he was hurt, but I did not know what to say, wanted to say something, to ingratiate myself, to stop his hurt; I said nothing, began to cry. He led me away after the meeting, did not buy me an ice cream cone as usual, did not try to gain my favors as usual, at the expense of my mother. In the following days, he said very little to me, seemed to be trying to push me closer and closer toward my mother. Once when I came near, he had pushed me away, saying, "You're not my boy; you're your mother's boy, aren't you?" With my mother sitting on the other side of the room, staring at me, he, sitting distant on the other side, staring too. I had stood looking from one to the other, head down, confused, bewildered. A few days later, when he and my mother were scrambling, wrestling over his wallet, the wallet fell to the floor and I picked it up. Both began to admonish me to bring them the wallet and I stood in the middle of the floor again, looking from one to the other, staring first here, then there, being pulled by one voice, pulled back by another, until, in total confusion, I threw the wallet in the direction of my mother, ran crying from the room. The next day my mother and I moved into a new house.

I wanted to tell him that I remembered those events, those days and others, that I was sorry for them, that I was, however, too little to be able to make choices, I could not decide between him and my mother, but I loved them both. I wanted to tell him, also, that though I admired him, I was angry with him too for forcing me to make such choices. I was enraged against him for deserting me, not protecting me as Alice's father protected her and her brother, but leaving me alone, defenseless—as I had then believed. As I grew older and sat in his living room, time after time, feeling terrified, cowering before him, and resentful, I wanted to tell him that he seemed more concerned with ideas than with his own son, more concerned with saving other people than he was with saving me, and that sometimes I hated him for this. But I also wanted to tell him that this hatred was not real, was only momentary, and that he could erase it forever, if he would only take me in his arms, hold me as before, ask me again if I was not proud to be his son. I could never tell him any of this verbally, but I could write it, putting it down on paper for him to read. By the time I had decided that I would do this, trying as best I could to explain what I knew and what I felt, he was dead—struck down by a massive hemorrhage of the brain.

Scott Minerbrook

EXCERPT FROM

"My Father, Myself"

In memory is the language of reconciliation.

My first memory of my father is an enthrallment of blind admiration for his simple ability to swim the cold waters of Lake Michigan. One afternoon when I was four, he took my mother, my brother, and me to the lake's edge in Chicago. We watched as he plunged in, and I remember his long, dark arms rising above the smooth, blue waters, then dipping below the surface. His feet churned up small fountains of white foam like you see at the bottom of a waterfall. My mother called to him as his form receded into the distance but he was even beyond the reach of her voice. Long minutes later, the liquid surface brought him back, dripping and smiling, and ready to eat.

My second memory is of terror. Later that summer, again at Lake Michigan, my dad took my older brother, Mark, and me to the same beach. But the sand was too hot for my feet, and he hoisted me on his shoulders and waded into the water to his waist, then his chest. He asked me if I knew how to swim. The water was smooth and cool and reflected clouds, and I told him that I did, which of course, was a lie. I don't know if the events that happened next were part of some careless punishment adults sometimes use on their children. I don't know if my lie came from mistaking a desire to be like him for being him. But I know that I assumed an innate ability to swim as he did.

Surely he knew I could not. In the next moment, my father took me by the wrists, held me over the calm blue water and as I kicked my feet and laughed, he dropped me. I remember claws of ice on my skin, which felt as though it had been turned inside out as the liquid burned into my lungs and nose. I opened my eyes and saw my father's legs floating upward, the grotesque blue patterns tattooing his legs. I saw the wavy surface of the water above. I saw the sand under my sinking feet, and then I blanked out. Just as suddenly as he had plunged me in, my father pulled me out, laughing and telling me not to cry. I was ashamed to cry but I did, not because I was in physical pain. In that moment—call it carelessness, lack of consideration—a bond of trust between us was severed and it has taken nearly four decades to begin to mend. One day four years ago, he asked me jokingly if I remembered it, and he was stunned when I said I did and that it had changed my life.

As anyone knows who has relived episodes of childhood terror, something else was broken in me besides trust, particularly my ability to trust male authority. It was the fear that I wasn't worthy of my father's love, that I was not valuable to him. No amount of reason could convince me otherwise. Knowing this wounded every contact my father could ever make. Even though I loved him, my love was mixed with fear that any small happiness I might feel could be snatched away if exposed to him. So many years later, I see him as someone much like myself. Someone who grew up, as many of his generation did, unable to show weakness, unable to express his pain except in acts of violence, afraid and ashamed as a man, not only as a Black man, but as an exile from life's feast. Unable to acknowledge his own emotions, my father could never allow others to show emotion, and his murderous rage became the mold upon which I shaped my world.

Today, I hunger for reconciliation with him on mutually agreed upon terms, because I am tired of the old bitterness between us. I hunger also for the language of reconciliation, which does not seem to exist between many Black men who are like me and their fathers who are like mine. Our wounds seem to run too deep. Some say the cause of this is the terrible legacy of slavery that has sundered the bonds of alliance not only between fathers and sons, but of Black masculine culture itself. This lack of language between African-American men most often seems a cultural flaw. The issue of the wounds African-American fathers unwittingly bring into their relationships with their children influence every aspect of our lives. It influences everything from how we perceive our relationship to authority, to our capacities for harm or for good, to how we hear the music of love, and choose our mates.

But it is never discussed openly and only rarely except in hours of private sorrow. That relationship between African-American fathers and their sons is, in a very special sense, beyond politics. It runs to the bone of what we are afraid to say: that we need our fathers desperately, and frequently, we feel we are not men because we have not been so in our fathers' hearts. I believe current African-American politics is tormented by this lack of father-to-son bonding. And yet we lack any language to create these bonds.

I believe that if Black men are to find our way out of the emotional wilderness we have created, which goes far deeper than the issue of race, if we are to teach others to have faith in us, we must learn to keep faith with each other, and this means repairing the old, wounded relationships with our fathers. There is no political coalition that is more powerful. Accusation won't heal those wounds. Neither will blame.

There is no book to teach fatherhood. I know now what I did not know as a child—that my father's relationship with his father was tainted by loss, which he found too painful to discuss. He brought this pain into his relationship with me. All I knew as a boy and even as a younger man was what any child wanted to know—whether I was wanted, safe, loved, and valued. I never felt I was any of these. I don't think this was ever given to my father, and it is only now as an adult that I know how hard it is to give something you have never received. My father, I believe, was tormented by what he had never received. . . .

Dad always worked hard. Often, he held two and three jobs at a time. But even after the episode at Lake Michigan, when so much of my trust for him simply disappeared in the sudden shock of knowing that I had to survive by myself, I felt something was missing in him. He could be charming and often was. He would sit me on his lap and pull silver dollars out of my ears or out of my older brother, Mark's, nose. He would park his old Ford in front of a store on a hill and not put the parking brake on, and then chase the car as it rolled downhill. He would take Mark and me to the circus—I still remember the wonderful sight of watching an acrobat balancing on his finger on a tightrope—and then, on a walk with me, he allowed me to gesture to pet a dog I didn't know. When I got bit, he blamed me for my clumsiness. "He feels that way because you are so much like him," my grandmother would say. But I still couldn't understand what that meant.

Later, after we moved to New York City, Dad took us to ride horses at a stable near our home on West 88th Street, and I rode a pony for the first time. Then, he would subvert the happiness he gave by beating my mother with his fists, sending his whole family into numbing chaos. This was the pattern of my childhood. When my mother was in the hospital recovering from the birth of my third brother, John, who was born blind in 1957, my father was entertaining a prostitute named Lucky in our apartment. When I ran to greet my mother's return from the hospital, my father was sleeping in his bed with Lucky in the kitchen. Mom was so angry, she began slapping him. Dad slapped her back and soon Mom was telling me to get the police. As I was running downstairs and about to open a huge glass door of the brownstone where we lived, he slammed me into it, knocking me unconscious. When I came to, the fingernails on my mangled hand were missing. This was the quality of my relationship with my father—of deep admiration and fun coupled with a deep sense of dread that he would suddenly lose control. It went on this way for years until I grew old enough to run the streets myself. And I did. My father once told me, after we moved from Manhattan when I was ten, that the main reason for the move was that I was becoming a thug. Maybe I was. . . .

One of the things that seemed miraculous about my father was his ability to teach himself new skills. He was, in most respects that count, self-made. After he and my mother, who is white, moved to the city of Norwalk, Connecticut—we were one of the first Black families on the street where we lived—Dad began the process of rebuilding the house from floor to ceiling while holding down a job as an insurance salesman. He and Mom bought new furniture, he installed a new kitchen, tore through walls to create space, carpeted and painted like a madman in a pattern of overwork that in some measure contributed to a loss of the very identity he seemed to strive for. He worked until it exhausted him, and so did Mom. Money slipped through their fingers.

Work to him was something he used increasingly to put himself beyond anyone's reach. Who could take him to task for trying so hard for his family? By degrees, he removed himself from us even more behind his work. At the same time he worked on the house, he would take extra jobs for various defense contractors in machine shops, or, to earn extra money, he would work in bakeries until the early hours of the morning.

I remember the smell of the fresh rolls and pastry he'd bring home. But I also remember the feeling that this was a substitute for acceptance. In school, I excelled at basketball and football to gain approval. After getting left back in the fifth grade, I excelled in my studies. But it didn't seem to please him. He didn't seem to notice. As he rebuilt the house, it seemed that he was chasing shadows and ghosts—of his family in Chicago, of his own—and soon I believe he lost sight of why he was working so hard. He was soothing something in himself, as much as providing for his family. My heart went out to him, but he seemed to need something to soothe his own sense of loss that went far deeper than anything I could ever give.

In those years in Connecticut, my father began to medicate himself by drinking heavily, not sleeping adequately or resting for years at a time. Restlessness doesn't describe the quality of his driven momentum. He plunged from one project at home or at work into another. One day, I came home and was looking for an envelope in his desk and found a loaded .38 caliber handgun. A pattern of grotesque violence emerged as he worked and drank and refused to take care of his health. All that he was accomplishing seemed to be slipping away from him and into an escalating pattern of assaults on his family. As soon as I was old enough to defend myself, I fought him back, hard.

Eight years after we moved from the city, my father began buying rifles. Except for one or two hunting trips, he didn't use them for hunting. He used them to beat my mother. All this happened, ironically, just as the dreams he once held were coming to fruition or were close to being accomplished. My older brother, Mark, was a pre-medical student now, and I was about to leave for Harvard University. But Dad seemed unable to feel anything or taste anything but bitterness that all this had been denied him earlier because he was a Black man and had been held back because of his race. It fed an even deeper sense of rage in him and we all caught it, like a bad bout with pneumonia. Everything was overshadowed by that rage. . . .

Between 1971, the year after I left for college, and 1987, my father and I didn't speak. These were sixteen important and eventful years for us both. During my first year in college, Dad returned to his family in Chicago and seemed to be doing quite well in business. He sold millions of dollars worth of life insurance on the South Side, but gradually he drifted deeper into a cycle of drinking and using cocaine. During my junior year, as I tried to do all I could to avoid getting drafted, he was arrested and convicted of a larceny charge in connection with writing bad checks. I tried to cut myself off from my feelings about any of this, something I grew increasingly adept at, and soon I could feel nothing myself. In a sense, I was imitating what he'd taught me. When I graduated from Harvard in 1974, he was in jail. In 1977, when I married, he didn't call. When my first son, Aaron, was born the next year, the silence continued. In 1983, when my second son, Terence, was born, this stony, heart-rending silence continued.

It was only after I began experiencing a series of violent and nearly disabling panic attacks at about that time, that I began to understand that my fears were connected to the relationship I'd had with my father. Aaron was 6 at the time, a few years older than I had been when I'd experienced near drowning at my father's feet, and the attacks were a great deal like the horrible sensations of strangulation a person experiences under water. I knew that unless I did something to try to see my father and confront him about the violence I'd experienced at his hands, I might never be free of the cycle in which I was tormented. While seeing a therapist for the panic attacks—a Black woman to whom I owe my life—I began writing him a series of angry letters describing what I had experienced and telling him my feelings about it. He was living again on the South Side of Chicago. Most of the letters were not answered. Some were. They expressed irritation that I should be holding him accountable for things that happened so many years ago. Why couldn't I just grow up? Forgive and forget. "When you ain't got nothing," he wrote, "you ain't got nothing to give." All hope of reconciliation, much less forgiveness, seemed worlds away.

For the next four years, I persisted. His letters grew defensive. We still didn't speak on the phone. He sent me a book about alcoholics in recovery. I wasn't an alcoholic. I threw the book away. Then I realized that he was trying to get me to think about what he'd been through so we could begin to talk about the context of his behavior when I was growing up. He had been an alcoholic. I thought I recognized in his gesture a need to begin to ask for understanding of what had happened to him. As a father myself, something responded in me, and by 1987, I was ready to see him face to face.

That year, the newspaper I was working for sent me to Chicago to cover the re-election of then-Mayor Harold Washington. My older son was nine years old, a cinnamon-brown, lean, tall, curious, shining, beautiful boy who wore glasses and played a saxophone in school and showed me not to be afraid in the presence of my own ghosts. In a way, he reminded me of my father and my admiration of him. My second son, Terry, was four, a robust, blue-eyed, blond-haired child who taught me to smile. He reminded me of myself and of the perfection of childhood. I wondered if I was like them when I was a boy, and wondered if my son could help restore my memory of who I was then. I knew that if I was ever going to be for them the father I didn't have, I would have to see my father sooner than later or I might lose out on my own children's childhood, as much as my father lost out on mine.

I called Dad on a whim to let him know that I was in town on a reporting assignment, which was my way of lifting the burden of making the first physical move toward reconciliation. I didn't know it then, but I'd waited for this my entire life. I was a man now, and had the protection of a career, a family, a home, a life. I was still angry, almost too angry to talk, but my excuse for calling him and inviting him to a meeting was that he would interpret any failure to call him when I was in his city as a failure of respect. I called.

With such gestures, we began a long and painful process that today is just beginning to heal old wounds. We first met in a downtown pizza parlor. He wore glasses. He was still thin, slightly frail and worn looking. After my reporting duties were done, I called and agreed to meet him the next day at a cafeteria. I remember that the place was sundrenched even at 7:30 in the morning. He was late. He waltzed into the room in worn blue jeans and a loose pullover and a pair of Italian shoes that made his feet look like they were wrapped up in webbing. He complained of problems with his arches and toes and the pains in his muscles. He sat stiffly at the stool at the counter, and before he looked at me, he took off his glasses that looked exactly like the ones my son, Aaron, wore. His gestures were a great deal like my son's. We ordered coffee, drank none of it, and had to order a second cup. We inquired about each other's health.

I asked him why he felt he could never be there for me, and why he had become so entangled in violence that had stolen so much of my childhood in a nightmarish thrall. He said he was glad I asked this question. I wanted to strangle him. I thought he was trying to be evasive, but what came next surprised me.

He said that his own father had died of a heart attack one day—just collapsed—at an age when most men are just beginning to enjoy their retirement. "I was afraid I was going to die that way, at an early age, myself and so I drank away my fear. It did terrible damage and I'm sorry."

I didn't know how to accept this. I don't think I did for many years. It didn't feel like an excuse, but I was 36 years old then and I knew nothing of what I know now, at 43, about waking up in the morning and feeling that if I don't work to raise my children, no one will. There are other things: the need to concentrate on the things that give me joy; the need for forgiveness and to forgive; the need to understand and be understood; the hope that my children will not judge me in the harsh ways I have judged my father.

I think of my father during those long years when he must have felt so alone and afraid in a place like Norwalk, Connecticut, which does not suffer Black men any better than Chicago does. My father was successful, but he never was able to enjoy his success. He was too driven by his own ghosts—his abandonment by his father, a rocky relationship with his mother—to ever be happy. The result was that he destroyed the things that could have given him joy. But what man is ever able to fully escape this fate? All of us have our ghosts. When we recognize these ghosts as being similar to the ones that haunted our fathers and our forefathers, cut free of every other consideration but what it means for a man to become a human being unto himself, it is possible to forgive and to recognize that in forgiving, one lifts one's own burdens. One recognizes the first grain of hope for the first time in life. It is a sweet moment to know this.

After we spoke a little more about his childhood, we parted, and it was a year before I saw him again. At least we weren't hurting each other with words any more. I stopped writing the letters. I saw him again at the graduation ceremonies of my younger brothers, Mike in 1990 and John in 1992.

He lives in an apartment that seems comfortable enough. He has renovated it himself. In our conversations, we've talked about his heroin addictions, about his life as a young man, of his fears and hates and how they consumed him, much as mine consumed me. He told me about the drinking and the ghosts that haunted him—of failure, of disappointing everyone, of love gone sour—and somehow these words changed my life. I am still trying to understand them now as I enter a phase of my life so different from any I've lived before: one without the terrible burden of silence between myself and my father and all that passed between us.

I don't think my father has made peace with the world. He is a Muslim now. He tries to help brothers in need, brothers out of prison, women in need of help. He gives his life to others in a way he could not when he was my age. He has suffered and I know that I have been part of his suffering. Conscience is like that. But now I want him to stop suffering and I know I am beyond that power if I cannot show that I am beginning to forgive the suffering he brought into my life.

Memory is a curious thing. It has the power to alter the feelings we have about the past. When we remember, we also forget so much about the particulars that once made us suffer. But this cannot happen until we face ourselves and the people who have given us pain.

I am a different man today than I was even five years ago because I have begun to talk to my father, and have been willing to see myself in him and him in me. I find that my relationships with other African-American men are a little easier and a great deal more straightforward, less covert, less protected, less defensive than they have been. This is because I am coming to know my father and, in him, myself. If he was brutal with me, I was not the one who was hurt the most. And in those moments of kindness are the material of a far more articulate future between me and him and between me and my own children. One must choose love over fear, understanding over hate, or life becomes an endless, haunted wasteland.

Patricia Elam Ruff

Dancing on My Father's Shoes

When I was a little girl, four or five perhaps, I used to dance on my father's shoes. We did this at family events—weddings, anniversaries, birthdays—but sometimes we danced in the living room to Ella Fitzgerald or Nat King Cole. I would slide my Mary Janes onto his shiny black tie-up shoes and lean close to him, holding on tight and wrapping one short arm partway around his legs. He'd put one of his gentle hands down on my shoulder, clasp my free hand in his, and extend our arms out, tango style. And then we'd dance in one sweeping motion, as if my shoes were glued to his. When my feet slipped off occasionally, he'd quickly scoop me back up onto his toes. It was the thrill of a merry-go-round or a Ferris wheel, as he spun me, rippling my dress and petticoat like an unexpected summer breeze. As the creases in his smooth brown face gathered into a slow smile, he'd laugh from way down low, deep, rich, and strong.

My mother told me that he wanted a daughter first and couldn't have been more delighted when he got me. He didn't call me his princess but I knew I was. I have a picture of us that's over thirty-five years old. For a community parade, I dressed up as the Little Old Lady in the Shoe, my father's idea. Magically, he created a huge shoe out of my tricycle, using cardboard boxes and poster paint. I know he spent a great deal of time and energy fashioning that shoe on wheels and in the picture he stands behind it proudly. I stand beside it rather nonchalantly, taking for granted my father's amazing creation.

So I was unprepared when my princess status, quite without warning, was ripped away raggedly, like a sheet of paper torn from a notebook. Suddenly, it seemed, I was no longer invited to dance on my father's shoes, or sit on his lap. Something happened that no one explained to me. I became a teenager and he no longer touched me. I felt

as if I couldn't touch him either. I didn't know whether I had done something to bring about these changes or whether something or someone
had directed him not to touch me.

I had no voice for my feelings and was without words for the anger
and pain over his being suddenly beyond my reach. I didn't know how
to approach him, how to question the subtleties, and soon I didn't want
to. I started not liking what he had to say, no matter what it was, and it
became easy to only speak to him when absolutely necessary.

Without knowing what I was doing, I tried to fill the void. I started
letting boys touch me. Lots of them. I lied about where I went and what
I did. Sometimes my parents found out. Sometimes they didn't.

Back then, I wanted things from my father that he couldn't give.
Later I came to understand that he gave me everything he had. Back
then I wanted my father to love me in the loud way that my girlfriend's
daddy loved her. Kim's daddy, who dressed garishly in pink suits and
pink shoes, gave her hugs that enveloped her, announced his love in a
booming voice, and paid for the two abortions she had before she was
sixteen.

My father (a meticulous dresser also, but one who wore dark suits,
white shirts, and ties with soft, muted stripes) was shy, quiet, hesitant,
and mostly silent about his love. His hugs were as brief as his brisk
kisses, given only when he or I had returned from a trip. He didn't discuss my burgeoning sexuality directly with me, but he tried, in vain, to
slow me down. I knew he was always watching me and maybe that's what
fueled me to be as promiscuous as I dared.

When I was fifteen, crowing about how I was a woman, my father
wasn't having it. I remember once I was on my way down the street, going somewhere with my friends when he came out on the porch. "Come
in here and put on a bra," he yelled. I screamed at him as I marched past
him, back into the house, tears blurring my vision. I was furious that he
had control over my body, but felt weird that he had been looking at me
so closely. How could he embarrass me like that? I told him how much
I hated him, put on the bra, and then slammed the front door. When I
got to my destination I removed the bra, and crumpled it down into my
purse until I went home. This is my body, I thought, and I'll do whatever I want with it.

As far as I was concerned all my parents' rules were stupid, devised only to humiliate me and hold me back from any chance at happiness. When I went to parties, I couldn't walk home with my friends. Instead, I had to meet my father out front well before the party ended.

One night I decided to test the limits and kept dancing. After all, the party was just getting started and I was working my body to the cool groove of Archie Bell and the Drells. Next thing I knew one of my friends began chanting, "Here comes Harry. Here comes Harry." Before I could turn around, there he was on the dance floor looking mean and evil, refusing to speak to anyone. He was in his trench coat, the flimsy legs of his pajamas flapping below like bedraggled flags. He was wearing his slippers, shoes that had no backs to them, and a brimmed hat hastily placed on his head, like an afterthought. Now that I have a fourteen-year-old son, I realize he was probably tired, ready to go to bed, worried, and pissed. Back then I just knew he was trying to mess up my life.

"Why'd you have to come in? I was coming right out," I ranted. He never answered, just drove straight ahead in the rain, occasionally pushing his hat back from his forehead.

I was a rebel without a name for my cause. I wanted the exact opposite of whatever my father wanted for me. I dated guys I met randomly in front of liquor stores, at basketball courts, outside of train stations, nightclubs, concerts, and parties, usually after they had made overtures like, "Hey, baby," or "You sure got some nice legs." The prerequisite was they had to be missing something: teeth, education, brains, common sense, and/or home training. Guys who wanted to do well in school and make something of their lives were boring nerds, cornballs, and weirdos.

Oddly, though, some of the guys who met my "missing something" test started pulling disappearing acts before our first date. I remember running into a guy named "Punchy," eighteen and home from the service for a couple of weeks, whom I had met at an outdoor concert. (I was fourteen at the time.) "What happened? I thought we were supposed to go to the movies," I said.

"Oh, man," he said. "Your father is what happened. He called me down to his office and told me I better never go near you again or he'd have me arrested for statutory rape. I'm sorry, baby, but I couldn't take no chances."

I was dumbfounded and enraged. When I confronted my father, I disregarded the pain carved on his face. He listened while I railed on and on about the violation of my privacy and the purposeful destruction of my social life. More than anything, I hated that he had the upper hand.

My father worked hard at the law practice he shared with his brother. When we were small, we didn't see him until dinner time during the week and often he went out again while my mother was reading us our bedtime story. "Sometimes he has to chase his clients down to get his money," I once heard my mother saying to my grandmother. Later he became the first black judge and then chief judge of Boston Municipal Court, and was well known for his fairness and integrity. He was also an institution builder in his community and a pivotal member of his church. On weekends he mowed the lawn, fixed our bikes, and took us for Sunday drives in the old station wagon my brother fervently wished he would trade in for a Mercedes.

He and my mother presented a united front: he supported, honored, cherished, and worked with her as an equal. I remember being surprised to learn that all couples did not behave this way. And although my father didn't squander words, I noticed that he talked to my mother, even laughed with her, gave her cards with mushy messages, and came home to her every night. There were times even with her, though, when he seemed to hold back. On Saturday mornings when he was reading the paper, she'd bustle around him cooking breakfast and talking, without taking breaths in between, about us, her friends, her reading, whatever was on her mind. His eyes wouldn't leave the newspaper, but he'd mumble an "Uhhuh" or "Umhm" at enough appropriate intervals to keep her going.

In those days my mother didn't work outside the home. She taught us that our father was a king for whom we often had to wait dinner, no matter how hard we pleaded or how "really starving" we were. She was the quintessential Black version of the mothers in *Ozzie and Harriet* and *Father Knows Best* who baked cookies, took care of all our needs during the day, and if we were naughty would say, "Just wait until your father gets home."

As children we always sought our father's approval far more than our mother's. We especially wanted him to see the A's on our report cards, notice the rainbows we made from construction paper, watch the way we rode our bikes with no hands. This continued well into adulthood. "Did you tell Daddy about my promotion?" I'd ask my mother long distance.

I don't know whether it was a conscious decision on her part, but it seemed as if my mother tried to make up for the physical affection I sought but didn't receive from my father. I felt as if I could have o.d.'d from her hugs and kisses. I felt smothered and enveloped by her kind of love, like thick cloudy air surrounding me, making me cough and sputter. I'd send her away rudely and she'd still come back for more. And what I would have done to have a fraction of that from my father.

I remember seeing the movie *Ordinary People* with my younger sister. The mother in the movie has great difficulty showing love to her children. I had recently graduated from law school and was living at home again. My sister was sixteen, ten years younger than me. We both cried uncontrollably several times in the dark theater. "Who did the mother remind you of?" I asked her once outside.

"Daddy," she said. We cried some more. "We have to tell him. We have to let him know how we feel," we both decided. Fueled by the movie's power, we couldn't get home fast enough. My parents were still up. We burst into their bedroom, threw ourselves on our stunned father who remained stone still and speechless as we cried all over him, grabbing him, holding on, not wanting to let go. "Daddy, please hold us, tell us you love us, we love you, we need you to love us," we begged. My mother, visibly shaken, cried, too.

We didn't really talk much that night but, perhaps several days later, while driving with my father I asked him to try to be closer to my sister. I didn't want her to go through my questioning of his love and subsequent pursuit of bad relationships. He promised to do better. And he did. I noticed him being more physical, more at ease with her. I was glad for her. In later years, I asked him to hug my sons, instead of shaking their hands the way he did with my brothers.

As I grew older, I came to see that my father showed his love in other ways. He has always been there for me, no matter my choices. When I opted to take a year off after high school and move into my own apartment instead of going to college, my father took a deep breath, asked if I was sure, and helped me fix up and move into my new place. The next year I did go to college and, after graduation, went on to law school. When I left the practice of law last year to write full-time, he wrote me that he was pleased I was able to "follow my dreams."

I didn't realize it then but I know now that I went to law school to get closer to my father, trying to grab onto the part of him that seemed un-reachable. Prior to beginning law school I had a lot of misgivings and self-doubt: Was it the right decision? Would I be able to handle it? The first assignment was to "brief" a case called *Marbury v. Madison* that clarified which branch of government has the final say in interpreting the Constitution. I read it but had no idea what it meant. All my fears were confirmed. I burst into tears in the living room with the book, which weighed a ton, sitting on my lap. My father stopped what he was doing and sat down beside me. He patiently read the case aloud to me, explaining until I understood. He assured me I could handle law school and I did. During the sixteen years I practiced law, I did acquire some-thing in common with my father and was able to talk to him more in-tensely than before. More often our conversations were able to spill over into social, political, and racial dialogues, especially with the Clarence Thomas, Rodney King, and O.J. Simpson melodramas coming back to back. Through these spirited talks I learned how similar our politics were and that there was some of him in me.

By the time I finished law school I wanted to get married and have children and had only my parents' marriage as a role model. I had no idea how difficult such a relationship would be to emulate. Because of the sordid choices I made early on, it was important for my father to ap-prove of my choice in a husband. I had been with the dregs of society all through high school and college and felt that he had little if any expecta-tions of me in this area.

My first husband was a long-time Bostonian and from a family my parents respected. He was a recent med school graduate with an upcom-ing internship in Washington, D.C. On the surface our future looked bright. I had on blinders, though, ignoring the shadows and cobwebs dangling on the periphery of this union. A year and a half into the mar-riage, other than the birth of my son, it was clear that a mistake had been made. Because I didn't want to disappoint my parents, my father in par-ticular, I didn't tell them about our problems until they got so serious I could no longer avoid it. My father, who like me expresses himself more intensely through the written word, wrote a letter to my husband, detailing his concern over the demise of the relationship. The letter stressed his love for me and how important I was to him. My husband skimmed the letter and tossed it aside. I retrieved it and read it hungrily, perching on the sentences that described how he felt about me. I kept that letter folded in my purse for more than a year, reading it again and again until it yellowed, tore at the fold, and eventually was no longer decipherable.

Four years after that marriage erupted, I brought my next husband-to-be home to meet my parents. I could see that my father thought highly of him. This pleased me. And when I walked down the aisle again with my father, my arm through his, he whispered with a chuckle, "This is the last time I'm doing this."

So, in the gray mist of separating from my second husband, I now wonder whether my father will think I'm a total failure at this thing he and my mother made appear so effortless. Intellectually and rationally I know my choices made sense to me at the time. With the help of therapy, I also know that, looking for men like my father, I chose men who were, for various reasons, still "missing" something. I chose men who were out of my reach because I misunderstood my father's example. Although I know I was affected by it, I do not blame my father for not touching me as much as I craved. It feels circular and somewhat simplistic to argue that had my father touched me more as a preteen I might not have needed the groping hands of young men. I always had a choice. While difficult to comprehend as a child, and with lasting effects, I understand now that my father loved in the only way he could.

Sometimes I am startled at how much I have become my father. I have nut-brown skin like him and am nearsighted as well. My grandmother told me that he used to read late into the night without adequate light and damaged his vision. I, too, am not naturally physical with my children. I have to remind myself that I need to hug them or hold them. It is hard work. I make the effort because I know how I interpreted my father's inability to do this. I don't want my children to suffer the same anguish if I can help it. We're alike in other ways too. Neither one of us "suffers fools gladly" and we can be impatient when things aren't as we think they should be. Both of us tend to express our disapproval through weighted silences.

As I stare at the two recent photographs I have propped up on my computer to help me reflect, I see the creases in my father's forehead, that distinctive "Elam" forehead, I, too, own. He is smiling in both pictures, the way he always does, full lips pressed smoothly back to show only his top teeth. His head sinks back proudly into his neck as he leans over slightly to the side he favors when he's in the groove of his distinctive walk. In one picture he wears a beige walking suit with a jaunty matching cap and sunglasses. In the other he is relaxed, leaning back in a chair at the airport, relieved at having just sent my sons back to me.

In these pictures and in reality, he seems to be content with his life and choices. He and my mother have been retired for six years. They have two homes they travel between, visiting us en route to either. At these times I look at him closely. I see that the creases in his face are deeper, that he's ready for my children to take their naps earlier, and that he falls asleep while we're watching a family movie. He is getting older and I fear what his absence will feel like. I haven't had enough time with him, I wasted so much. There are still many things I don't know about him. I've never seen him cry although I know that he's suffered major losses. The lawn mower cut off his right index finger and he had to drive himself to the hospital because no one was home; he's the one who discovered my mother's mother after she hung herself; and one of his children, my sister Alicia, died in her sleep when she was only three months old. But I was a small child when these things happened so I don't know how he managed his pain. I don't know if we'll ever talk about it.

Now, I try to meet him where he is instead of pushing him where I want to go. He isn't impulsive like me and I have learned to respect that. He, too, has risen, grown, and expanded to meet me somewhere in between. He reaches out to me now, he hugs me, he hugs my sons. He hugs his sons. He still writes what he feels in letters and cards but they are addressed to me now and come more often. He's changed what he could, what he felt he should.

My father still loves to dance. At my cousin's wedding he's the first one up for the Electric Slide. He licks his lips and sticks out his tongue, sliding it to one side of his mouth. He sways back and forth, snapping his fingers in front of him and lifting his eyebrows. He closes his eyes dreamily. Bending forward slightly he makes his moves, cool and dapper as always. "Go, Harry," folks shout. I like to dance, too. On the next record he reaches his hand out to me. We hold each other by the waist and glide around awkwardly at first, and then more smoothly until we hit our stride, circling the dance floor. I think about being a little girl, again, dancing on my father's shoes. I blink my eyes several times to keep the tears in. That was a long time ago, I tell myself. I've come a long bumpy way since then. So has my father. And most of our scars, collected along the way, have healed or are in the process of healing.

Pinkie Gordon Lane

Poems to My Father

VI. FINALE
I meant to tell you this, Papa,
I've divorced myself
from your memory.
The years never happened . . .
only the times when we
laughed
and strolled through the York Street Park
your sweaty shirt
and owl-shaped pants
caught up in the wind.

The trembling jaw and glassy eye
(pale mirages). The
foaming of your blood and
tears that never formed,
gathering like dark clouds.
Your skull melting
in the hollow of my hands
while I waited to grow up.
The years dissolving into a stream of
darkness and your face
a specter
of the mind.

You never happened,
Papa.

You were a shadow
a low light

a lost love
folding into the oval
of your night.

Lucille Clifton

forgiving my father

it is friday. we have come
to the paying of the bills.
all week you have stood in my dreams
like a ghost, asking for more time
but today is payday, payday old man;
my mother's hand opens in her early grave
and i hold it out like a good daughter.

there is no more time for you. there will
never be time enough daddy daddy old lecher
old liar. i wish you were rich so i could take it all
and give the lady what she was due
but you were the son of a needy father,
the father of a needy son;
you gave her all you had
which was nothing. you have already given her
all you had.

you are the pocket that was going to open
and come up empty any friday.
you were each other's bad bargain, not mine.
daddy old pauper   old prisoner,   old dead man
what am i doing here collecting?
you lie side by side in debtors' boxes
and no accounting will open them up.

3

Praise-Songs

. . . Daddy was a sure thing in a world of maybes, probables, hoped-
fors, and failures.   KALAMU YA SALAAM

My father was a warm, loving, caring man who was often called in the
middle of the night to get someone out of jail by posting his bond or
vouching for his character. This strong, hard-working African-
American businessman was also not averse to rolling up his sleeves in
the kitchen and cooking, or taking my sister and me to buy shoes if it
was more convenient for him to take us than it was for our mother.
                                        JOHNNETTA B. COLE

That I chose this topic was not accidental, for that was the text of my
father's life-loyalty to one's convictions. Unbending. Despite
anything. From my youngest days I was imbued with that concept.
This bedrock idea of integrity was taught by Reverend Robeson to his
children not so much by preachment . . . but, rather, by the daily
example of his life and work.   PAUL ROBESON

Born and raised on a farm in Sumter, South Carolina, my father
worked for thirty years at the New York City Housing Authority.
When I was a young girl, I would hear him early in the morning
preparing for another day of fixing elevators, stoves, windows,
refrigerators. . . . The whistling sound of the kettle would wake me
and I would walk, sleepy-eyed, to the kitchen and see my father
pouring boiling water into a coffee mug and stirring in freeze-dried

Maxwell and two lumps of sugar. He was "Daddy" then, but when I became a teenager, he was "Pop," and the sound that drew me to him was Motown coming from the hi-fi in the living room of our Brooklyn apartment. We would lipsinc the words and dance with our hands and hips the way the Temptations did. When I graduated from college, I called him "Dad" and what I began to hear was his voice telling me stories about life that left me thinking. Always thinking.

ANGELA GETTER

The dominant figure of my youth was a small man, five feet two inches tall. In my mind's eye, I am leaning out of the window of our apartment, and I spot him coming down the street from the Intervale Avenue subway station. He wears a coat and tie, and a small fedora is perched on his head. He has a newspaper tucked under his arm. His overcoat is unbuttoned, and it flaps at his sides as he approaches with a brisk, toes-out stride. He is whistling and stops to greet the druggist, the baker, our building super, almost everybody he passes. To some kids on the block he is a faintly comical figure. Not to me. This jaunty, confident little man is Luther Powell, my father.

COLIN POWELL

[My father] worked hard in a paper bag factory, but he'd still come home full of energy and call out for my brother and mother and me. We would follow him to the fields where the grass grew tall as wheat, and the four of us would play hide and seek there. . . . When it was time to go home, my father would reach down and pick me up under one arm, my brother under the other, lean down so my mother could crawl up his back, and then run all the way home . . .

BILL RUSSELL

My father was a race-man, proud, courageous and insistent on racial progress. He was an educator who exacted exemplary performance from his students both in academics and in character. I remember as a young girl attending a school assembly he had called when a student's tennis shoes had been stolen. "If there is a child in this school so desperate for shoes that they would steal," my father said, "come see me and I will buy you a pair of shoes." My father meant that. His wallet was open for those in need, and so was our home. Because there was no high school for blacks in small Texas towns, Daddy, and

Mother, too, invited students from rural areas to live in our home during the school year. We just pulled up extra chairs at the dinner table, made pallets on the floor and space in our beds.

BRENDA COLE

Other colored men, sometimes in soiled work clothes, sometimes in rumpled, ill-fitting suits, would regularly come to see my father, carrying school books in hands soiled from a day's work. He would escort them into his study where they sat for an hour or more in private, reading the Bible or a first-grade primer together. Through the walls I could hear their murmuring voices hesitating and stumbling over word after word. I thought it strange that these grown-up visitors had such difficulty pronouncing easy words like "the" and "men." I did not understand until I was about six years old that my father was in fact teaching them to read—and especially to read the Bible. He explained that I should not belittle them because of their illiteracy, telling me how hard their lives had been in the South, how they had been forced to leave school early to help support their families. He continued to have students at home until his death, quietly teaching scores of black men to read. SHIRLEY HAZLIT

Gwendolyn Brooks

EXCERPT FROM

Report from Part I

Home meant my father, with kind eyes, songs, and tense recitations for my brother and myself. A favorite of his, a wonderful poem about a pie-making lady. Along had come a man, weary, worn, to beg of the lady a pie. Those already baked, she informed him, were too large for the likes of him. She said she would bake another. It, too, was "large." And the next was large. And the next, and the next. Finally the traveler, completely out of patience, berated her and exclaimed that henceforth she should draw her own sustenance from the bark of trees. And she became, *mirabile dictu*, a woodpecker and flew off. We never tired of that. My father seemed to Gwendolyn and Raymond a figure of power. He had those rich Artistic Abilities, but he had more. He could fix anything that broke or stopped. He could build long-lasting fires in the ancient furnace below. He could paint the house, inside and out, and could whitewash the basement. He could spread the American Flag in wide loud magic across the front of our house on the Fourth of July and Decoration Day. He could chuckle. No one has ever had, no one will ever have, a chuckle exactly like my father's. It was gentle, it was warmly happy, it was heavyish but not hard. It was secure, and seemed to us an assistant to the Power that registered with his children. My father, too, was almost our family doctor. We had Dr. Carter, of course, precise and semi-twinkly and effective—but it was not always necessary to call him. My father had wanted to be a doctor. Thwarted, he read every "doctor book" (and he remembered much from a Black tradition) he could reach, learning fine secrets and curing us with steams, and fruit compotes, and dexterous rubs, and, above all, with bedside compassion. "Well, there, young lady! How's that throat now?" "Well, let's see now. This salve will take care of that bruise! Now, we're going to be all right." In illness there was an advantage: the invalid was royalty for the run of the seizure.

Audre Lorde

EXCERPT FROM

Zami: A New Spelling of My Name

Except for political matters, my father was a man of few words. But he carried on extensive conversations with himself in the bathroom every morning.

During the last years of the war, my father could be found more often away from home than not, or at best, sleeping a few hours before going back out to his night job at the war plant.

My mother would rush home from the office, market, fuss with us a little, and fix supper. Phyllis, Helen, or I would have put on the rice or potatoes already, and maybe my mother had seasoned some meat earlier in the day and left it on the stove with a note for one of us to turn on the fire low under the pot when we came home. Or perhaps there would be something left on purpose from last night's supper ("Leave some of that for your father's dinner tomorrow!"). On those afternoons, I didn't wait for my mother to come home. Instead, I packed the food up myself and took off downtown on the bus, headed for my father's office.

I heated each separate portion until it was piping hot. Carefully, I packed the hot rice and savory bits of meat stew or spicy chicken and gravy into scoured milk bottles which we saved for that purpose. I packed the vegetables separately in their own bottle, with a little pat of butter if we could get it, or margarine, on top. I wrapped each bottle in layers of newspapers, and then in an old towel, to keep the food warm. Placing them in a shopping bag together with the shirt and sweater that my mother had left for me to take to my father, I set off by bus down to the office, heavy with a sense of mission and accomplishment.

The bus from Washington Heights ran downtown and across 125th Street. I got off at Lenox Avenue, and walked the three blocks up to the office, past bars and grocery stores and small groups of people in lively conversation on the street.

Sometimes when I arrived, my father was downstairs in the office already, poring over receipt books or taxes or bills. Sometimes he was still asleep in a room upstairs, and the janitor had to go up and knock on the room door to waken him. I was never allowed to go upstairs, nor to enter the room where my father slept. I always wondered what mysteries occurred "upstairs," and what it was up there my parents never wanted me to see. I think it was that same vulnerability that had so shocked and embarrassed me the day I peered into their bedroom at home. His ordinary humanity.

When my father came downstairs, I kissed him hello, and he went into the back of the office to wash his face and hands preparatory to eating. I spread out the meal carefully, on a special desk in the back room. If anyone came in to see my father while he was eating, I wrote out a receipt, proudly, or relayed the message to him in the back room. For my father, eating was too human a pastime to allow just anyone to see him at it.

If no one came in, I sat quietly in the back room and watched him eat. He was meticulously neat, placing his bones in even rows on the paper towel beside his plate. Sometimes my father looked up and saw me watching him, and he reached out and gave me a morsel of meat or a taste of rice and gravy from his plate.

Other times I sat with my book, quietly reading, but secretly waiting and hoping for this special treat. Even if I had already just eaten the same food, or even if it was some dish I did not particularly like, these tastes of my father's food from his plate in the back room of his office had an enchantment to them that was delicious and magical, and precious. They form the fondest and closest memories I have of warm moments shared with my father. There were not many.

When my father was finished with his meal, I rinsed out the bottles, and washed his dish and silverware. I placed them back upon the shelf especially cleared for them, and covered them with the cloth napkin that was kept there for that purpose, to protect them from the dust of the back room. I carefully repacked the bottles into the shopping bag, and took the nickel carfare that my father gave me for the bus trip back. I kissed him goodbye and headed for home.

Sometimes no more than two or three sentences passed between us during the whole time we were together in the office. But I remember those evenings, particularly in the springtime, as very special and satisfying times.

Anthony Walton

The World According to Claude

"You can get by, but you can't get away." I kept hearing my father's voice, and it was annoying. Here I was, spending a beautiful Saturday morning in a Santa Monica hardware store instead of driving up the California coast or sleeping in.

I was sorting through aisles of plastic pipe connectors, all because someone had tried to get away with building a sprinkler system on the cheap. The system had ruptured, flooding my friend's yard and side-walk. To avoid a hefty plumber's fee, we had to do the repairs ourselves. I couldn't help hearing my father again: *"Do it right the first time."*

I've grown accustomed to hearing Claude's voice. As I've gotten older, I hear him almost every day. *"You're penny-wise and dollar-foolish."* *"You got champagne tastes, but a water pocket."* *"Don't believe everything you hear."* As my friends and I run into brick walls working our way into adulthood, I am increasingly amazed at the sometimes brutal truth that my father has imparted in his seemingly offhand way.

One Christmas Eve, he and I were working on the furnace of a rental house he owns. It was about twenty below outside and, I thought, colder inside. Tormented by visions of a family-room fire, cocoa, and pamper-ing by my mother (I was home from college), I wanted my father to call it a day and get on with the festivities. After all, it *was* Christmas.

"We can't," said my father. "This is these people's home. They should be home on Christmas." He continued wrenching and whang-ing on a pipe.

I saw an opening. "Exactly. *We* should be home on Christmas."

He shook his head. "It ain't that simple."

"It'd be simple to call somebody."

"You got a thousand dollars?"

"No. But you do."

"The reason I got it is, I don't give it away on things I can do myself."

A couple of hours later, when we had finished and were loading our tools into the car, he looked at me. "See? That wasn't so hard. But nobody can tell you nothing. That thousand dollars will come in handy. In fact, I'll probably have to send it to *you*." He shook his head, closed the trunk and said, "Boy, just keep on living."

"Just keep on living." I often thought it sounded like a threat, but now I see that he was challenging me to see the world as it is and to live in it responsibly. I was like a lot of kids I knew, middle-class, happy, successful at most of what I attempted—but largely at the expense (literally) of my father and the world he created. Now as I contemplate creating a world for his grandchildren, I gain more respect for such an accomplishment and the unblinking steadiness it takes.

My father is the kind of man overlooked or ridiculed by the media. His values—fidelity, simplicity, and frugality—are spurned by younger people, but I am beginning to see that these are the very values that keep a society functioning.

"Boy, you got to get a routine." He has gone to a job he does not like, in a steel factory, for thirty-six years. One day I asked him why, and he looked at me as if I had rocks in my head: "That's where the money is." And he has been married to the same woman for thirty-one years. "Marriage gives you a reason to do things."

As I gain more experience in a world where, it seems, virtually everything is disposable, I begin to appreciate the unsurpassed values of steadiness and limited objectives. I'm reminded of the television comedy *All in the Family*, and how much of the humor was directed at the willfully uninformed, purposely contrary Archie Bunker. It occurs to me, as I contemplate buying my first house, that everyone else, including his son-in-law, Meathead, who gloried in putting Archie down, was sleeping in Archie's house and eating Archie's grub. I'm increasingly aware of how much security my father has brought to my adventures.

They were adventures he rarely understood. My father was born into excruciating poverty in rural Mississippi during the depression. He had very little formal education, leaving school early to support his brothers and sisters, and bounced from Holly Springs, Mississippi, to Memphis to Chicago to the Air Force. But along the way he acquired a worldview as logical as Newton's.

The first and most important law of the world according to Claude is *"Have the facts."* God is the only thing he takes on faith. Recently, searching for a new lawn tractor, he went to three different dealers and got three different prices for the same machine. *"I'm from just outside Missouri; you got to show me."* He then went to a fourth dealer and purchased a larger tractor for less money.

I used to laugh at one of his hobbies, analyzing financial tables. He would look up from half an hour of calculating and announce: "Did you know if you put five cents in the bank when Columbus came to America, at $5\frac{1}{4}$ interest compounded daily, today you'd have $1,000,565,162 (or some such figure)?" Now I phone him for advice about financing a house or a car, and I'm beginning to understand how he can own real estate and several cars, educate his kids, and regularly bail those kids out of jams. *"Boy, a nickel only goes so many ways. But nobody can tell you nothing. Just keep on living."*

And I've kept on living, and surrendered a lot of illusions, one by one. Claude says, *"You reap what you sow."* I call this idea karma, that what goes around comes around. Claude cautioned me one night as I went out to break off with a girlfriend, "Remember, you got a sister." The notion that there was a link between my behavior and how I could expect my sister to be treated has served as a painfully clear guide ever since. And, in the current romantic and sexual climate, I like to think it's saved me some trouble. *"You can get by, but you can't get away."*

Claude values experience. I remember going with him in search of a family attorney. He decided against several without saying why, before suddenly settling on a firm right there in the office. On the way home he explained: "I was looking for a 'Daddy' kind of man. Somebody who's been through some battles, who's raised children. He had those pictures up of his grandchildren. That tells me what he values. And I think he's already made most of his mistakes." When I asked him where he had acquired all this insight, he laughed. "I didn't get to be fifty and Black by being stupid. You go around enough times, you begin to catch on."

Claude doesn't put a lot of stock in what he calls book learning. He says, "College never made anybody smart." But he has financed about $100,000 worth of book learning—and endured its being thrown in his face until the thrower had to return, hat in hand, for one kind of aid or another.

This leads to another basic law: *"Be realistic."* Claude sees the world very clearly, and what he sees is often not pretty. "It was like this when I got here, and it's going to be like this when I leave, so I'm not going to worry about it." I'm coming to see the wisdom in this. Young people often have to experience the world for many years before they have a hint of understanding human nature and, more important, history. For this reason, they often misread the world. They do not understand that poverty, war, and racism have always been conditions of human life. Worse, when confronted by the unrelenting intractability of these problems, they often abandon smaller, but equally worthy, goals.

Claude likes to say, *"If everybody would clean up his yard, the rest of the world would take care of itself."* That statement verges on oversimplification, but as a way of recognizing one's true responsibilities in the world it makes irreproachable sense.

This is probably the key to the world according to Claude—the power of limited objectives. By being realistic about our goals, we increase our chances of success in the long run. "Anything we do is going to be hard, and if it isn't hard, it's going to be difficult. But that just means it's going to take us a little longer." To me, this acceptance of the world and life as they are, and not as we would have them be, is the key to becoming an adult.

And so I am forced to acknowledge that the world according to Claude is increasingly, in my experience, the world as it is. I realize you *can't* put a price on a clear conscience, as Claude loves to say; very often the ability to live with one's self is all one can hope for. I'm beginning to see the power in, to spin a metaphor, not needing to play every single golf course on the planet; Claude has built a putting green in his back yard and mastered that. He has made his peace with the world, and that is enough.

Most of all, I realize that every time Claude said, *"Nobody can tell you nothing,"* he went ahead and told me something—and it was always the truth. Except maybe once. We were arguing, and I took exception to what I perceived as high-handedness. "You should respect me," I said. "We're supposed to be friends."

He looked at me gravely. "We are not *friends*. I am your father."

I haven't quite figured this out, because he is far from being my best friend. Sometimes I'm not sure we even know each other. But it seems he is the truest friend I have had, and can expect to have.

Sandra Y. Govan

The King of the Duke's Mixtures: Memories at the Corners

I. JUNE 28, 1996   *The Birthday*
When I open my eyes this sunny morning, stretch, and look at the clock
radio, it is 6:45 in Charlotte, one hour earlier in Chicago. "Is it too early
to call Daddy?" I ask myself. Then I answer, "Nah, he should be up." So
I call.

Today is my father's birthday. Born in 1919, the "Bloody Red Summer," he is seventy-seven on this day. Naturally, as his best girl, I need
to wish him a happy birthday and sing one, or both, of the ritual birthday songs on his day. I know to call early in the morning because training, experience, and instinct tell me that if I do not catch him before day
breaks, I might not catch him at all. My daddy, with the accent on the
first syllable of his last name, Govan, will not be sitting around on his
birthday, no matter the years the calendar records for him.

In his Hyde Park apartment the phone rings only twice before he
picks it up. His alert, cheery but gruff, "Hello?" evinces no trace of
sleep, no old-folks, tired-and-weary blues on this first day of the
seventy-seventh year. I have indeed just caught him for he is already up
and moving. Breaking first into the up tempo, upbeat, jazzy Stevie
Wonder version of the birthday song, which for me is largely chorus, I
sing "HAPPY BIRTHDAY TO YOU, HAPPY BIRTHDAY, HAPPY BIRTHDAY. HAPPY
BIRTHDAY TO YOU." Then I hit the ritual questions daughters ask when
they live eight hundred miles away and have to check in every week. "Hi
Daddy. Whatcha doing? How you doing this birthday morning?" His
expected response, "Oooh Sweetie, I'm doing fine," carries the soothing reassurance that all is still all right in my father's world. His answer,

however, to my first question is somewhat less comforting yet very typical of this indomitable man, my father.

At the crack of dawn Daddy is dressing to go downtown to the Greyhound station, preparing to catch the bus from Chicago to Cedar Rapids, Iowa. There, he will pick up a car for the auto transport company which hired him last fall and drive the car to Racine, Wisconsin. At seventy-seven, following a thirty-year stint as a bus driver for the Chicago Transit Authority, or the CTA, my Daddy is still on the road, still doing as he pleases and going where he chooses—the pleas of associates, friends, and relatives "falling on deaf ears" as my mama would have said, or considered saying and then dismissed, which is a wee bit more accurate. As his only daughter, it falls on me to be supportive; I do not fuss about such trips, nor do I question him to death about the itinerary and his health, or worry over much about his vision or his reflexes. Instead, I have enlisted ministers and friends around the country to pray for him; and I regularly plead with my mama, asking her to tell St. Peter to put his best squad of guardian angels to work watching over my dad, and those in his path, while he is on the road. I have made my peace with the fact that age notwithstanding, my Dad is a tensile-tough, sturdy and steady, small brown Iron Man. Indeed, Tanzel R. Govan is a man of many facets; a newly made church deacon and a poker player, an avid fisherman, an affable and charming cross between the highly prized Timex watch (that takes that licking yet keeps on ticking) and the celebrated Energizer bunny who keeps going and going and going, marching to his own drums.

I know when I call on his birthday that whether it means working or not on this special day, he is going to do what he wants to do—always has, always will. And, I know he will frame a story afterward about his newest adventure. Always has, always will. These peculiar road trips are nothing if not more grist for his mill. "Sweetie, the fog was so thick all morning—you could barely see the taillights ahead of you; yet fools were flying. And dadburnit, don't you know, just as I got to the Ohio Turnpike junction, I turned left instead of right because I just couldn't see the sign. I didn't go too far out of my way though before I got off and turned around."

Although African-Americans did not know the word "griot" until

Alex Haley gave it to us in *Roots*, my Dad always provided that role in our family. His stories about his life and his adventures always figured prominently in our relationship, and when I was a child, I would sit mesmerized for hours by the tales of Daddy's exploits. As a consequence, I did my best to model my life on his, with minor adjustments to allow for differences from his "old days" in Forrest City, Arkansas, during the twenties and my own childhood in Chicago in the fifties. One of his stories, about his 1929 arrival in Chicago, so stirred my imagination that I cast my father as a Black Huckleberry Finn and myself as Huck's Black sister.

II. SPRING, 1929/SPRING, 1957   *The Runaways*
The picture stirred powerful emotions—Daddy as conquering hero. Daddy as a ten-year-old child warrior—wiry, slight, standing astride the top of the still-moving freight train, having hoboed in the boxcar from Forrest City to Chicago, alone. Daddy taking in the city from atop the freight newly arrived from the country, determined to shake Arkansas dust from his feet. Daddy miraculously dodging the high-voltage lines carrying electricity through the rail yard. Daddy, quickly climbing down from the train, avoiding the rail yard bulls harassing the hoboes, to make his way to the streetcar line. With only a fragment of an address he started the search for his Aunt Mary, canvassing strangers to find this long unseen aunt who lived, as he intoned, "on the 5200 block of Lafayette Avenue"—and that was all the address he knew.

Audacious. That was the word that fit my Daddy, fit him as a child and fits him now. Whenever I heard the arrival story, my father's audacity, his bravery, his depiction of a marvelous adventure, resonated within me. At nine I finally asked him, "Daddy, why did you run away?" He merely said then, "Sweetie, I was tired of the whippings from my stepfather." Now, I never had a mean stepfather, and I was certainly never whipped so that the welts and scars remained forever. But, as a child, I sometimes *felt* abused so I determined to be like my Daddy. I could have adventures like his. I, too, could be brave. Like him, I could run away too—despite the fact that I was a girl and there were no slow-moving freight trains to jump near our home in Morgan Park. It was thirty years later before I ever heard the story's darker underside, before

I ever knew the more complex conflicts which caused my father to flee his home and his family to come to Chicago and be in the world.

But in the spring of 1957, when I left home for the first time independently, my reasons for leaving were a poor parody of my father's. Call it second child syndrome or sibling rivalry, but as a nine-year-old fourth grader, I fostered the belief that my mother loved my brother more than she loved me. He, I believed, was her privileged favorite and I was merely her burden, her handicapped child whom she would "have to take care of for the rest of her life." I'd heard her say this on the telephone to one of her friends and it wounded my pride and made me angry. I became determined to show everyone that I could take care of myself, that I had the courage of my father to make my own way in the world, and that I didn't need nobody to take care of me." I could do it myself. I also knew that my brother, just eleven then, was always threatening to run away but that he, lacking real character and true resolve, never made it further than camping on the steps just inside the back door. Because I had Daddy's genes and had really heard his stories, I had more courage. At nine, I carefully prepared to escape a home where I felt stifled and "unloved" by the principal power broker, my mother.

The short version of my tale is that I took my brother's Boy Scout canteen and filled it with water; I put clean underwear in a blue bandanna and tied this to a stick; then, I put a newspaper in the window to signal the school bus driver not to stop for me because I would not be bussed to the Jane A. Neil Handicapped Children's school that day. My preparations complete, I slipped down the steps and out the back door while my brother was frantically calling mama at her job to tell on me. While he was dialing, I made it to the garage and hid behind the door. When he came to the garage to check my whereabouts and then returned to the phone to report, I scooted out the garage, made it down the alley to Aberdeen, and then over to 111th Street to wait for the bus. I even bought the Chicago *Sun Times* at Fillmore's corner store. No one questioned me; no one stopped me. And when the big green CTA bus came, I boarded it and rode off. My river was 111th Street. I was going to have me an adventure, just like Huckleberry Finn, and just like my daddy.

Now, Chicago in the fifties was a highly segregated city, as Martin

Luther King, Jr., was to discover a decade later. It was a city divided by whites into ethnic enclaves—Irish, Italians, Poles—and covertly hostile racial camps. It was also bifurcated by railroad tracks; and invariably, the Negroes (as we were called then) lived on one side of the tracks, and the whites lived on the other. We met at the schools and the shopping centers but we never crossed into each other's territory without specific business intent. At nine, I knew that only vaguely. Because I encountered helpful white people at my school all the time, my teachers and my physical therapists, whites neither frightened nor intimidated me. When I got off the bus after riding a long way, across the railroad tracks and maybe two miles from home, I was in white territory but undaunted by my surroundings. I rang the bell at what seemed to me a nice house— the yard looked neat and there was a swing on the arched red brick porch. When the white woman answered the door, I politely said, "Hello. I'm running away. Do you have any cookies?" In the stories I'd read runaway children were always given sweets.

That poor housewife, whose name my family never knew, must have gone into shock upon seeing her visitor; but she was also a parent, at home with her own small child, so she quickly recovered her aplomb. She invited me in and offered the requisite cookies and milk; after some small talk we discussed my reasons for leaving home. She utterly dismissed the notion that my mama did not love me, pointing to how pretty I was ("But you look like a brown China doll; your mommy must love you to take such care.") and how neatly I was dressed and how nice my hair was braided. And then, she slipped away to call the police on the pretext of going to check her clothes dryer. Of course I overheard her call, and slick little me was on the way back out the door just as the cops arrived.

The police officers who took me away in the back of the squad car that morning were not the gentle caring cops of any story I'd read. They were massive and white, with blotchy reddened skin, scraggly hair, and fierce beaked noses. They were also callous and indifferent. I was just another small colored child whom they stuck alone in a corner chair and thought they could ignore while they typed reports on huge high desks. Although my wails and lamentations finally produced at least an ice cream cone, they did not talk to me nor offer comfort as television policemen always did. The sought-for solace finally came from my daddy who arrived to fetch me home. Called off his bus route to search for me ("She's your daughter. You go find her," Mama had said), he found me in the squat grey concrete Monterey Avenue substation, just above Vincennes Avenue. He claimed later in retelling the story that he could hear me from down on the street, wailing and crying between laps at the cone. By the tone of my cries he knew I was unhurt and was therefore reassured. And although I was truly glad to see him walk through that door, after huge hugs and weak smiles, we nonetheless had to engage in a bit of plea bargaining before I agreed to leave the police station. When Daddy said, "Sweetie, let's go home now," because I was afraid that this time, somebody would actually use a belt or a brush on me—despite the fact that I had largely sane parents who seldom were driven to spank, I actually replied, "No. Mama is going spank me. She doesn't really love me like she loves Tanny." Then my father explained how parents love all their children, whether they are first or last, boys or girls. And he added, "If you promise me never to run away again, I'll talk to your mother for you and you won't get a spanking this time. But if you ever pull this stunt again . . ." Bargain made, he gave me his handkerchief, dried my eyes, wiped my nose, signed some papers, and hand in hand, we went home.

III. SUMMER, 1962   *South to a Very Strange Place*
I will tell anyone who asks that the ages between twelve and twenty-two are hardest on mother/daughter relationships. Even when a good father is there to act as referee or intermediary, the going is going to be rough. Certainly, in my house it was like that. Ma and I seemed to have it particularly hard, the fallout from our unequal contests of wills filtered over the family. So when Daddy announced that he was going to go visit his family back in Arkansas, for the first time since he was grown, Mama told him she would pack my bags because I was going with him. My brother could not go; he was in summer school studying math. It would just be Daddy and me. Actually, this was not a problem. I loved being with my daddy, going anywhere.

When Mama threw me out of the house to go with Daddy, I was fourteen. The Freedom Rides had started but the movement had not impacted upon me yet. Dad and I were driving together back to the Forrest City I'd only heard about. In the long white Bonneville we had a

picnic basket packed full of fried chicken for Dad, and baloney and peanut butter sandwiches for me, plus bottles of pop. We were going to visit
Grandma Bertha and to meet assorted cousins I'd only heard tell of. I
don't remember the whole route or all of our many hundreds of conversations. I do recall we stopped in St. Louis to see Aunt Eva and her
daughters, Aramenter and Jean. I know that we took route 67 from Missouri to Arkansas. And I recall quite sharply that once we arrived in Arkansas, my Dad stopped telling stories and grew quite somber. "You're
going to see some things unfamiliar," he sternly warned me, "maybe
hear some things a little off color; but, whatever you do, whatever you
see or hear, don't say anything, you hear?"

He had never given me an injunction like that; questions, conversation, pointed observations, and words were the hallmark of our relationship. I honestly didn't know what to make of his command to be silent. Then came the test. A gas stop at an Arkansas filling station. And
there they were, my first sighting of the terrible tangible signs denoting
racial status. "COLORED, WHITES." Before the forbidden question could
emerge halfway out of my mouth, "Daddy, why . . .?" my father told me
to "hush" and that he would "explain later." Baffled as much by the mystery as I was subdued by his tone, I grew silent for a while in the car as
Daddy "explained" the tense and convoluted race relations circa 1962.
My anger did not develop then; it took me a year or so, and the first of
the Freedom Rides, to become truly angry.

When we arrived at my grandmother's and I saw the family enclave,
Daddy had much more explaining to do. My Chicago eyes had never
seen the grinding poverty of Black rural or small town America. I had
not then read Richard Wright and was unaccustomed to dilapidated
houses pitched crazily on stilts with holes in the roof even I could see.
Walls in my part of Chicago had no chinks in them and yards in Morgan
Park had grass in them, not dirt. And by the early 1960s, all of our
neighborhood streets (and many of our alleys) were paved, not red dirt
roads. I liked the few cousins I met and I loved combing Grandma Bertha's long silver hair as she sat in her rocker, but I did not like the oppres-
sive air of Forrest City. At that point, I knew instinctively why my father
had fled and why my mama had never come back to this place after she
and my dad married. My inquiries "Daddy why?" "Daddy how?" were
met with the constant injunction, "Sweetie, don't say anything."

In retrospect, I suppose that my dad was afraid that I would embarrass his family or hurt someone's feelings. Our conversation on the way back to Chicago was not lighthearted. Daddy shared no more stories about his adventures as a golf caddy. Now we talked quietly and seriously about class and race and the importance of a good education in America.

IV. 1950s — 1990s   *The Traveling Man*

We went frequently to Toledo, Ohio, when I was a child. Daddy had some terrific uncles there, Uncle Andy and Uncle Burns, big genial Black men who were warm to small children. And Grandpa Fred, Daddy's long-absent real father, lived there with Grandma Govan, his third wife. Grandpa Fred, the former railroad porter, dipped snuff from a coffee can on his front porch, and short round Grandma Govan was always playfully threatening, "Child, I'm gonna hurt you," if I did not eat all the overcooked cabbage she placed on my plate—yet I loved going to see them anyway. Part of my joy was the arrival adventure because Daddy never took the same route twice from Chicago. We saw various aspects of Toledo, and sundry other parts of northern Ohio, while trying to relocate Grandpa Govan's house. Somehow Mama found this inability to use the same tollway exits twice as less than endearing; I always saw it as another great oportunity for a scenic tour. Daddy just drove.

This peculiar habit of my father's to just drive until he finds it—the right road, the right vicinity, the right house—has remained with him over time. It is a charming character trait if one has time to meander or a serious character flaw if one is a bit uptight. Daddy is a focused driver and once he settles in behind the wheel, adjusts his golf cap to the proper rakish angle, and finishes aligning his mirrors and his seat, he is good to go. He is also, unfortunately, occasionally oblivious to surrounding traffic. Recently, returning from Flossmore, Illinois, to Chicago, driving up I-57 in his small but sporty white Infinity M-30, Dad had a run in with seven Chicago cops. He may be the only Black man in America to face down seven police officers and emerge unscathed. He told me the story:

"Sweetie, it was night and I was coming back home. I wasn't speeding but I was driving with the traffic flow. Then, I noticed the car behind me had his lights in my mirror. So, I moved over a lane. He changed lanes with me. He didn't speed up and he didn't pass. I said to myself, 'What is this joker up to?' but I did not floor it. So, I just kept driving and he stayed right with me. Oh, Sweetie, I'd say he was behind me for about seven or eight miles. Finally, I pulled just far enough ahead of him to see the blue light. 'Uh oh, boy,' I said, 'now you're in for it,' and pulled over to the side of the road. The officer who came up to the car was a young Black policeman. He said to me, "Mister, I've been chasing you for the last eight miles. You've had seven cars tailing you and now you have stopped seven police officers. You've been leading a parade back here. Why didn't you stop? What is your problem?' "

Of course, Daddy's problem had been that he simply had not seen the blue lights of Chicago's finest. The cop was up so close behind him that Dad could not see his flashing lights in the mirror. But he was calm and collected as he answered the officer's questions. Once the other officers saw they had no Rodney King, just my unflappable father, with his un-impeachable diffidence and self-deprecating humor, they turned and left the scene, all that pumped adrenalin for naught. Though the chase officer was disgusted and probably mildly perplexed, my dad, as he usu-ally does, to borrow one of his favorite British phrases, came out of that one "a bit of all right." He did not even get a ticket.

V. SEPTEMBER 1991   *The Arrival*

Exactly one month after we buried my mother, my dad came to be with me in Charlotte, North Carolina, while I underwent my third hip re-placement surgery. He'd come to Charlotte in 1985 for the first two—left hip one week, right hip the next—until Mama could come down; but this time, September 1991, he was coming alone without a backup second shift. Since we were both veterans of my various surgeries and since I knew how utterly boring the recovery period could be—trapped in the house, unable to ride in, let alone drive a car, and unable to con-centrate on books or Scrabble because of the pain meds, I determined that I would interview Dad and record his autobiography. I had a three-fold purpose in mind—getting his story before anything happened to him; obtaining more details about his life with Mama before I came along to squish myself between them on the couch (no question but I was intensely jealous and felt he should have waited for me); and keeping both our minds from fingering the jagged wound of our recent loss.

Although I believed myself familiar with the details of Dad's early life and the arrival story was almost a totem for me, I nonetheless asked Dad to tell the story again, "this time for the record." So, we sat together at my kitchen table, me with two pillows beneath my hip and my right leg extended at the proper angle, and Dad just across from me, ever solicitous of my comfort. Then my daddy told the arrival story again, complete this time with details he had never provided before.

It seems my father was not a novice at slipping aboard trains. Two lines, the Rock Island, which ran from east to west, and the Union Pacific, which ran north and south, formed a junction in Forrest City. Dad had practiced hopping the freights; he'd ride the twenty-seven miles to Brinkley, Arkansas, for a test run or he'd ride a mile or two from Forrest City and jump back off. He liked riding between the first car and the engine. Once he rode to Pine Bluff, a distance of approximately 150 miles, and then back to Forrest City. Another time, he rode all the way to East St. Louis. Although he was scared to death by the tales hoboes told, Dad said he slept in the hobo camps and ate with the hoboes often, bumming food just as the hoboes did. In those days, obtaining food from strangers was not that difficult. "Sweetie," he told me, "I'd just go from door to door, asking for food; and if they had it, they'd feed you. Especially the Black cooks working for white families; they'd make you a sandwich or sometimes you would do an errand, but in most cases, they just gave you food."

By the time he turned ten, Dad was a restless high-spirited child rapidly becoming aware of his options. He'd already been to see his grandfather, walking the seven miles alone to Marianna, Arkansas, where "Governor Govan," a barber, was to the local Black populace a fairly big man in town. He knew he had a father somewhere out there who worked for the railroads, and he knew he had an aunt in Chicago. So, when his stepfather, who was the greens-keeper at the Forrest City Golf Club, went "to pay him for old and new" once more, Dad took off. He was tired of the hated whipping with elm tree or peach tree switches; he recollected too well being hung up in a burlap tobacco sack at age four and left in the barn all day.

Dad abandoned Forrest City with nothing more than the clothes on his back—no knapsack, no bandanna on a pole stuffed with spare clothing or food, not one red penny. He hopped the Rock Island and rode to Springfield, Illinois; sometimes riding the rods beneath the train, sometimes on top of the car, sometimes inside the boxcar, always careful to avoid being spotted by railroad detectives and to keep away from hoboes who might be dangerous. From Springfield, he jumped another train, bound south to East St. Louis; and in East St. Louis he finally climbed aboard the top of a high-speed freight that was headed directly for the Chicago rail yards. For a moment, as he reached this climactic point in the retelling, the two "arrival stories" converged and resonated again. My childhood memory of Daddy the conqueror returned and I saw him once more standing atop the boxcar as it clattered beneath the high-tension wires used by the suburban electric trains. I saw and heard the railroad workers on the ground, seeing him up there and "almost having a fit," afraid he would electrocute himself, yelling up at him to "Stoop down! Get down!"

Then, the story turned down an unfamiliar road. When Dad climbed down from the freight, the first person he talked to was a white man—a rail yard master who saw him, spoke kindly to him, asked where he was going. In Dad's words:

"He said, 'You want some food?' And I said, 'Yes.' So he apparently was something like a yardmaster. I'll never forget him because he was the first person I'd ever run into . . . or ever heard of . . . or known was a queer. He fed me, then molested me. Then he gave me fifteen cents and directed me to State Street from the Illinois Central yards to downtown in Chicago.

My dad caught the streetcar but missed his stop and rode another several miles into the south side of Chicago before he realized he'd gone too far. Someone helped this ten-year-old runaway from Arkansas with directions about how to get back, but even so my dad said "I was so dumb that I tried to board a northbound streetcar on the left-hand side. After several stopped and I saw people getting off on the other side, I finally got the right idea, walked around to the other side and got on. I told the conductor where I wanted to go and he told me to stand right there on the rear platform with him and he would show me where 57th

Street was." Dad finally found his way to Aunt Mary's house where he was welcomed, bathed, fed, and allowed to stay in safety.

This was the first time Dad had told me this full, dark version of the arrival story. I wondered briefly why—perhaps because it was "for the record," perhaps because my mother's death made him feel his own time to tell all of his story was running out. That day in my kitchen, I stretched out my hands and squeezed his, tyring to squeeze hard enough to reach the boy he had been.

VI.   *King of the Duke's Mixture*
In my unbiased estimation, my father was in many respects a man ahead of his time. To me, he has always been patient, gentle, thoughtful, nurturing; he was, perhaps, a bit too passive when strong feelings seemed necessary; perhaps a bit too quiet when, from my point of view or my mama's, verbalizing would have stood him in better stead. But, that said, he always shared with me, always talked with me, and up until the time I chose to pursue a Ph.D. instead of a law degree I would have crawled over quicksand to avoid hurting my daddy, to avoid hearing the stinging "Sweetie, I am so disappointed."

Rather than my mother, it was my daddy who alone brought me home from the hospital back in August of 1948. Eons before it became acceptable for fathers to hold major childcare responsibilities or to share in domestic duties, my daddy did it (Mama said she "trained him" but he did it nonetheless.). Perhaps it was a bonding experience, for in the era long before child safety seats, when he had to hold me in one arm and drive us home with the other, we became a father/daughter duo and I was forever imprinted as Daddy's child. It helped that neighbors and family friends always said, and I mean always, "She looks just like you, Govan," and as I thought him extraordinarily handsome (despite an absence of hair across the top of his cranium), it was extremely flattering to hear we looked alike because that meant I was cute.

I spent my early childhood tucked up under him when he was home, and he would cart me, casts on both legs, around the neighborhood in the much beloved red wagon. I spent my youth talking with him, learning to appreciate the supple versatility of the English language while we went fishing in Wisconsin lakes or played endless Scrabble games at the yellow formica kitchen table or drove across Chicago from south side to west (to see the venerable great Aunt Mayo, or the much adored Aunt Mabel and Uncle Sam, or the largely unfamiliar and therefore strange host of west side cousins); or when we sat at the kitchen table weekend mornings eating his scratch pancakes and sausage or scratch waffles and sausage or baked cheese and onion eggs à la Govan with bacon on the side, or scratch biscuits and rolled omelettes; or, tasting the grandly mysterious concoction, sometimes awful and sometimes swell, dubbed Daddy's Duke's Mixture. It was always, "Sweetie, taste this."

I spent the rest of my formative years garnering the bits of wisdom he earnestly dispensed about survival in the real world. Frequently these were offered over school day lunches ("Sweetie, when you must fight a bigger girl . . .") or on one of the long drives to see ancient Aunt Paralee over in Gary or huge Unlce Windy with his west side tribe. Later, the tidbits and pearls came on the short trips home from O'Hare after a trip, or standing by the car as I prepared to hit the road on my solo trips back to graduate school in Atlanta or to my first real job in Iowa ("Sweetie, don't go off and become an egghead, you hear?"), or the second job in Kentucky, or the third in Charlotte, North Carolina.

Unabashedly I can say that I have always been a daddy's girl; when I was small, I had Daddy wrapped around my baby finger, where I firmly believed he belonged. Whenever he changed a recipe or made one of his patented Duke's Mixtures, he came to me first to test the newly combined flavors: peanut butter and blueberry yogurt; pineapple ice cream sprinkled with coconut; lemon flavoring in the pancake batter; apple, banana, and strong yellow onion in a garden salad. On that fork, in that spoon, along with whatever else was so regally presented for my judgment, there was also abiding love.

Flora Wilson Bridges

A Seat at the Welcome Table

I'm gonna sit at the welcome table
I'm gonna sit at the welcome table
    one of these days
I'm gonna sit at the welcome table
I'm gonna sit at the welcome table
I'm gonna sit at the welcome table
    one of these days

I spoke with my sister, Tee Gee, long distance this afternoon and discovered that my father was on his way to Washington, D.C., as the national representative for the Black Lung Disease Association. To tell you the truth, I wasn't at all surprised that my seventy-seven-year-old Daddy was selected to do this. As a matter of fact, this is characteristic behavior for him. You would have to meet my father to understand why I say this. Let me attempt to explain.

My father was born in 1919 in Hueytown, Alabama, to a fifteen-year-old mother who was told by her father to "get rid of him." In those days (as in these days) it was a surefire path to disgrace and rejection from the Black community to bear a child "out of wedlock." Not only was my father born at the wrong time and in the wrong place, he was born looking more white than Black. So my child/woman grandmother summarily packed him off to be "taken in" by the Wilsons, the most prominent Black family in Logan, West Virginia, of that day.

Daddy told me that before he was three years old he knew he was "different." I asked him how did he figure that out at such an early age, especially given the fact that my fanatically jealous Muh Dear (his adoptive mother) would never tell him the true story of his origins? He said that he used to reflect upon the fact that not only did he not look like anyone in their household, he didn't look like anyone in the whole community.

In spite of this, my father, more than any person I have ever encountered, feels a profound sense of belonging wherever he is and with whomever he comes in contact. He is never an alien in a foreign land nor has he ever met a stranger. To this day I don't understand how he got that way; but I do know that somehow he passed that on to my sister and myself. For, just like Daddy, we, too, are children of the universe. For in our father's house we were taught, above all else, that we were not mistakes, nor were we born out of season, but that we belong.

I am pretty certain that this is the reason why, although we have four brothers (all of whom I feel are remarkable people), my sister ended up graduating from West Point Academy and is completing her studies to be a doctor and a lawyer; and I ended up becoming a preacher and a college instructor of religion. My sister and I always knew we were entitled to the same opportunities as our brothers. In the small south Georgia town where I was born, Bainbridge, Georgia, my sister's journey has already become the stuff of legend. A few years back, when my mother returned to this place of her birth after forty years of living on the south side of Chicago, she and I walked into a local furniture store. When I spoke, the genteel white proprietor said, "Y'all aren't from here, are you? Who are your people?" When my mother called my grandparents' names, he said, "Oh yes! I know about you!" He then proceeded to recite, in marvelous African griot style, the story of where my family members sat at my sister's graduation from West Point Academy.

This is what happened. My grandmother on my mother's side was the maid for the esteemed Rich family of Bainbridge, Georgia (and they *were* rich). She worked in their kitchen from, as our people say, "cain't see to cain't see" for a wage that barely managed to help feed, clothe, and put a roof over the heads of her two daughters (Mama and Tee). Yet at my sister's graduation, somehow (I say because God has a divine sense of humor) my family ended up sitting at the table with the Rich family whose grandson was also graduating. They looked at Mama. She could barely remember them. When it all clicked they said in utter surprise, "Is that you Agnes?!" The granddaughter of slaves was graduating with the grandson of slavemasters. My sister (who on a good day weighs one hundred and twenty pounds) in one fell swoop made possible what it took Dr. King, the Movement, and the National Guard to do elsewhere in our nation. For instead of serving the Rich family, we sat at the same table.

I have my own small family legend. I am an ordained minister in the Black, Baptist church, a church where the saints are still inclined to say, "God ain't called no woman to preach." Nevertheless, preach I did and I later went on to achieve a second ordination status in the United Church of Christ, which is an overwhelmingly white denomination.

My sister and I are who we are because my father, early on, liberated us from our own fear of not belonging whether it was in our own household, the Black church and the Black community, the United States, the broader world and—indeed—the entire universe. When I was a very little girl, my mother finally had to spank me before I would stop calling Daddy "Freddie." After repeated warnings, although I was a reasonably intelligent child, I still could not fathom why I could not call him by his first name. I cannot recall my father ever making me feel that I was somehow "less than" because I was a child. He was, as I can recall, the only father on the block when we lived in Chicago's Altgeld-Gardens Housing Project to come home from work and roller skate with us up and down the sidewalks. Yes, our sense of belonging in the universe, our sense that we were important to the entire scheme of things even though we were poor, female, and Black, must have somehow begun in those glorious early evenings of whizzing down the sidewalks with Daddy while the other parents looked on from their porches and acted "proper."

Here I cannot remember one instance when I felt that my opinions were not being taken seriously by my father. If he thought I was wrong, which wasn't often, he would carefully dissect where he thought my thinking was faulty and where I had gone astray. When this happened, I was permitted to heatedly disagree without ever being cautioned that I was only a child. Daddy never pulled rank as an adult thinker. This fostered within me, at an early age, a certain confidence in my own intellectual abilities, a tremendous love for the art of dialogue, and the ability to appreciate the beliefs and opinions of others without feeling in any way that my own opinions and beliefs were being compromised or threatened. In other words, I grew not only to respect but also to celebrate and love difference. In the light of this kind of permission to be my small, Black, female self on the part of my father, it does not surprise me that I would later be able to withstand the pressures of being in a male-dominated vocation, the ordained ministry, and to pursue without much fear and trembling what has traditionally been a male-dominated degree—a doctorate in religion with a minor in philosophy.

My father is amazingly literate and well read. Although life did not permit him to attend college beyond a single year because he went to work in the mines in West Virginia (the same mines that took the life of my grandfather in a terrible accident and severed the little finger on my father's left hand), I remember that he constantly read. Indeed, when I later went to Yale Divinity School, following my call to the ministry, he invariably had read all of the works of the world's great theologians before I even knew they existed. Sometimes, though I should have long known better, I would call myself introducing him to some theory by Barth, or Bonhoeffer, or Tillich. Invariably, he would proceed to quote some part of their theology that either supported or negated my views. He was always tremendously excited by their ideas, in contrast to my own disgust that Barth had written so much and that I had to learn it all in order to pass my exams.

On many, many evenings while he sat at the kitchen table and we talked as I washed the dishes, the dishwater would grow cold as I forgot the dishes in our discussions of world literature and culture and in the simple stories he told me of the years of his own growing up in what he called the time of "quasi-slavery." When I was in the fifth grade, in our predominantly Jewish elementary school, our teacher asked us to name our favorite book. She was quite surprised when I said *War and Peace*, but then she never knew my father. In the same year I remember my teacher's astonishment when my siblings and I held literally all of the positions on the Student Council—elected positions in that almost all-white school. There were two other Black students in my class, the twins Max and Maxie. I remember I hated that the teacher assigned our seats by academic rank. Max and Maxie always had the last two seats. I traded off with a boy named Jeffrey all during those years in competition for the first seat. Alison, who let it be known that she had a Black maid and didn't have to carry a key like I did, sat in the third row. Her father may have had money, but my father gave me the gift of knowing how to beat the odds and feel at home anywhere on the planet.

When my father entered his seventies he decided to attend Chicago Theological Seminary as a special student. True to form, he excelled academically and was perhaps the most beloved student in the class. Our family found this out when he became ill enough to be hospitalized. All of his classmates visited him in the hospital and none of them was anywhere near his age.

My father was no stranger to pain and sickness. In his fortieth year he was diagnosed with cancer. I believe the fact that he worked two jobs for as long as I could remember (the second job was delivering packages via bicycle at night for a store on the south side) contributed to the breakdown of his health. He was so ill that he did not see natural sunlight as he languished in a hospital room in the Veterans' Hospital from autumn to autumn for a solid year. His weight went down to less than eighty pounds. The doctors told my mother, who was expecting my sister at the time, to be prepared for the worse. My father told me years later that once he heard the nurses, who counted him almost out of the land of the living, say, "This one won't be around much longer." He underwent more operations than anyone should have to endure, the kind of surgery that cuts off and cuts away. The Christmas after my sister was born, we went to visit him. My mother warned me to "straighten my face" so that shock would not register. But despite the cancer and the surgical violations, he beat the odds and lived.

For more than a year after my father's hospitalization, I secretly observed him fight a battle with another kind of illness. This illness was depression. Inside, I knew he grieved for the parts of himself that the surgeon's knife had slashed away. He would sit quietly, hardly ever speaking—something that had been impossible for my sociable, humorous, gregarious father before—on the front porch in his slippers, robe, and pajamas. I couldn't get him to talk. There were no more discussions about politics, books, and the state of the world. There was only silence. Then one month after many months, slowly, almost imperceptibly, the words, the humor, the love of life returned. He found his undeniable place in the universe once again. He conquered cancer and the resulting surgery by making himself at home in a body that was no longer like the one God had originally given him.

I'm gonna feast on milk and honey
I'm gonna feast on milk and honey
    one of these days
I'm gonna feast on milk and honey
I'm gonna feast on milk and honey
I'm gonna feast on milk and honey
    one of these days

Last year, when Daddy was seventy-six, my sister told him that she is lesbian. She had told me when she figured it out for herself some five years before. My father then proceeded, at her quarter-of-a-century mark, to escort her to a local lesbian bar. As usual, he was the social success of the evening. Many of the people there, so different from him in terms of age, race, class, educational status, and gender, had tears in their eyes because an elder designed to grace their place with his presence. Again, my sister was unintentionally involved in creating a small legend. Again, my father did not feel like an alien but was secure in the universe.

For as long as I can remember, my father taught me a form of power that did not come out of the barrel of a gun. He taught me a "resistance of the heart" that fought any notions of inferiority. He taught me how to "be" and how to let other folks be. He set an example of speaking his mind and insisting, with dignity, that he has a right to be heard, an example he continues to hold up today in Washington while speaking for the Black Lung Disease Association. These days, in the class I teach young college students, entitled African-American Spirituality, I tell his stories and introduce them to this gentle but powerful worldview of inclusive and radical community. For he taught me, a long time ago, to experience the "seat at the welcome table" that my enslaved ancestors sang about. They did not see it, but it is realized in me.

Gail Bowman

Expressions of His Love

If our mother hadn't died in her early fifties my sister and I might not have been led to make such a study of how our father expresses himself. If I hadn't gone into the ministry I might not care so much about what we mean when we say God is our heavenly Father (heavenly Mother/ Father, heavenly Parent). Nevertheless, because of events, I am inclined to "study" my dad "like television" (as he would say), with particular attention paid to the expressions he is known for using. He is a very well-educated man, but he is often at his best in simple truths, stated simply.

The first expression I remember hearing was spoken not by my father but by his father, Floyd, also known as Pop-Pop. Over a Sunday family dinner the adults had been talking about someone expending a lot of ill-considered energy on a project, largely ignoring the possibility of asking for a helping hand from any of a number of community people who would have been happy to assist. "Oh, yeah," Pop-Pop commented about the rather self-impressed worker. "He's busier than a one-armed paper-hanger in a high wind." My sister, Linda, and I, little kids at the time, collapsed into gales of giggles. It was our first clue that our grandfather had a way of collecting popular expressions, inventing some and using all on good occasion. Daddy does it too; he "came by it honest."

Both of our parents worked outside the home. Daddy was a teacher and didn't work in the summers, so he, my sister, and I spent the days together—weeding the garden, cleaning the house, and letting the time pass. In the proper mood, Daddy could be talked into storytelling, so we heard about him having to bail out of a Tuskegee Airman training flight and spend the night in a northern outgrowth of the Okefenokee Swamp. We also heard about the early days of our parents' romance, when our self-controlled and very stylish mother had leaned out of an upper story apartment building window in Chicago to invite him, a handsome and uniformed virtual stranger, to a party she and some other young women were giving.

Spending as much time with us as he was, Daddy was the main source of discipline. Even then, he had a way of using expressions as a way of making his point while also taking the sting out of the chastisement. When a visitor came to chat in threadbare clothing so long out of style that Linda and I couldn't wait for him to leave so we could begin making fun of him, my dad simply commented, "Well, you know he's about as poor as Job's house cat." Enough said. Some expressions, however, were clearly intended to smart. We could tell that a guest who passed a long afternoon listing the many things he refused to provide for his family had lost our father's respect. Daddy's comment after he had left: "My God, he's tighter than Dick's hat band."

Despite the fact that my sister and I were both adults when Mom died, Daddy has ended up doing a lot of things which most people would consider women's work. He flew to be with me when I had "female" surgery, is my niece's babysitter of choice, and flew again to take care of me when I had the chicken pox. On the morning he was due to arrive during the chicken pox experience, I used my fingers to number the huge, blistering, oozing pox I had on my face and in my ears, mouth and hair. I lost count after passing 125. I had not looked into a mirror for two days; the last glimpse of myself had disgusted and almost scared me. No one had seen me like this. Even the mail carrier who had brought an express package which required a signature had seen only my pox-covered hand.

When my Dad arrived, I made certain no one else was outside the door, then let him in. I braced myself for a reaction, but he only commented that I seemed to have been having it pretty rough, then moved to the kitchen to check for homemade chicken soup ingredients. He stayed with me for five days, eventually drawing me back out in public, so by the time he left I was ready to return to work and was almost nonchalant about the stares of my students. Only months later, when cocoa butter had faded almost all the scars into memories did my father finally make his comment about his true reaction when I appeared from behind the door in the full throes of the disease. "She looked," he laughed at a family dinner, "like somebody had turned her inside out."

So it is that Linda and I tend to wait for Daddy's comment, preferably an invented or adopted expression, before making important life decisions or deciding how best to react to life events. When my sister came up against a mean-spirited person on her job and began plotting ways of striking back, Daddy drily commented, "You know, it never pays to get in a —ssing contest with a skunk." Wisely, she reconsidered her plans. When I called, devastated, after an ill-fated job interview in which a church deacon had issued a haughty dismissal of my academic credentials which clearly had more to do with my being female and in ministry than with anything else, Daddy remarked, "Well, he was probably a man with a room temperature I.Q." and the world righted itself again.

My dad can sum up a person's appearance in concise eloquence which is equal parts affection and ribbing. When my nephew decided to change his "look" and I was asking about it (yet unseen) over the telephone, Daddy described it nicely for me: "He has about as much hair as there is dust on a piano." A family friend visited after an extended period without dental care, and Daddy commented after his departure, "He could eat an ear of corn through a picket fence."

It should not be surprising that Linda, Daddy, and I tend to trade expressions back and forth among ourselves. When someone is expending an inordinate amount of time and effort hassling me, I tend to use Daddy's expression: "She's on me like a cheap suit." When my first effort at banana nut bread met with mixed results, Linda borrowed one of Erma Bombeck's favorites: "He who hesitates gets the burnt piece." I ran across an apt description of an aimless lifestyle which has become part of Daddy's repertoire: "When you don't know where you're going, any road will take you there." All three of us use "Even a fish wouldn't get caught if he kept his mouth shut." And I remember Mom by using one of her expressions: "He who maketh of himself an ass should not take it ill if others ride him."

When I was younger and heard God referred to as parent, I would think of the things parents do for very young children—feeding them, clothing them, and admonishing them to stay away from the stove by teaching them about "hot." As I have matured and my appreciation of my father has continued to expand, my understanding of God has also grown. Now when I think of God as Parent I also think of needs we never outgrow.

I have always been told God is "generous" and I had thought that I

understood this. However, a few years ago my father gave me something, and then, a few weeks later, he offered me another of the same
gift. "But you already gave me one, Daddy," I said. "I did?" he said,
"That's okay. Why don't you have another. You know I love you." And
in that instant I finally understood—God is *generous*, open-handed, giving to us each day, not counting or tallying what has already been given,
then giving again and out of love.

Following our dad's ways, studying his wisdom and collecting his expressions, my sister and I are both reminded of Another who was at his
best in simple truths, stated simply. "He who is without sin, let him cast
the first stone" is one of His best ways of quieting a judgmental spirit.
When we are feeling sorry for ourselves and thinking of giving up He
asks: "Do you *want* to be made well?" And in the midst of trouble, "Be
not afraid, only believe." For us, wise and well-chosen words are characteristic of both our heavenly Parent and our remaining earthly parent.
We see similarities between Jesus and (our father) James in terms of
God's loving kindness, understanding, and humor.

Among the many inexplicable aspects of the cosmos I would include
the mystery of blessing. Almost twenty years later, I am still not prepared to say why our mother died when there was still so much for her
to do and experience. Likewise, however, I am not prepared to say why
my sister and I are given a father of such wisdom, loyalty, humor, and
love. Job (the man with the house cat you have already met) probably expressed it best: *The Lord gave and the Lord hath taken away. Blessed be the
name of the Lord.*

Ellen Finch

A Master Craftsman of Love

I was born and reared in Philadelphia, a cosmopolitan and historic city whose several exits are well-marked for tourists from around the world, but I have lived vicariously in Caroline County, a small farm community located midway between Fredericksburg and Richmond, Virginia, a place without exit markers on Interstate 95. This is the birthplace of my father, William Washington Byrd Nixon, and it was the focus of stories that entertained me as a child. Even as an adult, I value my father's stories about the best techniques for successfully milking a cow, moonlight trips to the watermelon patch, numerous encounters with snakes, the jokes of men working at the sawmill, skinny-dipping in the South River, and the courage of his grandmother who was born into slavery. Aunt Jane, as she was called, *walked* from North Carolina to Richmond with her six sons. My father postponed going to college for two years in order to care for his grandmother when she was ailing. It would be the first of many times he would demonstrate compassion for elders in failing health. Values of caring and sacrifice, gifts of his country upbringing, shaped the relationship my father had with my mother, whom he married in 1942, and with the three children born of their union. Indeed, out of a desire to recapture the feel of Caroline County country life, my father chose for our upbringing an area in Philadelphia that rescued us from the imprisonment of city life.

My mother taught elementary school. My father ran wood and machine shops in schools located in Philadelphia's poorest neighborhoods and targeted for children, most of them Black boys between the ages of twelve and sixteen, considered "retarded educable." He made himself indispensable to every school in which he worked by building teaching materials for other teachers, repairing machines, and helping members of the staff with their most difficult fix-it problems. From jewelry to scenery for plays, he could handle almost anything. And he did it all with a smile. He was simply too good to be true! The down side was that my father was never appreciated until he retired.

My mother earned a master's degree while working and raising three children, an achievement that was merely a stepping-stone on a career path that would take her through a doctorate in education and eventually land her in the principal's chair of a large elementary school. Her professional career was enhanced by a parallel laundry list of impressive church and civic credits. My father's willingness to help out in virtually any domestic area was critical to my mother's professional attainments. He was the one who chauffeured the three children to and from all of our activities. I always felt that because he was so directly involved with our many activities, Dad was closer to understanding many of the things going on in my life than my mother, particularly when I entered my teens and my mother became increasingly bogged down by work, school, and care for an ailing mother. It seemed that Dad was always the one who dried the tears and boosted me with encouragement. He was always in my corner, perhaps even when he should not have been, which left my mother to play "bad cop," at least for my sister and me. It was not a role she enjoyed playing.

I was a good student in school and because of my family's reputation, particularly my mother's achievements, I was expected to set and achieve high goals for myself. My choosing the traditional roles of housewife and mother came, understandably, as a surprise to my college and childhood friends. For twenty-four years, I have struggled with the tension between the achievement-oriented identity I was raised with and left behind, and the traditional maternal one I have assumed in my marriage, but I have always been clear that in the role of my choice, I am my father's daughter. I am the support mainstay.

My husband often jokes that my father and I share an almost archetypal father-daughter relationship. The eldest daughter, he says, is an extension of the mother and almost becomes a kind of "second wife" to the father. I have resisted picturing myself in this way because ours is not a culture that handles even the vaguest notion of polygamy well or any hint of the Freudian "Electra Complex." But the archetype precedes Freud. It takes us back to the beginning of human history, to a time before taboos and morality were introduced to regulate human behavior. While such regulation was absolutely necessary, it didn't erase the natural attraction which existed in the wild, so to speak, and which yet survives in what Carl Jung calls the *Collective Unconscious*. In spite of my resistance to the idea, however, I have come to realize that my relationship to my father is increasingly one which follows the archetype. I am my father's eldest daughter. He and I are psychically linked.

One of the aspects of the archetype is the father's attraction to attributes in the daughters which are different from any the mother possesses. I think about that when I remember receiving at the age of ten a cookbook for young girls as a gift from my godmother. I was thrilled and excited by the prospect of baking and within a short period of time began to take over most of the baking at home. Because Dad loved home-baked goods, the kitchen became that special room in the house where we bonded. To this day I know that the best way for me to tell Dad "I love you" is to bake a cake or pie. (Biscuits will do if there isn't much time for the involved work of cake batters and pie shells).

My father also has a tremendous love for antiques, influenced, I am certain, by his appreciation as a craftsman for workmanship, style, and durability. I remember his going to a house that was to be demolished and asking if he could have the solid oak flooring. He took up the floor board by board himself. Later, he and my brother put the oak boards down in our house. As a young adult, I accepted his gifts of old chairs, tables, and bookcases because everything new was simply out of the question, a financial impossibility, but what began as a necessity soon became a love affair I was having with antiques. I especially treasured old pieces which belonged to my female ancestors from either side of the family tree. Most of them came to me through my father who stored them away, sometimes moving very large and heavy pieces by himself. He can rarely pass by a flea market without at least taking a look. Together we have spent many hours poring over each other's treasures.

When I was younger, I leaned on my father for emotional support and he was always, unconditionally, there for me. Since my mother's death in 1992, the roles have been reversed. For a year after her death, my father telephoned me, calling long distance from Philadelphia to Atlanta, and I was there for him. I became his close confidant, his advisor, his friend. Our shared interests and our bonding, planted deep years ago, keep us going in spite of the void created by my mother's death. It appears that Jung is having the last word!

Manning Marable

In My Father's House

I.

James Palmer Marable was born November 16, 1921, in a wooden cabin deep in the piney woods of east-central Alabama near the small town of Wedowee. He was the third child and second son of Manning Marable and Fannie Heard Marable. Manning and Fannie would eventually have thirteen children in all, the last child born in 1944. Manning was essentially a rural entrepreneur. Although he was the son of slaves and had attended school less than six years, Manning was determined to make something of his life. With his growing family as his primary labor force, he cultivated several hundred acres of land, mostly planting cotton and corn. On the side, Manning constructed a whiskey still and peddled corn liquor to rural farmers, Black and white, during Prohibition. With the extra cash from selling moonshine, Manning purchased more land, farm animals, cattle, and timber. My father recalls that even during the depression, Manning had boundless confidence in his ability to make money. Manning would "buy anything!" my father still exclaims. "He'd buy a mule, whether we needed or not. He'd see an old mule and say, 'We'll buy it! How much you want for it?' . . . He was always successful in negotiating, in buying and selling."

Life in rural Alabama was fairly predictable. Work began well before dawn, milking the cows and feeding the livestock. The boys were assigned various outside chores, from sawing timber to ploughing. At home, Fannie was the dominant presence: cooking meals, sewing, mending and washing clothes, supervising a rapidly expanding number of children, cousins, nieces, and nephews, and managing the household budget. The older girls helped with the cooking, cleaning, and supervising the younger children. "We'd all work in the field," my father remembers. On weekends, Manning and his sons went fishing or hunting.

On Sundays, the entire family attended church services in the morning, and often invited the preacher and his family to their home for Sunday dinner.

White people usually seemed peripheral to the daily routine. "We were usually just around Black people," my father explains. "We rarely came out of those hills. We went to a Black school close by." Of course, direct contact with whites was inevitable. Several times each year, my father traveled with Manning carrying a load of raw cotton or fresh produce from their farm to Wedowee. "When we'd go there, when I was a kid, I soon learned that white people were 'white people.' These were the bosses and the people you bought groceries from."

It was during these visits to Wedowee and the larger neighboring town of Roanoke that James first encountered the harsh reality of racism. "White people were pretty much in control of everything," my father observes. "When you walked down the street, you'd hear Black people say, 'Those little white girls are coming down the street, and you have to get out of the way!' And I'd see other Black people move over. . . . Everybody just moved to the right or to the left. You didn't get in their way." Whites were a privileged caste, and demanded to be treated deferentially.

You had to learn at an early age to avoid situations where confrontations with whites might develop. About once each year, the Marable family would go to Roanoke's department store to purchase shoes and clothing. My father states, "I remember the white clerks would say, 'You can't try that hat on!' You'd buy a shirt or a pair of trousers and you'd have to guess at your size." Once my father was taken by his parents to the local white dentist to have a tooth removed. Walking into the dentist's office, he was immediately forbidden to sit down. "And they said, 'You go over in this room. We take you all over here in this room.' And *that* was where they pulled the teeth of Black people." The room was dirty and poorly lighted, and the dental equipment had been used. Blacks came to expect inferior treatment and second-class service. Sometimes the humiliations were public and vulgar. "I never remember any whites calling me 'nigger,'" my father says. "They'd just refer to me and my brothers as 'boys.' But I'd see other white men walk up to Black people in the street and kick them." For whites it was humorous just giving "niggers a boot in the butt." In the classroom, the conditions for

Black learning were always substandard. "It was just common knowledge that we would get used textbooks," my father states. "But nobody ever questioned or challenged racial segregation. I don't remember anyone protesting it. I don't remember any of my teachers or my parents' friends talking about it. It was just sort of the rule of doing business for everyone: whites were in charge." This was the omnipresent reality that Manning Marable could never forget, not for a single moment. In private, my grandfather's constant was *"never* to be under the white man's thumb."

Coming of age in a racially segregated environment, opportunities were limited for my father. But on the Marable farm even as a boy, James excelled at fixing household appliances and farm implements. "I was always tinkering with things, tinkering with cars, tinkering with machines," my father explains. "I was always building something." With his younger brothers, my father would construct wagons for hauling farm machinery and produce. "You'd cut off a log that's round—maybe twelve inches in diameter—knock a hole in it and you got your wheels." James watched and learned how every piece of machinery around the farm worked. By the age of thirteen, he could repair and service the family model A Ford and drive the tractor.

My father's experience operating and maintaining vehicles led to what he now describes as his "glorious opportunity." As a high school student, James would walk one mile each way down a dirt country road, where the school bus stopped for Negro children. The bus slowly meandered about twenty miles each way between the village of Malone and Roanoke every morning, taking more than one hour for the journey. At the beginning of James's tenth grade, the owner of the school bus asked my father if he would be interested in driving the vehicle every day. "I'd been driving everything else," my father thought, and replied quickly, "Yeah, I'd like to take a shot at it." The pay was twenty-five cents per day, about five dollars a month. Throughout his tenth-grade year, my father got up early before dawn every morning, walked several miles to pick up the bus, and drove twenty miles each way to and from Roanoke.

Since the school bus was never completely filled with students, my father would pick up additional passengers, who would simply wave the bus to a halt. "They gave me a nickel or a dime to ride the bus," my father explains. "You'd really be surprised how that added up. I didn't spend it. I didn't have to because I carried my lunch from home." Soon James was earning more than five dollars each month from the extra passengers on his bus route.

"This was the beginning of really being an entrepreneur, understanding what money was all about," my father reflects. By his final year in high school, "I basically hit the jackpot. By that time I was the senior driver. I had a perfect record driving without any accidents." When the high school football team scheduled its games away from Roanoke, James was asked to drive the bus for several extra dollars. He earned a reputation for being reliable and trustworthy. Soon the high school principal's wife asked James to be her regular driver: "A lot of times she'd go to the high school and would ask me to come to the principal's office. The principal would hand me his keys and say, 'My wife wants you to take her downtown.' I'd say, 'Yes, sir.' And I'd get tips like that. I'd drive her. She'd want to go home or shopping. It was quite an honor to drive the principal's car." James's financial independence directly influenced his relationships with other students. "I was rather shy, as I recall, and not all that aggressive," my father relates. "But I had money, and everybody knew it. I would loan money to people even then because I had money. And they would pay me back."

James's new privileged status also had a direct impact upon his social life. "I sort of fancied and played around with some of the girls in high school," my father admits. "They chased me because I had money, you know, and because I drove the school bus." James and his older brother Morris often accompanied each other on "dates" with young women from church or high school.

"In those days you actually sat in the living room with the girls on one side and you sat on the other," my father explains. "No hanky-panky stuff, not in that living room! You'd go over there and sit until about nine or ten o'clock, when the old man (of the house) would either start coughing or he'd say, 'BEDTIME!' Either way, you got the message loud and clear, to get ready and go home."

II.

James graduated from high school in the spring of 1942 and briefly began working full-time on his father's farm. During his senior year, Pearl

Harbor was attacked by the Japanese, and the United States entered World War II. So it was not surprising when on July 20, 1942, my father received his draft notification. After basic training, my father was part of a racially segregated unit in the army air corps. Because he had graduated from high school, he was assigned to a special training school for mechanics and engineers. Throughout the remainder of the war, my father was a staff sergeant and head mechanic of a flight crew which repaired and serviced airplanes. The routine of army life was easy for the farm boy. "I was sort of gifted with having worked with tools and cars and trucks in my background," James recounts. Checking the fuselage of an airplane or making sure that the nuts and bolts were properly tightened "was very easy to do." The biggest adjustment my father had to make was in the context of race relations. The U.S. military was racially segregated, and would remain so until 1948. But within the military bases and during wartime, African Americans were often treated better than they had ever been before. For nearly two years, my father was stationed just outside Detroit, where he had the opportunity to experience a large urban environment without legal Jim Crow. During the war years, my father's expectations and attitudes concerning segregation subtly but fundamentally changed.

By 1946, when James was discharged from the military, it was difficult to relearn the social etiquette of Jim Crow. Leaving Detroit, my father traveled south, headed home to Alabama. James recalls that as the train passed through Cincinnati and crossed the Ohio River, the conductor walked down the aisles of each car, shouting: "The Maxon-Dixon line, all of you people must move to the rear." "No one said 'Negroes,' but everyone knew what he meant," my father comments. When the train arrived in Birmingham, James walked up to a lunch counter in the station. He failed to notice the sign which read "whites only." "When I went in to get a sandwich, the white girl said to me, 'You have to go to that window.' She thought I was just ignorant." But my father bristled silently inside himself. "I'd been up above the Mason-Dixon line, in places where they didn't pay too much attention to race," my father observed. But despite his sergeant's uniform, plus his good conduct medal, flight wings, "and all that good stuff," he was still treated as a second-class citizen. It was this realization that prompted James finally to decide to leave the South.

Back in Roanoke, James once again began working full-time for his father. But some of his high school friends who had also served in the military were already talking about enrolling in college, either at nearby Tuskegee Institute or in the North. One of his buddies mentioned that there was an all-Negro college "up there in Ohio, Wilberforce University, a fine school where there's no segregation." My father thought about attending Tuskegee Institute, but decided against it, largely because it was in the South. "Anyway," my father reasoned at the time, "all they do down there is teach you about farming. You could teach agriculture maybe with a Tuskegee degree, but if you wanted to be a schoolteacher or doctor of something like that, you ought to go to that Negro school in Ohio." By the time James and three of his high school classmates finally decided to apply for admission to Wilberforce, it was almost Labor Day: "Somebody must of told us to call the dean of men at Wilberforce College. We got him on the phone. We said, 'We've got four veterans down here and we'd like to come to your school. We want to know if you'll admit us?' " My father remembers: "I got my bag and collected my other personal items together in a paper sack. With my buddies, we caught a bus and headed for Ohio. Somehow we figured out how to get from Dayton to Wilberforce." They arrived only one day before classes began for the fall semester.

The segregated curriculum of the all-Negro high school in Roanoke had not prepared James adequately for a northern college. In math and the sciences, my father continued to excel. But in English, he struggled below a C average. "I should have asked for help, but I didn't," he says. "It was very difficult to write and it always bugged the heck out of me." James could answer questions in class, and was able to discuss ideas with confidence. But in his written assignments he was completely unsure of himself. He began spending more time in the library, asking other students to help him.

It was in the library at the beginning of his sophomore year that James began to notice an attractive young woman who always seemed to be studying. Occasionally she would assist him in locating books and reference materials. She was a minister's daughter, very pleasant and somewhat talkative. "But I could see she could write and do all that kind of stuff," my father observed. One Saturday evening James attended one of the college dances, and he recognized the young woman from the library. Ten months later, they were married. Within a year James, Jr., was born.

In an old automobile he had purchased, James drove thirty miles each way to go to work. He obtained a job in a tool and die industrial company, but it was anything but pleasant. "I was called a 'utility man.' In the plant, there were machines that were grinding the tools out— where you poke iron through the machines to make bolts or screws or whatever." The waste from the tool machines, irregular chips of metal, grease, and oil fell to the factory floor. "My job was to shovel it up, put it in a wheelbarrow, roll it, and dump it someplace." Here, as elsewhere, racial segregation was the general pattern of employment. Whites held the higher-paying jobs as managers, machinists, and technicians. All of the utility men "were Black people," James recalled.

By my father's senior year in college, June was again pregnant (this time with me). My father was deeply concerned about his future after graduation: "I wanted a better job and I was going all around (to find work). My highest hope at that time was to get on as an airplane mechanic or even to become an airplane pilot. I still loved planes and I knew that I would enjoy working on them. I knew we were coming into an age of commercial flying, the airlines at that time were expanding, and that there was money to be made." But getting an equal opportunity for employment for Negroes was rare in the late 1940s. My father explains, "Every time I went out to Wright Patterson airbase (near Dayton) to apply for the job, I was always told that I was a finalist. Sometimes they'd say, 'It's down to three of you.' But they always picked one of the whites." After applying for different positions and being turned down a half dozen times, my father's dream of being a pilot or a flight mechanic finally died.

It was about this time that my mother, who had graduated from college in 1948 and was now working full-time, had the idea for her husband's future. James had one year's eligibility remaining of his GI educational benefits. Why not enroll in the master's program at Ohio State University, in nearby Columbus? My father resisted the suggestion, telling his young wife: "I didn't really feel I could hack it. I knew I could talk in class, but I never felt comfortable putting it on paper. Never did." June replied: "You take your notes in class, bring them home to me, and I'll fix them up." So James reluctantly agreed to enroll in the M.A. program in education at Ohio State. Throughout the next year, my father attended classes during the day and held down a job after school. June revised his rough drafts and lecture notes into excellent essays. But successfully completing homework assignments was only part of the challenge. "In those days, there were very few Blacks in graduate school," my father states. The white professors "would constantly watch me and they would ask me questions. But I always read their books, and knew what to say." My father's basic strategy was to read carefully the books written by his instructors, and to ask specific questions based on their own publications: "I'd read their old books. And I usually would say, 'Doctor So-And-So, in your chapter on so-and-so, what did you mean? Now sometimes I really knew the answer. But they were always impressed, and they loved that." By the summer of 1951, at the age of twenty-nine, James Marable received his M.A. degree in school administration with a minor in counseling.

III.

June and James moved to Kansas City for several years, both working as teachers in the public school system. As before, my father held down a second job at night, and they saved that salary to purchase a home. They moved to Dayton, Ohio, with two growing boys in 1955, the year my brother went to the first grade. James continued working sixteen-hour days for years, teaching at predominantly Black Dunbar High School during the day, and working as a laborer at Dayton Tire factory on the second shift every evening. Finally at the age of forty, my father collapsed from exhaustion in a suburban department store. It was my most traumatic experience as a boy, watching my father, who had always been so strong, being taken away in an ambulance. After a short time in the hospital, my father recovered. But somehow I could never look at him in quite the same way. Now I appreciated just how hard he worked, and had always worked. As an adult years later, I would search to find the words to tell my father just what he had meant to me. But the words did not come.

Do we ever really comprehend the world of our Black fathers, the factors which made them who they are? Do we hear their personal stories, understanding their hardships and mistakes, difficulties and triumphs? There are many Black men who bore the weight of racial oppression without surrendering to bitterness and alienation. They worked at multiple jobs to care for and to support their families. They quietly sacrificed their own chances for upward mobility to improve the material conditions for their daughters and sons. No one mentions their sacrifices in the pages of African-American history books. Their names are largely unknown and their voices rarely heard. But it is in our fathers' houses, in the world they courageously helped to build with our mothers and sisters, that we are able to affirm ourselves.

In their personal stories, we can listen to the quiet dignity of our men. We can bear witness to the simple sacrifices and day-to-day experiences of our fathers, which create new possibilities and new visions. Through their voices, we begin to learn about and to find ourselves.

Cheryl Clarke

A Father Scarce as Hen's Teeth

My father is the second son of an only child, on his mother's side, and of a father who had seven siblings. I am his first daughter. My mother was his first wife, and he was her second husband. He was a stepfather, uncle, cousin, brother, brother-in-law, son-in-law, grandfather, Mr. Clarke, and Popsi—the last, a name I gave him in my young childhood after hearing others call him "Pops" because of his prematurely graying hair. All the children in the neighborhood called him "Popsi." The only time he lived away from his family and his hometown of Washington, D.C., was during his four-year stint in the army during World War II. My father taught me arithmetic, how to print my letters, took my sisters and me to the library every week during the summer, and monitored our progress in grade school. "Do your lessons!" was the sternest thing he ever said to me.

Because he was home during the day and worked nights, he was responsible for homemaking and childcare from eight to five during the work week. My mother took over at five and on the weekends. I often think that working from eleven at night until seven in the morning for thirty-five years, five days a week—never with nights off on the weekend—was a great sacrifice for my father. His day began at 8:00 A.M. with breakfast for my two sisters and me, after which he drove my sisters and me, our various and sundry friends, and some stragglers to our particular schools. While we were in school, he shopped, cleaned the house, did the laundry, raked the leaves, mowed the lawn, and made preparations for our return. Between 2:30 and 3:00 P.M., he picked all of us up from our different schools, depositing us at our different homes. He made sure that my sisters and I practiced piano, did homework, played a bit, and ate the dinner he had prepared for us. All this by 5:00 P.M. when my mother would come through the door from her government job: beau-

tiful, frazzled, hungry, and stern. After her arrival, my father would re-
tire to my basement room for his five hours of sleep. I would wake him
at ten so that he could get to his job as a security guard at the Bureau of
Standards, a government agency.

When my teachers, Catholic nuns, encouraged students to talk
about how the aphorism "Man is the head of the household and the
woman is the heart" was practiced in our families, I always sort of
ducked out of sight, not quite sure what to say. When I was ten, I asked
Popsi, as he wrung the clothes through our wringer-washer, what
should I say if "Sister Julia Maria asks me what Mother does?" He
frowned and answered dismissively: "Tell her *your* mother does more
than your average mother. Your mother is a housewife and a government employee. She is heart *and* head. That's all." Still, I felt a degree of
anxiety that I couldn't say my mother did just the one thing—the
"heart" thing—and that it was my father who taught me arithmetic,
showed me how to print letters, took my sisters and me to the library
every week during the summer, monitored our schoolwork, and performed other household tasks rarely associated with fathers? Besides, I
knew that my mother was not into the "heart" thing. She'd never been
into it even when she had to do it.

As I look back on it now, being far less judgmental, I see that my father had his way of raising us and didn't meddle in my mother's way (but
that did not work the other way round). His way was definitely easier.
My mother brooked no sass, eye-rolling, or pouting over her executive
mandates. My father, on the other hand, let me talk back to him for the
balance of most days, countering only with a "Why do you have to be
so disagreeable?" Being able to be "disagreeable" with him at such an
early age helped me later to disagree with any kind of rules—particularly those regarding a woman's so-called proper place, meaning, heterosexuality, marriage, and the family. And he helped with that resistance: "Get a college degree instead of a marriage license. You'll get
fu'ther" were his cautionary bywords to me.

My maternal grandmother described my father as a "good man," a
putatively rare species among the "trifling mens 'vailable to the average
colored woman" in D.C., an extremely heterosexual town, and predatory, too, where women are supposed to be worried because they out-
number men. The night I waited in my prom dress for two and a half

hours in my parents' living room for Freddie, my date, to pick me up was the night I swore off male-dominant heterosexuality, made myself a promise that I would not be sitting around in Washington, D.C., waiting for some man simply because men were supposed to be as scarce as hen's teeth. "Take the hen's teeth," Popsi had told a confessional niece who was rationalizing her marriage to a deadbeat. I wanted neither a husband nor hen's teeth. Because of his influence in my life as nurturer and as friend, my father pushed me to a larger world and a larger self.

Dilla Buckner and Jennifer Hicks

When the Subject Is Fathers: Two Daughters Reflect

D.B.: Pop, Father, Daddy, Dad, Grandaddy, Gramps,—the list could goes on, with each of these titles rendering chapters, books even. Names like Velt, Uncle Velt, Roosevelt, or "Lulee," his calling card for his cousins, aunts, uncles, and friends from the country who knew him way back when. It took me fifty years to figure out how anybody got "Lulee" out of Roosevelt. About three years ago, I asked everybody at the family reunion if they knew the origin of this name. I was told that Aunt Phoe ("Fe"), his aunt and his mom's favorite sister, had called him "Little Lee" because he looked exactly like his mom, Grandma Olivia, whose nickname was "Lee." It didn't take long for Little Lee to turn into Lulee.

Dad has such a multifaceted past and history that I almost don't know where to begin talking about him.

J.B.: God, D. B., What can *I* say about him? We love him. I love him. I guess I have always seen him as larger than life, an "icon," and I just learned that word. I'm not even sure I know what it means. But I love him. "Icon," I guess (without a dictionary) it means big and respected in his area, his field. Not like God. Because no one is God, but God. Although, he *is* close, especially, so he thinks. And it seems the closer he gets to "going to be with God," the more it is important to him to be like Him.

D.B.: Yet, Dad, in *his* mind's eye, has a flaw. This father person—cotton picker, chopper, boot strap laborer, lumberer, still has a personal, self-inflicted flaw: lack of education. Yep, Pop still feels and has often been reminded of the fact that he is, with his fourth-grade education, not educated. To me, he is among the most brilliant Black men that I know; yet, America awards the Blacks with the "cents" and not the "sense." For that, we lack in true education because without the latter "sense" we know not what to do with the cents we may make.

J.B.: Father was educated in his career by a higher power as much as either of us was educated in schools that he "provided" for us and for Mother. He was gifted with carpentry, spirit, and vision that not only has helped him survive for eighty-eight years against "The Depression," his in-laws, the Baptist Deacon Board, cancer, and sometimes his own insecurities and jealousies to thrive over almost nine decades. I pray (like you Dee) that his "heart" and caring for people who don't deserve him don't destroy him. (But who really knows how much giving is enough?) Dad always taught us to give and to care. I appreciate those traits, virtues. I have learned, however, at this age and stage in my life that there is a point at which I think a person should "get off!" after being given and given. That is the users, the takers, the "supposedly needy." I think they should "get off!" because they have some perception of how much they *will* take, not just can take. Dad seems to be able to give forever. My question is why should he have to? Why does he feel so strongly that he has to, that it is his calling to do so?

D.B.: Dad made more money carpentering than his schoolteacher wife (whom he assisted in getting her college degree), helped Saturday drunks (who were superb workers) get out of jail on Sunday after church, bowed with polite "yes, sirs and mams" to southern whites to get jobs, favors, and whatever else he wanted done or thought he needed, bought (by borrowing from a white) his present house and land for $1500. He sent or offered three daughters the opportunities to obtain college degrees. They did what his (and mom's) common senses (with cents) allowed. One daughter did three years, the other two completed their doctorates; each fed on or learned from the other. Dad told me, "I will send you to school for as long as you want to go and do well." He and mom had only to pay for my bachelor's degree because they had instilled common sense in me that allowed for the other cents to come from scholarships, grants, and the "Jim Crow money" (as we called it) Black students received from the state of Mississippi for attending Black colleges. Now, I ask you, is this a man who should even consider his education a handicap?

J.B.: I, his baby daughter, have indulged him with adoration through fishing trips—very early complete with worms and ticks—through his spoiling me, through growing into a woman and his indulgence of me in my horrible taste in men. He always believed in me, even when I "fucked up." I didn't even know my father was a "mane," "main," or, "man" until I was an educated professional with a daughter of my own. Honey, the look of disdain he gave me when seeing me in hot pants! He didn't think I was dressed like a doctor. He still doesn't think I dress like a doctor sometimes; and sometimes it comes across like I'm not dressed like a lady. But, he has been patient and watched me carry myself. Now that I've somewhat proved that I am a woman and a lady, I have almost earned his respect. After all, neither one of us, his daughters, is a son. But it doesn't bother me, and I have never gotten the impression that it bothered him either.

D.B.: I always believed, and still do, that Dad is one of the smartest men that I know. The wisdom that this man has exhibited throughout my life makes me consider him an Einstein in terms of his discoveries, a King in terms of his dealings with society as a whole, a Booker T. on the practical issues, and a Du Bois on intelligence.

J.B.: Mother has often said that Dad was a much better father than he was a husband. As a mother, and two times a divorcée, I think I understand what she meant. It's the "mane" thing. He came up in a time when a "mane's got to do what a mane's got to do" whether it's right or not. She should be canonized for living with him for sixty-one years! It aggravates me sometimes when I see him act so strong-willed, dominating, and plain-assed obstinate. Sometimes I make a point to tell him to chill, but I know he's too old to change. I just settle for saying my piece and stepping around him. You know, to do what I want to do or what it is I think is right to do. After all, he (and Mama) gave us that independence. He (and Mama) taught us to take care of ourselves. I also know when he's bad it's his own fear of losing her, his helpmate, his rock, to aging decay. It reminds him of his own mortality, his age and his cancer (did you know this old carpenter calls it his "termites"?). He's scared. He is a tender, tender soul. He loves us and our mother. He loves his work and church and people (all peoples of the world). I always think of that flame, red face at the head of the Deacon Board; that face full and brimming with tears. Full of life and love and the glory and blessings of God. I blame him for making me a cry baby. I love him for giving me a heart full of love although a lot of times it makes a fool of me. I wouldn't have it any other way.

D.B.: I want always to remember that Dad is not only a practical person and hands-on worker who could build a house out of leftovers from a house he helped tear down, but that he has also always been a believer in educating his own, in building their mind power, and in building a better community by active nonviolent work to end segregation and protect equal rights.

J.B.: If I never find a mate, it's his fault. I can't find a copy of him. They broke the mold and maybe that's good. After my last divorce, Mama said "Well, Jen, maybe you'll have to marry your dad." I agreed. But I probably couldn't live with him either!

I hardly think of him now though without thinking of him and Mama as a unit. I am so grateful to God almighty for giving him to me (to us). I'm even more grateful for God's giving him to my daughter, the only real father she has ever truly known.

Dolores Kendrick

What about Humphrey Bogart?
An Alleluia for Ike

Ike was his own man. Whatever that phrase means (one who carries his own weight; one who creates his dreams and nourishes them once they are born; one who defies a persona offered to him by a fretful world, but produces a persona of his own, made to specifications, tailored to his fragile ego)—Ike was it. Unlike the "own man" myth that ravished the young twentieth century in which he lived, he was not a prisoner of his own man Alter Ego. He carried his own baggage (his own hang-ups, what little there was to travel with), and when it became too heavy for him, he simply tossed it away, perhaps for some poor misfit stumbling upon it to rummage through. For with Ike there was always a little surprise hidden somewhere in the packing, and the poor misfit had to find it. It was one of the ways he kept himself from being a loser. In the end Ike wanted me to get into his dying. I couldn't do that, but I could help him across and I did.

As I write this I am reminded of a poetic work about Ike that I am trying to finish now. I had begun this work, *Johns a' Dreams*, before his death, but on a friend's advice decided to put it on hold at least until Ike had finished giving me his last and final gift, his journey through the world in all its Ikenarian dimensions of friends, and the politics of human commerce, and love, and loss, and abandonment and the silence and chaotic things and through it all an accommodating, almost archetypal humor that defied the laws of gravity for the seasons of hope.

As I sat by his bedside on one of his many visits to the hospital, I thought he was indestructible. There he was making jokes about his illness, going under in and out of the jokes, laughing to himself, and all the

time watching me to see if I had gotten it—the punch line, the line that
punches out doom and despair.

*You know, the devil is a crazy man, but he's smart. Never forget that. He
told me once one of his secrets. Wanna hear it? Know what he said? Ike, he said,
you're a good newspaperman, a good reporter. I want you to write about me one
day. And be fair. You know? People all think that I'm cruel, that I put people in
this terrible fire, consuming, hungry, all over the place. Well, you know, that's
not exactly true. I don't use fire, Ike, let's get that straight. I use a microwave,
just like everybody else!*

We both laughed that evil spirit away. And that was exactly what Ike
was up to. Nothing dare come at him until he was ready. Death would
have to stand at the door and knock, and when Ike was ready, he'd let him
in. Or perhaps there might be a phone call, which would give Ike time
to put him on hold while he closed another deal.

My father started his own newspaper in Washington, D.C., some
thirty-three years before he died. It was not the time of perennial success
for Black businessmen, but he had his vision and he stayed focused upon
it. The paper, *Capital Spotlight*, was the voice of the world of Black business, social life, and sports. It chronicled the comings and goings of
a world that was quietly vanishing even as the newsprint was pressed
freshly on the page. Ella and Chick Webb at the Howard Theater, Nat
King Cole and Lena Horne, too, Lionel Hampton, Duke, the supper
clubs, one called The Bengasi where most of the great jazz bloomed, Har-
rison's fine restaurant where the chicken salad was as gourmet as it could
get, the little businesses blooming and disappearing one after the other
as if to give nourishment to that sweet and sacred world of I will survive.

Ike recorded all of that—and more. He loved it; the by-play with the
man-in-the-street, the numbers players who often saved his day when
the office rent was due, the poker players, something he had mastered at
age fifteen and learned to put into his survival kit for a rainy day, learned
it with passion for something else, something more, something that
only Ike could render with oblivion, not an other force or other energy,
not a ghost hiding in the closet coming out now and then to chastise him
with a "peek-a-boo!" Not a wolf in sheep's clothing, or a disappointment
disguised as a fulfillment. When I left his bedside that winter evening,
the devil joke in my memory, I felt enlivenment. Even at the bottom of
his pain he had given me a little of his energy, and I wrote him a poem.

He's writing a check,
puts it in an envelope
takes a pill,
reaches for water,
gestures for a waiter
to come to his table.

And all the while there is nothing,
only air that he catches
creates with, shapes his horizontal
world as he swims midstream.

And the liquid air catches him
for a second, then spits him out.

He sees shapes, but they leave him
for ejaculations of little people drowning;
he talks to them in slurred tongue,
the strut of the language he invented
years ago when he found that he, too,
had to survive a Black man's skin,
with a Black man's soul,
and a dream that refused to come colored,
quitting that perfect job when his white boss
called him boy, quitting and coming back
alive in all his genius of gender
that made him something singular, sifting
his tailor-made profession from the shifting
sands of stars.

I touch his soft hands
and know the soft horror
that refuses to be hard enough
for him to break.

He goes under.
Out, back, sees me with his blind eye,
whispers something in that language
that owns him now, greets me gracefully

while the painkiller prompts him,
thinks he still has his leg,
which the surgeons took six hours before,
unknowingly knows the leg is gone,
thinks he can scratch it,
and something happens:

he reaches for a memory in the nothingness.

I grab his hand,
he tightens his grip,
the memory crumbles,
he goes out again,
comes back:

It's good to know you're here.
The hospital bed lies to him
about his limb, what he feels
as his fingers curl about his body
the blankets, cold sheets, the tubes.

I let him go,
it is his way I give him now,
but for a moment,
I try to bring him to me,
the gray head slipping off the pillow,
the mouth open,
the snoring of breath.

How are you, Ike? I call.
He must have found my voice
somewhere in his uneasy exile
as he switches to something familiar,
that chemicals can't correct.
See you soon, he whispers, moans,
screams, sings, and drifts upon
the back of a soft sound

that blankets him

drains out the infections,
punishing his horrors, purifying,
making him holy.

My father was practically orphaned at age twelve. His mother, Hattie Akers, was one of the first Black actresses in American musical theater, and she was on the road most of the time. Consequently, he was raised by his maternal grandmother in a three-story brownstone-type house in LeDroit Park, then one of the most affluent neighborhoods for Blacks in Washington. Quite a few of the people "on the hill," faculty at Howard University, lived in LeDroit Park as did a few people in the music world (among them, the well-known opera star Mme. Evanti) and most of Ike's tennis partners, though his favorite tennis partner and friend was Sterling Brown. After Hattie's death at age twenty-seven from tuberculosis, Ike was more or less on his own, except for the guidance of Mother Akers. His father had long since deserted him and his mother, and he saw Bobby Tut (the Tut was a taken name since my grandfather apparently loved the mystique of glory of the young Egyptian, King Tut, and claimed a little of that for his own) just once in his life when he was seventeen years old.

Bobby Tut owned a restaurant which apparently thrived for many years in Asbury Park, New Jersey. Ike did not have fond memories of Bobby Tut, perhaps because he knew there was too much of his father in him, too much with which he couldn't reconcile himself: the possibility of surviving at the expense of family. As it turned out, it was the women in his life who gave him their energy for his wholeness, his completeness, and in the end knowing such wholeness cannot be borrowed he turned to his spiritual self and found his own gravity.

I remember Mme. Justine she pronounced it Mme. Joostine. Sounded sort of French. She ran a brothel, but she insisted upon her dignity—and I admired her for that. She'd dress her girls up in Sunday-Go-to-Meeting outfits, reserve three front rows of seats for them at the Howard Theater for the evening show, wait until everyone was seated, and down the aisle she'd come with all twenty-four of her women behind her—like she was going to church or something. There wasn't a sound in the place, just all those Negro eyes escorting Mme. Justine to her seat. She had it all, and she knew it—because how many husbands in the audience had been her customers? Justine knew name, rank, and serial number. All that in her little white book. Oddly enough, that kind of power endeared her to the community. She was too dangerous.

Ike chuckles, and suddenly without knowing it (or perhaps he does), he has given me a healthy respect for all creatures great and small.

My mother loved him even in the pain between them. He was not lovable as a family man, too many ghosts to squander, but his appetite for life knew no bounds and nourished him to the end of his days. She knew and understood that appetite, but she also knew that she could not allow him to devour her whenever he was hungry. She was her own person, whole and incredibly free even though she became his wife at age nineteen in order to have someone "take care" of her. They tried three times to make their marriage work, "for the sake of the children," but how can a man who was never taught how to love be a caretaker for anything or anyone but himself? "I come first," he often said. "If I go, everything goes."

And that kind of logic seared his smothered seed for compassion and generosity, sensitivity to pain. What remained was what he owned: a random self-empowerment. When they divorced, my mother paid him great tribute. She told my brother, sister, and me that no matter what happened we were always to remember that he was our father and we were to respect that. Whatever went on between the two of them *was* between the two of them, and we were never to forget how special Ike had been to us in good times as well as bad. We were family. No divorce could change that. We were in God.

Ike went on to marry again. My mother never did.

In his dying days he often speaks of my mother who passed on seventeen years before. He, my brother, my sister, and I had long since stopped calling her Mama. She was Gaga, an abbreviation of Grandmother that her grandson had given her. After all, "Gaga" took "grandmother" out of her vocabulary. Neither my mother nor my father was ever confined to the structures of aging. It simply didn't exist. You are who you are and in between that is a life. In tune with the good Lord, you grow into that life with a certain steely stealthiness and breeding. Well, he says, Gaga should be praying for me. I've got a deal coming up with the paper, and I need her prayers.

Prayers?

Walter, an old Black man with one eye, rejected by his upper-class family because he is retarded, sits at our kitchen table holding forth about God and religion with my father. My mother is making hot milk for Walter. It is his mid-morning snack.

Suddenly, he begins to sing.

I will guide you,
I will guide you,
I will guide you
with my life.

On the way from
earth to heaven,
I will guide you
with my life.

No, Ike says, you've got the words wrong. It's I will guide you with my knife, Walter.

No, Mr. Kendrick, it's life.

No, Walter it's knife.

But Mr. Kendrick . . .

Listen to me, Walter, it's knife.

But Mr. Kendrick, God don't carry no knife. He's a peaceful man.

Yeah, but sometimes the only way peace can be captured is with a knife.

Aw no, Mr. Kendrick. Ya never get peace with a knife. God knows that.

My father, realizing that he has pushed the joke as far as it will go, steals a cautious look at Walter and starts the hymn again.

I will guide you . . .

The words fluttter across the room. Suddenly, Walter picks up on the last word, the word he believes in, the word God made especially for him: Life . . .

My father joins in. You know, Walter, he says, jokingly, feeling the spirit passing through his jaw. Maybe you're right. God doesn't need a weapon to protect us.

He loves us, Mr. Kendrick, Walter says simply.

Ike, who never knew how to love, whose parents had denied him that gift of gifts, and who had yet to to learn the mathematics of loving, finds himself one with Walter (something like the numbers on a payroll?) and surrenders to his first lesson in love and prayer—from this old, abandoned, retarded, one-eyed

*man whose vision transcends his just long enough to give himself to Ike as
Father.*

Yeah, Ike says, and looks around for a grin.

Now he is dying. He sits in his wheelchair (because diabetes has
taken one leg) dressed to the hilt. In that wheelchair he has gone to
black-tie formals honoring him for his contributions to the community. He has directed his newspaper from his office in the National
Press Building from this wheelchair, and he has held court with me
countless times from this wheelchair. He is dying and he knows it. But
Ike is a good poker player and death wouldn't dare take a peek at his
whole hand of cards. That spirit has to pay to see.

I remember so well his final moments with me. He needed embraces.
Over his eight-five years he had finally learned the mathematics of love,
though he had not mastered the timetable. He had become a wonderful
grandfather, though he had hopped, skipped, and jumped the idea of
himself as father. I came to visit him in his small apartment to bring
him communion, as I had become a eucharistic minister, a ministry
that allowed me to give communion to shut-ins, and Ike, being the newest shut-in in the parish since he had connected to Catholicism two
years before his death, was consumed by these Sunday communions like
no one else I had administered to. I knew at that time that he felt himself going under, more frequently than he wanted to admit—leaving a
room, a thought, a conversation somewhere in the energy of now and
going out into the universe alone in the spirit of his hope and tenacity,
a kind of regal roaming through locks and doors and barriers, while his
body sat trapped in a little leather chair with wheels, and brakes, and
footrests. When he returned to that body he would rise from his sleep
and command: "Let's talk about the movies. What about Humphrey
Bogart?"

Maybe Bogart was out there seeing him across. Ike was always a fan
of films—particularly those made by Warner Brothers. Maybe Bogart
had peeped at his whole hand and knew that Ike was just bluffing, and
any man who had the imagination to bluff death deserved a proper
escort.

I don't know.

Lenard D. Moore

My Father's Ways

I.
You perch me on a stool
like a blackbird on a branch,
teach me time tables
that multiply like rabbits.

II.
You take me to football games,
coach me, draw plays
in symbols
on metal bleachers.

III.
You walk through your garden,
farmer, witnessing crops;
you name plants, show me
how to harvest.

IV.
You mold me into
a potter spinning clay
in circles,
shaping bowls and vases.

V.
Now, full-grown,
like a tree rooted deep,
I bend forward into the light
of your voice in prayer.

4

Fare-Thee-Wells

In Honor of David Anderson Brooks, My Father

JULY 30, 1883–NOVEMBER 21, 1959
A dryness is upon the house
My father loved and tended.
Beyond his firm and sculptured door
His light and lease have ended.

He walks the valleys, now—replies
To sun and wind forever.
No more the cramping chamber's chill,
No more the hindering fever.

Now out upon the wide clean air
My father's soul revives,
All innocent of self-interest
And the fear that strikes and strives.

He who was Goodness, Gentleness,
and Dignity is free,
Translates to public Love
Old private charity.   GWENDOLYN BROOKS

So as we bid farewell to Dad, I want you all to know that I am looking forward to a family reunion. I am looking forward to union together on the other side of the Jordan. I am looking forward to seeing Dad in a place where the wicked will cease their troubling and the weary shall be at rest. I tell you when I get there, I'm going down Revelation Boulevard to the corner of John Street, right around the corner from Mark's place. But I want to go to Nahum's place. I don't want to be in Jeremiah's house, it would be too crowded. I don't even want to be down on Peter Street, too many people there—I want some quiet time. I want to sit down with C. L. West, I want to sit down with Nick Bias, and I want to sit down with Aunt Juanita, and I want to sit down with Aunt Tiny. And I want to sit down with Dad!   CORNEL WEST

Since his death two years ago, memories of Dad are gifts my brother, my mother, and I open in rituals of healing that are sometimes planned and other times spontaneous. The gift I open with special delight is the bedtime game inspired by my favorite story about Father Bear putting Little Bear to bed. My mother would bathe me, dress me for bed and then call out to my dad, "Little Bear is ready." That was Dad's cue to lift me onto his shoulders and begin "looking" for Little Bear. "Is she in this room?" my dad would ask. "Nooo!" I would answer. "Have you seen Little Bear?" he would ask my mother. "Nooo!" she would answer. We would move from room to room, looking under beds and in closets, going upstairs and downstairs. Each time Dad would move in the direction of the bathroom he shared with my mom, I would scream, "Little Bear's not in there, Daddy." I knew that the game would end when Dad would stand in front of the bathroom mirror and "discover" Little Bear sitting on his shoulders. "There she is," he would say and lift me down for a tight embrace. Always I would say, "Do it again, Daddy. Do it again." Sometimes he would. It is Dad's face of love I see clearly in the reflection of my memories.   JANINE-BARBARA ANTHONY

Miriam DeCosta-Willis

Looking toward Arbutus

> The future does not exist, the Indians of the Altiplano say,
> we can only be sure of the past—from which we draw
> experience and knowledge—and the present—a brief
> spark that at the instant it is born becomes yesterday.
>
> ISABEL ALLENDE

My earliest memory of my father is of that sweltering summer day when he came into my room—the one that Uncle Herbert built for me at the far end of the second-story porch—smiled down at me tenderly in my crib, and asked, "How's my little girl?" Still groggy from an early-afternoon nap, I giggled with delight at the sight of the tall, slender man in the blue tie and stiff white shirt who looked at me with such affection. When he picked me up, I put my arms around him and snuggled my nose into the crook of his neck, where I detected the familiar smell of tobacco, English Leather, and Vaseline hair tonic. This was my daddy, my very own daddy, I thought, as I touched his face, feeling the slight tickle of his beard against the palms of my hands. Like other images of childhood—the sight of bats at the window, the cry of shrimp vendors in the streets of Charleston, and the taste of Uncle Herbert's silver bells—that loom large in my imagination, the touch of my father's face is one of the most important memories of my early years because it evokes feelings of love, warmth, and tenderness.

Another image, dark and painful, haunts me. On another hot summer night, I walked into the back bedroom of my parents' home and saw Daddy stretched out, quiet and apparently asleep, on the twin bed under the window. In the dim light of the lamp, he looked so small and frail and old, this man who, at six feet one, usually towered over me but who now lay motionless on top of the covers. It was quiet in his room that

night except for the ticking of the clock by his bed, the sounds of
Mother stirring in the kitchen . . . and Daddy's heavy, labored breathing. While I sat with him that night, I mumbled the usual bedside nice-
ties—"The children came to see you." "I know you'll feel better tomorrow." "Can I get you anything: water, a glass of juice, your pills?"—but
what I really wanted to do was to put my arms around him, snuggle into
the crook of his neck, and whisper, "I love you, Daddy." But I couldn't,
I just couldn't . . . because of my natural reserve and emotional coolness.
At thirty-seven, I was a different person from that little girl whose world
began and ended with her father: I had grown up and away from him,
and there were others in my life—a husband from whom I was now divorced, four children aged eight to sixteen, and a man whom I loved beyond reason—all of whom laid claim to my heart, but the memory of
that night and the guilt that I felt over my failure to reach out and hold
my father have haunted me through all these years.

The long years and the emotional distance that separate the girl's
touch from the woman's guilt underscore the complexity of my relationship with my father, a relationship that was so deep, so profound
that even now I keep returning—in my memories, in the pages of my
journal, in the walking-around hours of my daydreams, and in the
tossing-and-turning hours of my nightmares—to the past with questions, the answers to which I am now only beginning to understand:
Why is love so demanding? Why do we hurt the ones we love the most?
Why do we withhold love, rationing it out in bits and pieces, afraid, perhaps, of giving too much or of revealing too much of ourselves? This
summer, I have had the extraordinary experience of revisiting the past
and getting to know, really know, my father, while researching his life—
reading his letters, articles, and books; examining his papers, docu-
ments, and photographs; and talking with other family members, particularly my mother.

In long, late-night telephone calls, Mother has spun golden tales
about my father and me, confirming what I have always known: that I
was a daddy's girl. A sensitive and perceptive woman with a delightful
sense of humor, a sharp memory, and a love of people, my mother, at
eighty-two, is the family storyteller. A month ago, Mother laughed, remembering, "You were so funny looking," she told me, "with such a
long, pointed head that Dad called you 'Skoodle Head.' He bought a

frilly dress and a fancy bonnet to cover your baldness." Five minutes later, she called back to tell me, "And another thing, Dad took over your care after Frank was born. Our house was next to his school, so he'd run home between classes to see about you. He always wore starched white shirts, and it was so funny, one day he came home to find that you had had a bowel movement and wiped it all over the wall. Well, you should have seen your father: he rolled up his sleeves and proceeded to clean up you and the wall with his usual precision." My father's partiality for me survived my infancy and was still evident when I was a young girl. On another night, my mother told me: "When we were living in Orange-burg, you did a lot of the cleaning, which you liked, but you didn't care anything about cooking. I told you, 'You need to learn how to cook.' You started fussing, just running your mouth and running your mouth. I got angry and slapped you. When Dad came home, I told him what had happened. He said, 'What! You slapped *my child*?' He was very upset." Daddy never spanked me because he didn't believe in violence or corpo-ral punishment; all he had to do was to raise his voice and give me a stern look. When he said, "Now, *Mi*-riam," with an emphasis on that first syl-lable, I knew that I was in *deep* trouble. The story above points up some of the tensions that surface in a family when a child feels closer to one parent than to the other. Although Mother and I are very close (at least we have become so as adults), she must have been aware of my devotion to my father and of my antipathy toward her during that difficult growing-up period. There's a folk saying, "Mama's baby, papa's maybe," but it was the other way around in my family; last year, I told some friends, in front of my mother, "I'm my father's child. My mother adopted me," and we both laughed, knowingly.

When I was a little girl, I loved to watch my father shave. He'd stand over the bathroom sink in his white boxer shorts and sleeveless under-shirt, decked out in a battered felt hat, yes, a hat, to keep his hair from falling in his face while he shaved. After he finished, he would take off his hat, pour a few drops of Vaseline Hair Tonic in the palm of his hand, rub his hands together before raking his fingers through his hair, and then comb the tonic through his heavy, dark hair. He seemed totally un-aware of his good looks: the height, the handsome face with the high forehead and penetrating eyes, the athletic build and finely shaped legs, his large calves curving down to thin ankles and high insteps. (To this day, the first thing that I check out is a man's legs!) An older family friend once told me, "I saw your father getting off the train in New York. I just turned around and followed him because he was the most gorgeous thing I had ever seen."

But looks didn't mean a thing to Daddy; what mattered to him was what was in your head. Of all the gifts that he gave me, the one that I treasure most is the love of learning, which he nurtured through books, quiet afternoon lessons, long discussions at the dinner table, and, through example: writing at his desk by day and reading late into the night.

I must have been about four when he returned from graduate school, but I remember the two presents that he brought me from New York. He photographed me, resplendent in the first gift—a pink wool coat, trimmed in rose velvet, with a matching cap and muff—standing at the top of the stairs outside our house at 54 Montague Street. Daddy's little girl, proud and pretty in pink! He also brought me a set of books, which I have kept all these years, books such as *Adventures in Geography, The Turned Intos*, and *Runaway Rhymes*, in which the rhythm of the words, the beauty of the illustrations, and the wondrous adventures of the characters fired my imagination and kindled dreams of travel to distant lands. My favorite was *Little Peachling*, a collection of Japanese tales told by Hanashi-ka, who recounts the miraculous story of the little boy who was found in a peach and became a famous warrior.

My father, who taught me how to read long before I went to school, was a consummate teacher, exacting and sometimes impatient but always thorough. A perfectionist. During my first semester at Westover, a preparatory school to which I was sent at age fifteen, I failed algebra after making the highest grade—99.5 percent—at the segregated high school in the small South Carolina town where I'd grown up. I was devastated. And I didn't have a clue as to what was going on in class, so, when I came home for Christmas vacation, Daddy, who had been a mathematics major in college, took matters into his own hands. Every day, I would go to his office and there, surrounded by books and papers, sunlight streaming through a bank of windows and smoke curling up from his Camel cigarettes, Daddy and I worked through the afternoon. He would carefully explain the logic behind the various operations and then give me problems to solve until—miracle of miracles!—everything became perfectly clear. When I returned to school, confident in my newly acquired skills, I made straight A's in algebra to the teacher's utter amazement.

Once, I told a friend that I had sprung, Athena-like, from the head of my father, who was my teacher, mentor, and guide. Sometimes, according to Mother, my special status worked to his detriment. She told me this story by way of illustration: "One summer while Dad was working on his Masters at Columbia, we went up to visit him. You were four then. He came home one day with a very important term paper that he had been working on. You threw it in the bathtub and by the time he found it, it was ruined. I was outdone, but all he said was, 'Oh, that's fine. That's probably where it belongs.' Then he sat down and wrote the whole thing over."

Although he was a very kind and loving man, Daddy looked and acted like the college professor that he was, and he had fairly traditional ideas about marriage, family, and women. ("It's very unlady-like for a woman to smoke," he'd tell me, although he was a chain-smoker; and he told my fiancé, "Leave the dishes alone. That's women's work.") I never heard him curse—he was very proper and always correct—but he liked his "highballs" in the evening, because, I think, bourbon took away his inhibitions, smoothing the sharp edges of his reserve and allowing him to loosen up and express himself more freely. A strong and forceful man, he was definitely the head of the house (though he and my mother had an amazingly egalitarian marriage); I respected his strength and looked for it, expected it even, in the men I have loved. Because he had grown up in a house full of strong, determined women—a stern and puritanical grandmother, widowed mother, and four older Victorian sisters—he must have struggled hard, I now realize, to assert his maleness in contradistinction to females, while engaging in typically masculine coming-of-age rituals: working as a carpenter in the summer, playing baseball, captaining the basketball team, and pledging Alpha. And so, he taught me the power of femininity (lessons which I sometimes ignored), but he also encouraged my feminism by challenging my ideas, respecting my opinions, and praising my academic achievements. Although he must have assumed that I would marry some day and have a family, he also anticipated that I would go to college and graduate school, have a career, and make my own way in the world because he raised me to be independent and self-sufficient.

In the evenings, after dinner, we would sit around the table and talk, Mother washing dishes at the sink, my brother and I indulging in chocolate milkshakes, and Daddy stirring the ice in his bourbon and coke. "Yes, I see what you mean," he would comment, showing respect for our opinions, "but have you thought about the impact that the program would have on the disadvantaged?" he would ask, challenging us to re-examine our ideas. In those long, enjoyable evening discussions, we talked about everything, current events, politics, education, Black history, and the strange antics of white folk. Those after-dinner conversations helped to shape my view of the world and of my place in it.

Some of my father's lessons, though, went unappreciated and sometimes unheeded; he was so funny trying to teach a willful little girl the facts of life. At three I asked, "Mother, where do babies come from?" and, sociologist that she was, she gave some clinical answer that I didn't understand, so Daddy told her, "Beautine, I'll take care of this." He went into a long encomium about the virtues of marriage and the beauties of motherhood, after which I asked, "But, Daddy, what's so *beautiful* about it?" When I was seven, he tried again, soon after I taught a little boy to do "artificial respiration" at a birthday party. (This was during the Second World War and I was doing my part for the Allies.) Daddy and I were sitting in the living room of the house in Philadelphia that we shared with Aunt Edna and Uncle Petey, when he handed me a book about the birds and bees, saying, "Your mother and I think you ought to read this book. If you have any questions, I'll answer them." The book described the growth of the fetus in the mother's uterus, which left me totally confused, but I was fascinated by a round photograph of little tadpoles called "sperms" that swam across the page like a school of very confused fish. "This is strange," I thought. When I finished reading, Daddy asked, "Do you have any questions?" "No," I answered, very shyly, because neither of us was comfortable talking about sex, but my father taught me an invaluable lesson: if you want to find out something, get a book. So, by the time I was ten, I had read *God's Little Acre, Strange Fruit*, the *Kinsey Report*, and the "good parts" of the medical books that belonged to Dr. Pettus (my friend Yvonne's father), which answered all

of my questions ... and then some. My last "lesson" on that subject
came when I was fourteen and on the basketball team at Wilkinson
High School. The coach must have told my parents that I was seen kissing my boyfriend on the school bus when we traveled out of town because one evening Daddy sat me down for a heart-to-heart talk. "Be
careful how you behave on trips. Remember that you're a *DeCosta*," he
warned. That did it: I had visions of thirteen aunts and uncles glowering
at me from the dark shadows of the bus. My father would have been
quite surprised, no, traumatized, to know that, in spite of his teaching
about the beauties of motherhood and the importance of books, his little girl grew up to publish a book of erotica!

There were other things besides sex—our feelings, our fears, and
our insecurities—that we didn't discuss freely, and, as I grew older, the
silences became longer and the tensions became more apparent. One incident stands out in my mind: I was fifteen and away at Westover for the
first year, and Daddy drove out to the tiny Connecticut town (a village
square, two churches, several houses, and a school) to visit me. Westover
had strict rules about visitation, even by parents, so he could stay for
only a few hours that Saturday afternoon. We talked and talked:

"Do you like the school?" he asked.

"Oh, yes. I'm learning so much and I'm in all the clubs," I said, excitement in my voice.

"How do the other girls treat you?

"Fine," I lied. "I have lots of friends: Pepper and Beth and ...

I was so proud of my father that day, the way he looked, the way he
talked, the way he was ... but I was so ashamed of myself. I felt so ugly,
dressed in the drab, brown school uniform with no make-up or jewelry
("Young ladies should not adorn their bodies."). I had gained twenty
pounds from the rich meals, midday cocoa and cookies, and afternoon
"sit-sits" where we fixed peanut butter and jelly on toast, and my face
was burned from the neck up because I'd been receiving radiation treatments for acne. But I was talkative and ebullient, trying to impress my
father with my worldliness and sophistication (I'd begun to shave my
legs, curl my eyelashes, and smoke in the closet after lights-out). Inside,
though, I was miserable. I hid from him the daily assaults against my
self—the parents' insults, the teachers' slights, and the arrogant as-
sumptions about who I (the first Black student) was—because I didn't

want to worry him. Did he sense, for my father knew me better than I knew myself, that I was hiding behind a mask and putting up a front for him? When he left, I felt that the only man who really loved me had walked ever so gently out of my life, so I went into my room, locked the door, and cried long into the night.

Sometimes I wonder if my father ever really knew the woman that I eventually became because I was always very careful, as I grew into adolescence and then womanhood, to preserve the image of the "good daughter," hiding from him the problems: financial, marital, personal, and family. Why? Because he and I were both raised in fairly "traditional" families, where a genteel formality and courteous reserve were required. We were Charleston-bred in a place where and at a time when we were expected to dissemble emotions—whether impassioned cries in the night or shouts of sanctified joy—like so many nappy edges concealed beneath the silken contours of a nylon wig. As I have matured, I have fought against that formality, that reserve, and all those painful silences, encouraging open discussion of even the darkest corners of my life. But my father did not have that option, I now understand, because of the circumstances of his life. Born in 1910, the youngest of eleven children, Frank Augustus DeCosta always struggled to overcome: the death of his father when he was only ten months old, the limited resources of his family, the difficulty in obtaining an education (he went away to college with $32 in his pocket!). And what a price he paid for that struggle. In his later years, there was a sadness and a loneliness about him that I sensed but did not feel free to talk about. He seemed to distance himself from people, as he became more and more *ensimismado* (literally, "put into himself"; translated, "lost in thought" or "sunk into a reverie"). A friend once saw him, alone, at Atlantic City walking down the beach; when he had a heart attack at fifty-nine, my father drove himself to the hospital; and, finally, he died alone. He paid dearly for being a strong and silent man.

However my father might have struggled with his personal demons (demons that I can only intuit, because he lived a careful, guarded private life), he never, ever, failed me. Although I left home at fifteen, he wrote long, frequent letters that always ended "Lovingly, Daddy." (I write, though not so beautifully, with the same hand—a firm, deliberate script, characterized by open vowels and tall capital letters.) He and

Mother supported all of my educational endeavors, making space in their home for my two children and me when I was working on a master's, and turning their house completely over to me when I returned with four children to pursue a doctorate. Whenever Daddy visited me and my family in Memphis, he always left me a check because he knew, intuitively, that we were struggling financially. And he had an uncanny ability to sense when I was in trouble. I'll never forget the week in early January when he announced, "I'm planning to come to Memphis. I really miss you and the children." I believed him, because that Christmas—always special to Daddy—was one of the few that we had spent apart. Little did I realize that he was coming to check on his daughter. He must have felt the tension in the house, noticed my husband's absences, and heard my whispered conversations on the telephone, but he never said a word. I remember his final goodbye at the airport. We were standing in the parking lot, Daddy somber and serious-looking in a dark grey coat and felt hat, when he turned to me and asked, "What is this I hear about another man?" I caught my breath and swallowed hard in disbelief. Then I looked into my father's eyes and said without flinching, "But I love him, Daddy." In the years that followed, through my separation, divorce, and move to Washington, Daddy never asked questions about or commented on my personal life, but he had to have known that man, who was also married, was very much at the center of my life. He must have viewed that relationship as a betrayal of all that he had taught me, but he respected me too much and cared too much about me to intrude on my privacy. Thank you, Daddy.

I, on the other hand, still feel that I failed my father in so many ways. First, because I couldn't remain *his* little girl forever; I had to grow up and loosen the bond that had sustained me through all those important and formative years. Mother told me recently that my father was devastated and close to tears when I left home, at age twenty, with my new husband; he believed that he had lost his daughter forever. Insensitive and self-centered that I was, I never thought about *his* feelings. A year and a half later, Daddy came to visit us, in Memphis, a week after the birth of our first child. I had had a long and difficult delivery and was exhausted after several days of cleaning up, cooking for my parents, and staying up nights with a fretful, colicky baby. It was getting late. Daddy was sitting up drinking highballs and I was holding the baby, who was screaming at the top of his lungs. Daddy said something like, "You need to put that child down," in a rather stern voice, and I went off . . . I said, "Daddy, you need to go home. You're drunk!" My father walked out and, later, told Mother that he would never return to my house. I was devastated. My cruel, thoughtless words stood like a ten-foot brick wall between us for months. I was stubborn and Daddy was proud and so it took a long time for us to resume our close relationship. I have never forgotten the incident.

Nor have I forgotten my inability to comfort Daddy on that Saturday night when I found him quiet and still in the back bedroom. I drove back to Washington and spent the next day catching up on work around the house and seeing after the children because I had been away at a conference in South Carolina for a week. Mother called that afternoon to tell me that she had taken Daddy to the hospital but not to worry because he seemed better. Since he had been scheduled for routine surgery to have his pacemaker replaced, we did not think that his condition was serious. That night, I was out late because I had decided, after months of turmoil, that I would break up—finally—with the man whom I had loved for five years. It was a painful and heartbreaking dissolution for us both, so I arrived home at one o'clock in the morning.

I awakened with a start about five o'clock on Monday morning. At first, the room was dark, but, gradually, I began to discern the shapes of objects—the closet door, the dresser on my left, and the bureau across the room—as the sky outside my bedroom window turned from a plum-colored black to the palest grey. Everything was perfectly still except for the curtains that fluttered every now and then in the breeze blowing through the window. And silent: no doors opening and closing; no cars screeching to a stop at the corner; even the birds were quiet. The air was radiant and translucent: *"la región más transparente,"* I thought, as I watched the slow metamorphosis of dark shapes into shoes, books, photographs, and a dark blue dress thrown carelessly across a chair. Suddenly, I felt something tactile and physical in the room, enveloping me in waves and waves of . . . sensations and feelings. It was an energy force like bright, warm sunlight moving slowly across a wooded plain, engaging all of my senses: sight, touch, taste, sound, smell. Later, I must have drifted off to sleep, because the telephone awakened me. "Miriam?" It was my brother Frank. *I know, oh, God, I know*, I thought to myself. "Daddy died early this morning."

I have this uncanny feeling that, as I grow older, *I am becoming my father*. When I was growing up, I had the audacity to think that I was shaping my own destiny: I loved reading and writing, was drawn to academic life, and never considered doing anything else but teaching. I did not realize, however, until I began reconstructing my father's biography, that I have walked, however falteringly, in his footsteps: the academic achievements, degrees, college teaching, department chairmanship, direction of graduate programs, and publication of articles and books. Nor did I realize that so much about me is like him: the seriousness, reserve, emotional distance, fascination with numbers and words, aptitude for languages, and enjoyment of physical activity (he played baseball and basketball; I played basketball and field hockey). But what meant the most to me was to discover the deeper *kinship of the spirit*—in our values and beliefs, the way we look at life, our attitudes toward people . . . and, even, our dark sides.

Life is a funny thing, how it sometimes brings you full circle back to your roots no matter how far up to the sky you spread your branches. It is a very humbling experience. When we began making preparations for my father's funeral and burial in Arbutus, a cemetery on the outskirts of Baltimore, my brother said to me, "We should buy a family plot with room not only for Mother and Daddy, but also for me and you." I was divorced at the time and had moved with my children from Memphis to Washington. I had no real roots anywhere, but I still protested, "Oh, no, I couldn't do that. I'm still young. I may move away, travel, remarry, so I wouldn't want to be tied down to any memorial park." I did all of the things that I imagined: I moved to another city, traveled throughout the world, and married the man whom I had loved for years. But several years ago, when my husband died, I returned to Washington and took a job in a university outside of Baltimore, near the little town of Arbutus. On a clear day, I can stand at my fifth-floor office window and look out across the campus, over the parking lot and the playing fields, and, if I look very very hard, I imagine that I can see the flat marker bearing my father's name. And I whisper into the wind, "I love you, Daddy."

.

Georgene Bess

Plaiting Now My Daddy's Hair

My father was a strong man. He was never intimidated by anything, not even failure. His motto was "Get up and try it again." The first time he said that to me, I had fallen and skinned my knee. Crying, I ran to him expecting sympathy. I got none. Instead, I got those words and my feelings hurt because I couldn't understand why he would tell me to go fall and hurt my knee again.

My father, a farmer, worked hard, no matter the season or the weather. I remember him coming from the fields in late evening, tired and dusty. We—my sisters, my brother, and I—would run behind him on the tractor, our mouths watering for the dirt pulled from deep within the earth with the harrow, a piece of equipment used to turn up the soil for planting. He would chuckle at our hunger, and say, "Children don't grow up right if they don't eat dirt. That's what's wrong with city children. They don't eat dirt."

Daddy's large black hands were hard and callused. With pain I remember the time I told him they were ugly. They weren't soft and smooth-looking like the hands of fathers I saw on television. He only chuckled and said, "Baby, I got a working man's hands."

At night, he would ask us to plait his hair, a chore all of us hated. But every night, without fail, he would say, "One of y'all, come plait my hair" and each time, without fail, I combed and plaited to the rhythm of my anger.

Every Sunday, before going to church, Daddy would go up the road to Benny Montford's grocery store (a pit stop really) for the newspaper and a bag of penny candy for us. When he bought groceries, he would buy us cookies, either 'Nilla Wafers or True-Blue, both of which I still love today. And every Friday, he gave each of us a quarter to buy ice cream and soda during Fun Day at school.

When Daddy became gravely ill, our lives changed forever. Those hands that had mended fences, steered the tractor, ground the corn, fed the hogs, grew the crops, and provided food, clothing, and shelter for us were now covered with large pus-filled sores. He had cancer, and it spread rapidly throughout his body—lungs, back, brain. Admitting him to the hospital was painful for all of us because we knew that being away from the farm—away from work—would be devastating for Daddy.

When he came home from the hospital after an extended stay, the first thing he did was put on his overalls and brogans. He wanted to be useful again—to work on the farm again—but the brogans were too heavy for him in his weakened condition. Not being able to do the work he loved or wear the clothes he liked best was too much for him. I saw the pain in his eyes and realized that my "get up and try it again" father was already dead.

He was readmitted to the hospital only to come home a short time later a virtual vegetable. He could no longer put on his signature brogans and Osh-Kosh blue denim overalls. He could no longer feed himself or dress himself, or talk and laugh as he once had. I cried inside when I heard his scratchy, hoarse, and incoherent whisper. I wanted my daddy back again. I wanted to give him nightly kisses on his beard-stubbled cheek and I wanted to hear him say again, in a strong and clear voice, "One of y'all, come plait my hair." Unable to see him suffer, I wanted my daddy dead. The gods granted my wish. Daddy died quietly in his sleep at the age of sixty-four. With a strange calmness after his death, I reached under his bed for his broken-in brogans, a painful reminder of what Daddy had once been, and put them away in the closet—out of sight as Daddy was. I did not grieve.

Seventeen years later while teaching Robert Hayden's "Those Winter Sundays," I relived Daddy's suffering and revisited his death. Then it was I grieved. Seventeen years of unshed tears fell when I recognized my father in the quiet warrior Hayden writes about. My father, too, on "Sundays . . . made banked fires blaze," ridding the house of the "blueblack cold." He made our house, and our lives, warm, and yet he never got a thank-you from us.

Remembering the many times I had "spoken indifferently to him, / who had driven out the cold," I was so overcome by an acute sense of shame and sadness that I wept in front of a class of twenty-three students. Stunned, they didn't know what to do or say. In the silence of their discomfort (and embarrassment), I heard a voice say, "Take your time, Miss Bess. Take your time." Although I couldn't see the student, my eyes filled with tears, I knew immediately who he was: the only African-American student in the class. He responded to my pain in the way Black church congregations respond to ministers struggling for the right word in a sermon when they are overcome by spirit: "Take your time. Take your time." For seventeen years, I had been fighting the grief in large part because I could not face my guilt.

After I took my time and wept, took my time and remembered, I realized that I had winter, spring, summer, and autumn Sundays to celebrate with my mother. I resolved to be a better daughter to her than I was to my father. I will not take her for granted and at every opportunity I will thank her, and thank her again, for her love. I know Daddy smiles in heaven.

James Baldwin

EXCERPT FROM

Notes of a Native Son

There was a whistling sound in my father's throat; nothing was said; he
could not speak. I wanted to take his hand, to say something. But I do
not know what I could have said, even if he could have heard me. He was
not really in that room with us, he had at last really embarked on his
journey; and though my aunt told me that he said he was going to meet
Jesus, I did not hear anything except that whistling in his throat. The
doctor came back and we left, into that unbearable train again, and
home. In the morning came the telegram saying that he was dead. Then
the house was suddenly full of relatives, friends, hysteria, and confusion
and I quickly left my mother and the children to the care of those impressive women, who, in Negro communities at least, automatically appear at times of bereavement armed with lotions, proverbs, and patience, and an ability to cook. I went downtown. By the time I returned,
later the same day, my mother had been carried to the hospital and the
baby had been born.

III.

For my father's funeral I had nothing black to wear and this posed a nag-
ging problem all day long. It was one of those problems, simple, or impossible of solution, to which the mind insanely clings in order to avoid
the mind's real trouble. I spent most of that day at the downtown apartment of a girl I knew, celebrating my birthday with whiskey and wondering what to wear that night. When planning a birthday celebration
one naturally does not expect that it will be up against competition from
a funeral and this girl had anticipated taking me out that night, for a big
dinner and a night club afterwards. Sometime during the course of that
long day we decided that we would go out anyway, when my father's fu-

neral service was over. I imagine *I* decided it, since, as the funeral hour approached, it became clearer and clearer to me that I would not know what to do with myself when it was over. The girl, stifling her very lively concern as to the possible effects of the whiskey on one of my father's chief mourners, concentrated on being conciliatory and practically helpful. She found a black shirt for me somewhere and ironed it and, dressed in the darkest pants and jacket I owned, and slightly drunk, I made my way to my father's funeral.

The chapel was full, but not packed, and very quiet. There were, mainly, my father's relatives, and his children, and here and there I saw faces I had not seen since childhood, the faces of my father's one-time friends. They were very dark and solemn now, seeming somehow to suggest that they had known all along that something like this would happen. Chief among the mourners was my aunt, who had quarreled with my father all his life; by which I do not mean to suggest that her mourning was insincere or that she had not loved him. I suppose that she was one of the few people in the world who had, and their incessant quarreling proved precisely the strength of the tie that bound them. The only other person in the world, as far as I knew, whose relationship to my father rivaled my aunt's in depth was my mother, who was not there.

It seemed to me, of course, that it was a very long funeral. But it was, if anything, a rather shorter funeral than most, nor, since there were no overwhelming, uncontrollable expressions of grief, could it be called— if I dare to use the word—successful. The minister who preached my father's funeral sermon was one of the few my father had still been seeing as he neared his end. He presented to us in his sermon a man whom none of us had ever seen—a man thoughtful, patient, and forbearing, a Christian inspiration to all who knew him, and a model for his children. And no doubt the children, in their disturbed and guilty state, were almost ready to believe this; he had been remote enough to be anything and, anyway, the shock of the incontrovertible, that it was really our father lying up there in that casket, prepared the mind for anything. His sister moaned and this grief-stricken moaning was taken as corroboration. The other faces held a dark, noncommittal thoughtfulness. This was not the man they had known, but they had scarcely expected to be confronted with *him*; this was, in a sense deeper than questions of fact, the man they had not known, and the man they had not known may have been the real one. The real man, whoever he had been, had suffered and now he was dead: this was all that was sure and all that mattered now. Every man in the chapel hoped that when his hour came he, too, would be eulogized, which is to say forgiven, and that all of his lapses, greeds, errors, and strayings from the truth would be invested with coherence and looked upon with charity. This was perhaps the last thing human beings could give each other and it was what they demanded, after all, of the Lord. Only the Lord saw the midnight tears, only He was present when one of His children, moaning and wringing hands, paced up and down the room. When one slapped one's child in anger the recoil in the heart reverberated through heaven and became part of the pain of the universe. And when the children were hungry and sullen and distrustful and one watched them, daily, growing wilder, and further away, and running headlong into danger, it was the Lord who knew what the charged heart endured as the strap was laid to the backside; the Lord alone who knew what one *would* have said if one had had, like the Lord, the gift of the living word. It was the Lord who knew of the impossibility every parent in that room faced: how to prepare the child for the day when the child would be despised and how to *create* in the child—by what means?— a stronger antidote to this poison than one had found for oneself. The avenues, side streets, bars, billiard halls, hospitals, police stations, and even the playgrounds of Harlem—not to mention the houses of correction, the jails, and the morgue—testified to the potency of the poison while remaining silent as to the efficacy of whatever antidote, irresistibly raising the question of whether or not such an antidote existed; raising, which was worse, the question of whether or not an antidote was desirable; perhaps poison should be fought with poison. With these several schisms in the mind and with more terrors in the heart than could be named, it was better not to judge the man who had gone down under an impossible burden. It was better to remember: *Thou knowest this man's fall; but thou knowest not his wrassling.*

While the preacher talked and I watched the children—years of changing their diapers, scrubbing them, slapping them, taking them to school, and scolding them had had the perhaps inevitable result of making me love them, though I am not sure I knew this then—my mind was busily breaking out with a rash of disconnected impressions. Snatches

of popular songs, indecent jokes, bits of books I had read, movie se-
quences, faces, voices, political issues—I thought I was going mad; all
these impressions suspended, as it were, in the solution of the faint nau-
sea produced in me by the heat and liquor. For a moment I had the impression that my alcoholic breath, inefficiently disguised with chewing
gum, filled the entire chapel. Then someone began singing one of my
father's favorite songs and, abruptly, I was with him, sitting on his knee,
in the hot, enormous, crowded church which was the first church we attended. It was the Abyssinia Baptist Church on 138th Street. We had
not gone there long. With this image, a host of others came. I had forgotten, in the rage of my growing up, how proud my father had been of
me when I was little. Apparently, I had had a voice and my father had
liked to show me off before the members of the church. I had forgotten
what he had looked like when he was pleased but now I remembered that
he had always been grinning with pleasure when my solos ended. I even
remembered certain expressions on his face when he teased my
mother—had he loved her? I would never know. And when had it all begun to change? For now it seemed that he had not always been cruel. I
remembered being taken for a haircut and scraping my knee on the
footrest of the barber's chair and I remembered my father's face as he
soothed my crying and applied the stinging iodine. Then I remembered
our fights, fights which had been of the worst possible kind because my
technique had been silence.

I remembered the one time in all our life together when we had really spoken to each other.

It was on a Sunday and it must have been shortly before I left home.
We were walking, just the two of us, in our usual silence, to or from
church. I was in high school and had been doing a lot of writing and I
was, at about this time, the editor of the high school magazine. But I had
also been a Young Minister and had been preaching from the pulpit.
Lately, I had been taking fewer engagements and preached as rarely as
possible. It was said in the church, quite truthfully, that I was "cooling
off."

My father asked me abruptly, "You'd rather write than preach,
wouldn't you?"

I was astonished at his question—because it was a real question. I answered, "Yes."

That was all we said. It was awful to remember that that was all we had *ever* said.

The casket now was opened and the mourners were being led up the aisle to look for the last time on the deceased. The assumption was that the family was too overcome with grief to be allowed to make this journey alone and I watched while my aunt was led to the casket and, muffled in black, and shaking, led back to her seat. I disapproved of forcing the children to look on their dead father, considering that the shock of his death, or, more truthfully, the shock of death as a reality, was already a little more than a child could bear, but my judgment in this matter had been overruled and there they were, bewildered and frightened and very small, being led, one by one, to the casket. But there is also something very gallant about children at such moments. It has something to do with their silence and gravity and with the fact that one cannot help them. Their legs, somehow, seem *exposed*, so that it is at once incredible and terribly clear that their legs are all they have to hold them up.

I had not wanted to go to the casket myself and I certainly had not wished to be led there, but there was no way of avoiding either of these forms. One of the deacons led me up and I looked on my father's face. I cannot say that it looked like him at all. His blackness had been equivocated by powder and there was no suggestion in that casket of what his power had or could have been. He was simply an old man dead, and it was hard to believe that he had ever given anyone either joy or pain. Yet, his life filled that room. Further up the avenue his wife was holding his newborn child. Life and death so close together, and love and hatred, and right and wrong, said something to me which I did not want to hear concerning man, concerning the life of man.

Albert Raboteau

EXCERPT FROM

A Fire in the Bones

I was born in 1943, during the second war in this century to rack the
world with death and destruction and untold misery—a war that demonstrated the horrors that doctrines of racial supremacy can effect. I was
born into a country and a part of the country burdened by racism and
racial oppression. I was born Black in the American South, in the state
of Mississippi. I was born into a family of Indian, French, German, and
African ancestry in a small town on the Gulf of Mexico named after a
king of France, Bay St. Louis. I was born three months after my father
was shot and killed by another man, a white man, in Mississippi, in
1943. . . .

. . . I grew up without knowing the full story of my father's death. My
mother and my stepfather decided not to tell me until I started college
because they did not want me to grow up hating white folks. As a result,
I wondered if the story were shameful—otherwise they would have told
me. I never knew my father. I had no memories of him. I had no stories
of him—only one blurry picture. I knew only his absence. Several
months ago, I went back to Mississippi in search of my father. I didn't
know what I'd find after all this time, only that I needed to go. I talked
to aunts and uncles, cousins, and close family friends. I found two newspaper accounts of his death. I spoke with the son of the man who killed
my father. On the last day of my trip, I went to visit my father's grave. I
had been there many times before, but for the first time, I suddenly began to cry. I cried for him, for my mother, for my sisters, for a father and
son who never met. Then, as if in memory, I saw him. I saw him laughing; I saw him raging; I saw him shot, and falling, falling into my arms,

into my life. After all these years of waiting, my father and I have finally met. I bend down, pick up some dirt from his grave and rub it on my head. All the sorrow wells up inside me and merges with the joy of meeting him, finally for the first time . . .

It is fire in the bones.

Bettye Parker Smith

God Didn't Live in
Mississippi Then . . .

Somewhere between my infancy and the time I turned six years old, I deified my daddy. And, by the time I turned seven, I had taken small but giant ritualistic steps to canonize him. Inarguably, my young mind was already propelled by a set of facts and conditions that exceeded a lifetime of exposure to Jim Crowism and other Southern segregated contingencies. The stringency of the covenants which characterized the time and place when and where I entered this life was not just assiduous; indeed, it required of me a double-coated level of endurance. I wondered, for example, why my daddy's sharecropper-boss had been birthrighted as "Mr." Fred Carlyle while my daddy was referenced by this man and others of his hue and form as R. T. Smith; or, why Carlyle's six-year-old daughter was "Miss" Mary Jane and I was Bettye. The lessons I learned in the first few years of my life did not result from formalized textbook training; no one sat me down and diagrammed the parts of the two worlds that I quickly grew to know. It was simply the way it was that one little Black girl plus one little white girl did not equal just two little girls; that my daddy who towered more than six feet in height, who was very fine, robust, and virile, was not the bearer of a fully endorsed manhood card, in this part of the world. Instead, the results of this peculiar equation emanated from a far different mathematical concept.

By the time I turned six, I could dramatize the family story about the lynching of my cousin Cockeye, with the same gusto as my daddy often did. And, while, as a preschooler, I labored with the mechanics of reading and writing, I had no difficulty following the crooked road to the public toilet that neoned "colored." But, while on the one hand these contradictions were certainly baffling for a little person growing up Black and female in Mississippi, a lifestyle cushioned with lots of hugs and kisses, and long walks straddled across my daddy's shoulders searching for plump, juicy blackberries, shortened my negative memory span, and, in temporary junkets, took the sting away.

I am forced to admit, my resilience and grown-up sense of memory and balance notwithstanding, that the cruel and rapacious reordering of God's plan by mean-spirited messianic want-to-bes wreaked havoc on my young and tender soul and planted lengthy feelings of ambivalence within me about life and living. My ability to daydream at a moment's notice often rescued me from the pit of embitterment and there were times when reality matched my fantasy. Usually, I found solace in the winds; coming to terms with the Mississippi winds and the dregs of their baleful howls was one of the most intriguing challenges to which I bear witness. My daddy had a franchise in the winds and often reminded me that voices and other human descriptives could be recognized if I listened carefully. While these messages were not always philanthropic, they were indeed road maps for those fortunate enough to possess telekinetic powers. So, because my daddy had an investment in the winds, by February when I was age six, I had audited his course and could decipher the envoys and their messages.

It stands to reason, then, that on Tuesday night after having been tucked into my bed and having accepted my daddy's goodnight kiss, I was abruptly awakened by the sounds of the winds, intermixed with my daddy's exposed physical discomforts. The winds, on this bleak and chaotic evening, were not hesitating; they were talking to me; warning me of unwonted visits upon our house. A bang outside suggested that a limb had fallen from the sycamore tree and crashed itself against the back of our wood-framed house. Simultaneously, I eased out of bed, walked to the front room, and saw my daddy writhing in pain, bending low, and softly calling my mother's name. As her voice returned in subdued whispers, I crept up behind them and wrapped my small arm around his left leg. I needed him to help me unscramble the message in the wind that was playing havoc on my senses.

There were no black physicians in Hazlehurst, Mississippi, then, and all these years later, one has not taken residence there. So, it was old Dr.

McGreggor whom my mother awakened in the middle of the night to seek medical assistance for my father. He was a general practitioner, the town's leading medic, and while I had never seen him on my street, it was generally known that he made house calls. But it must be remembered that even though R. T. Smith had a close kinship with the first known physician, Imhotep, and was the distant cousin to other Africans who brought civilization to this world, in Hazlehurst, Mississippi, during these years, there was no value attributed to his life by those in decision-making positions. Dr. McGreggor prescribed, via telephone for my daddy, a dose of Epsom salt. I often wondered how he managed the rest of that night. Did he have bad dreams? Did he reclaim his sleeping position immediately? Which biblical passage did he subscribe to justify his system of belief on superiority and inferiority? Was he disturbed by the mighty winds? Did he own stock in Epsom salt? I wonder if he thought that this hydrated magnesium sulfate would wash clean the magic in my father's voice. The next morning when my mother reported to Dr. McGreggor that my daddy's condition had worsened, he prescribed—at a distance—a second dose of Epsom salt. Her third call to the doctor's office was intermixed with my mother's salient young tears and frantic pleas.

The nearest hospital was some thirty-five miles away, in Jackson. The ambulance driver would make this journey only if directed by the physician. Halfway along the two-lane highway my mother discovered that the form she carried showed that the doctor had "mistakenly" arranged for my daddy to be received by the state's charity hospital in Memphis. My mother had money which she and my daddy had strategically saved to buy our own house and open his own small business, and at this moment she never even hesitated about using this hard-earned money to care for my father at the Baptist Hospital in Jackson, where she knew he would receive the best care. The driver refused to return to Hazlehurst to get the doctor's form corrected, but he agreed at my mother's insistence to drive my daddy to the Baptist Hospital. I do not know on what day God moved to Mississippi, but on this February morning, she had not arrived. In fact, on this day, no force was functioning: my African ancestral spirits were on holiday; Mr. Willie Earl's mojo was inoperative; and Mrs. Emma Jean's voodoo cauldron had gone dry. The Baptist Hospital was under no pressure to accept my father and they just refused to admit him. Now, the driver of the ambulance performed as he was originally instructed: he had R. T. admitted to the charity hospital. Preoccupied with the pain in his stomach, my father had no voice in this matter. Distracted by the pain in my heart, I was reminded that he had left without kissing me good-bye. He didn't see my tears or hear my protests over his departure; a ritual which I performed each time he left me. Suddenly, I felt shivers moving up and down my spine.

The announcement about his homecoming a week later, after he had recovered nicely from the surgery for something-nobody-seemed-to-understand, brought me out of my hiding place under the bed. I put on my best behavior, picked some fresh wild flowers, and prepared to receive my daddy. You see, I was very passionate about his presence and was quite selfish about the dispensation of his love and attention. I was highly emotional, territorial, and disapproving about anyone, including my siblings, my mother, or my grandparents, who wished to receive a hug or a kiss. I thought my daddy could fly and when he held me tightly in his strong arms and hoisted me high onto his shoulders, I would close my eyes and envision the flapping of his wings. He set rules about my upbringing to which only I was privy and which made me feel very special. He loved my hair, enjoyed playing with my curls, and forbade my mother from cutting or straightening out my curls. I knew that I was the apple of his eye and as Cousin Emma has said all these years ith a big grin, "Bettye Jean is the spittin' image of R. T." And, when I grew up and developed a romantic interest in other men, they were required to have the physical stature and heart of my daddy. Any degree of deficiency in either of these two areas has always resulted in swift departure.

It took about two seconds for my mother to realize that the nurse at the charity hospital was not looking at or talking to her. The woman seemed human but her ultra-thick Southern accent along with some strain of "ism" she had contracted interfered with her ability to communicate with my mother, so she babbled to "Mr." Fred Carlyle, who had escorted my mother to the hospital, something about there being a death yesterday at five o'clock and she was sorry they had made this useless trip. Then she mentioned my daddy's name. In the past tense. Within seconds, my mother collapsed.

From the old "magnolia state"—"Mississippi Goddamn," Nina Simon calls it—there should have been an apology, some sign of penitence, some atonement. Not old age, an incurable illness or a tragic accident, but racism stole from my mother, and from me, an honorable man who had wings and could fly, a man whom we both loved, a man whom I idolized, a man who now speaks to me in the winds.

Toni Vincent

A Final Rite

I.

In the spring of 1951 my father left our home in the Bronx for a trip to West Virginia with Uncle Pete, who needed to spend a few days with his sick mother. Sharing the driving from New York allowed both men to visit family. Daddy could stay with Mama Lizzy in Beckley while Uncle Pete was in nearby Gary #6, and they would still be home in less than a week. Whenever possible, the two Black men preferred the arduous, fifteen-hour drive, with no possibility of restaurant stops, to the humiliation of riding Jim Crow trains in the South. Their visits over, they had braved the return trip in spite of threatening thunderstorms. At 12:15 A.M. while driving east in blinding rain on the morning of May 21st, just outside Rich Creek in Giles County, Virginia, on a curvy, mountainous stretch of Highway 460, a west-bound semi crashed head-on into their 1949 Buick. Uncle Pete survived, but my father, sleeping in the back seat, was killed instantly.

II.

As I approached our block, I was surprised to see my Aunt Mattie's eldest son, Cousin Marvin, entering our house. Usually, visitors only came to see Daddy, but he wasn't back from West Virginia—in fact he was already a day late. I trotted to the stoop, leapt up the front stairs, and bounded inside, curious, ignorant. Muffled sobbing sounds were coming from Mother's bedroom. Looking pale and trembling slightly, with a breaking voice, Marvin told me of Daddy's death. My gaze locked onto his reddened eyes and I saw his face and jaw moving, making sounds. The drone of his words stung my ears and my chest began exploding. My body inflamed, I turned away. Marvin repeated his message. I wouldn't believe him.

That day was a stopping point in my life. I would not believe that Daddy was dead, that such a cruel, outrageous horror had overtaken us. Consumed by disbelief, I never spoke of Daddy's death, or mentioned him at all, after that day. The void it created in my life was immense, for I had adored my dad and his influence on me was profound and sweeping.

Mother and I were not close. Daddy's death, which might have united us in grief and comforting, had the opposite effect. We never spoke of him. It was our way of avoiding the pain, but the result was deepened sorrow and separation. That evening, after Marvin left, our house felt much emptier than it had minutes earlier, when Daddy was only "away." I went outside, incredulous and numb.

III.

In 1982 I was living in Berkeley, attending a discussion group at the Unitarian Church led by a retired Baptist minister and theologian, Bernie Loomer. Predictably, I was irritated whenever there were references to God, Jesus, the scriptures, or the like. Most of the time, there were none. I liked our leader, but I could not have said what kept me there, every Sunday, faithfully drawn to the group.

After weeks of rambling, pointless (as far as I could see) discussion, Bernie suggested that members of the group share their religious journeys. Each week, we heard one or two personal "Odysseys," and before long, an interesting transformation occurred. The argumentative, competitive, ego-driven individuals who vied impatiently for center stage each Sunday turned into a tightly knit group of caring, sensitive, vulnerable, searching, friends. When my turn came, I presented a brief autobiography explaining that I had no religious journey. To my amazement, Bernie asserted that I had indeed experienced a spiritual journey, and that my father's death had been a religious event in my life.

IV.

Each time I tried to make a genealogy chart for my class, I fell into uncontrollable crying. I was more puzzled than irritated when I told my roommate, Concha about it. After a few insightful questions, she gave me the name of a grief counselor, Bob McDonald, who specialized in

Native American youth and suicide. It was 1984 and I was enrolled at Starr King School for the Ministry.

Bob was a very likable, strikingly good-looking, Native American man who lived just off the freeway in Hayward. When I visited his home/office he began by telling me about himself and his father's suicide, which had shaken his adolescence and caused him to pursue, professionally, the meaning and consequences of such events. I told him, hesitatingly, about my father's death, though I had very few details and even fewer memories of my father's life. I was nervous about expressing my distress over something that had happened thirty-three years earlier. Did it really make sense to rehash all that stuff now, I wondered.

Bob knew that I needed to grieve my father, and insisted on starting right away. He suggested my wearing a black armband, lighting candles, and employing other rituals to express mourning. We agreed on three more meetings, a week or two apart. I had assignments for each session. The first was to write letters to my father, to try to rebuild our severed relationship.

Over the next few weeks I constructed a small altar and wrote letters and notes to my Dad often, placing them before the few photographs I had of him. Through Bob, I learned that I was angry with Daddy for leaving me, and realized that I had lost nearly all my memories of him when I vowed—on the day of his death—to stop speaking and thinking about him. I tried to recall the things he liked and surrounded myself with them. We had imaginary conversations, where I revealed everything I had wanted to tell him over the past thirty-three years. We listened to music together. I tried to recall the antics he performed to make me laugh when I was a child. I thanked him for those memories and told him of my sadness and emptiness. I shared my teen-aged agonies with him, telling how lost I was without his guidance. I wept for his absence from my adult life. I told him how I wished he had been present for my children, to teach them the sports that he loved, to hear them laugh at his comic stories, to answer their questions.

After a few weeks of daily invocations, with discussions and shared activities, Bob asked me to make a likeness of a father. Initially, I spurned the idea because I cannot draw, yet the exercise proved to be very moving because it brought back to me a vivid memory of my father's appearance.

I was beginning to feel comfortable with this pseudo-fantasy world where my father was present, when Bob told me that it was time to do a final ritual and say goodbye. Regretting the end of the sessions and exercises, I brought in all my letters, notes, drawings, fetishes, and the various aids I had devised for invoking my father's presence. We performed a final rite, listening to some farewell music that I selected—a down-home blues which always made my heart ache as though a shaft had pierced it. At the end, all traces of our sessions were burned, ritually, in Bob's fireplace.

I had hoped for a clap of lightning, or parting clouds with radiant sunlight breaking through, but nothing spectacular happened. I thanked Bob for his help, for the experience of being with my dad for a while, and went home. I threw away the armband. The only clue I had to any change in my life, is that a month later I finally finished reading a novel I had been browsing sporadically for fifteen years: James Agee's *A Death in the Family.*

Dolores Stephens

Daddy's Little Girl

There is an African proverb which says, "Father's advice is like salt in your food." This is a suitable epigram for this heuristic, for this is my first formal reflection on my relationship with my father. Indeed, reflecting has caused me considerable stress because, though he has been dead for six years, I have not been able to come to terms with the nature of our relationship during the last ten years of his life. This, then, is an odyssey into consciousness to retrieve memories and meaning.

My father was a skilled furniture upholsterer and weaver of cane, rush, and rattan for chair seats. People came from miles around to his shop, for he was the only such craftsman in that part of the country. Business acumen he did not possess, nor the vision to attract his sons to share in the business with him. Instead, he was his father's son, for he taught those sons who would learn but his paternalism drove them from employment with him, and there could be no talk of partnerships. Belonging to an era in which a female would not be taught the family business, except in a hands-on way, he never offered his daughters the training. However, he did not deny us either, at least not me. As much as I hovered around him, I could certainly have learned the trade; after all, I watched and listened to all. I was the little assistant who passed tools, witnessed work orders, listened to the explanations of why work was not ready, and heard the laments about those who did not pay when it was.

As the youngest child and the youngest female, I undoubtedly was Daddy's "little girl." The runt of his litter as he had been among his own siblings, I was the companion on trips to rich folks' houses to deliver chairs from his shop or to deliver telegrams which had come through the Western Union substation at our home. Some of my earliest memories are of road trips—to "homecomings" at rural churches where he spoke to some conference and where the ladies' sweet potato pies ended a dinner under trees in the churchyard, to the home of cousins I did not know and do not recall, to towns some miles away to visit aunt or brother, or to "turnings out" of lodges which had mysterious rituals that I ignored then. Daddy was known wide and far as an orator and was highly sought after to participate in debates at church. He always elected to take the underdog position in debating on such topics as "Who was the greatest biblical prophet" (and he always won). Rather than beaming with pride at his victories, I was in those days rather embarrassed by the high-pitched, somewhat sing-song intonation of his delivery. And even though this delivery earned his children teasing from neighborhood boys, Daddy was the one usually invited to conduct the laying of cornerstones at some church or community building in Black neighborhoods in surrounding areas.

Such oratory proved an indelible print on me because after he rose through the Masonic ranks to the thirty-third degree and became Worshipful Grand Master, I was often witness to his chantlike recitation of the graveside ritual for a deceased Mason. I can see him under the huge trees in the cemetery (there were no grave canopies except their leaves). I *can* hear his cadence. I can sense the gravity of the role he held. And I later felt a small part of the ritual, for he would get me to call the local Black radio station to have an announcement made of the call for an assembly of the brotherhood. And it was I who would locate his white apron, white gloves, and (wow!) sword.

The curse of such popularity and recognition was that I could never escape the watchful eye of adults who always said, "I know your father." Little did they know it was my mother who would mete out punishment for breaches of good conduct or smears on the family name. Daddy was not the one waiting to deliver the wrath if word reached home of some infraction. I recall only one punishment from him, and I do not recall the reason. I can still see myself sprawled on the hall floor after a good thrashing (an illegal one by today's "standards" for parental discipline). He whipped me until I lost my shoe. I was more shocked at his action than hurt by the whipping.

My brothers and I learned early on that Daddy would respond to some misconduct with only a threat about what he would not "put up with." He simply wanted no part of trouble. Understandably, then, he was not the person I went to when one of my brothers frightened or bullied me. Nor was he my male hero. My oldest brother had that role for a while because he returned wounded from military service in World War II, and he was interested in pugilism. I hung around him and his friends to watch them pound punching bags and to hear them tell stories about Joe Louis.

What Daddy did exhibit for me was a persistent pride. I thought his pride in family an obsession until I came much later in life to understand it was what distinguished him from his siblings and that it may have been the impetus for his paradoxical "make-do" attitude so disdained by his brothers. No matter that his father, who had built what seemed an empire, was possessive, petty, and paternalistic and used material goods as whipping sticks for his sons. Only Daddy seemed to capitulate to the power. Other sons turned to their own lives, leaving the nest and signaling their belief in the adage, "God bless the child that's got his own." My daddy's inheritance of the "home place" carried a high price. He attempted to keep family records intact, but one failing my brothers and I saw was his attempt to overuse family as the salt in our food. We resisted. He persisted. We resisted. There was no truce.

By the time I was a teenager, I had fallen from grace. I was no longer my father's constant companion (a nephew was now in my shoes), and there was little reason for my brothers to tell me, as they often did, "Daddy will listen to you." I was as frustrated as they with Daddy's eccentric behavior, his intractability, and his resolve not to be child to his children—which meant not taking our advice—and I, too, had experienced the sting of his rebuff: "Miss" he had called me when I tried to get him to "listen." That was the last time I offered a daughter's advice to an old man who made decisions which he would not reconsider. For the remaining seven years of his life, I "put him in God's hands," my way of reneging on some filial duty that called me to reestablish the bond, to recall the days when as Daddy's "little girl" I listened rather than advised as we traversed the town and outlying areas on his missions.

When he died in 1988 at the age of eighty-seven, my daddy was an enigma to me. As I read the obituary which I helped compose, I was acutely aware that it presented facts about his life without capturing his identity. What do I know of this man, my daddy? That we did not understand him, nor did he understand us. That his relationship with his father, whom he apparently both feared and revered and who was his opposite—tall, authoritative, cold, and aloof—stamped him with a desire to please. That he was not an independent soul but a man anxious for parental approval, seeking it by being caretaker, provider, and loving son.

The pain of the last years of his life has not been stanched by time, but I have, finally, opened the book of my father and as Daddy's "little girl," I am now prepared to read it, to reflect on it, and to write about it.

Ntozake Shange

Dear Daddy

Dear Daddy, *"El amor que tu me das . . ."*

I guess I'm still up by sheer force of habit. Remember how you'd
come in from the hospital after ordinary people were long in bed? I can
still smell the steak sandwiches from Brunswick St & the fried shrimp
you'd pick up at Five Paints just when all the night people/gamblers
pimps whores B&E men 3rd shifters were satisfying their own wants.
The car made a whirring noise that would annoy somebody else. Yet,
even in the country, especially in the country in the vacant night absent
of music and gleeful conversation that old Cadillac sounded like a sweet
Miles solo, muted sweet, a classic. Why today we misst Muhal Richard
Abrams and the AACM at that place that caught fire during a reading
of mine!

I guess you should know I never refer to you in the past, even though
I know you died. But, you know, you died in the middle of the night,
your special time & mine. You were driving lonely Jersey highways on
the way from a wrestling match. I loved driving those roads with you,
listening to Louis Armstrong or Tito Puente; the distances were always
too short. The car, asphalt sliding under our laughter & tales of meeting
Dizzy Gillespie or Horace Silver. I met Horace Silver & got Son Seal's
to autograph my arm. So I brought something to the table, too. But, you
knew that.

Daddy, I hope I didn't embarrass you too much when I had you pick
me up at Black Jack's in South Trenton, so I could show you my photograph above the bar just when Tookie started to tell you her life story
since you brought her into the world & Black Jack come out of his private quarters since it was yr 1st time in his place even though he'd been
yr patient for years. But, Papa, I knew I cd go to Black Jack's on time, I
had to dance. Dance hard & fast. Loose & light on my feet. Dazzle any

colored say with brilliant feet & timing. Dancing how you danced with Mommy with abandon and grace.

You know what else? I don't like the way what they family calls yr grave site either. Not that it's not proper. I mean there's an impressive tombstone & some kinda heavy potted perennial. But Daddy, there should be an earlier installation, by David Hanmor, and a Howard Pindells tapestry should be floating over you to keep evil spirits away & let you feel the evening breeze as she comes to you. Damn, Daddy, I should have gotten Martin Puryear to craft you some sacred cypress wishing web so I cd come in & out of the realms of this world you cherished at will. Then Irma & I, that's Miguel's sister who always thought you were handsome, would get Ricardo the Dominican Santero to come "clean" the whole space. Irma, Miguel, Ricardo, & I swam clandestine in the Raritan river & Ricardo washed our heads with fresh coconut milk, right from the shell. That'd do you up just fine & protect you if you go haunting the lil joints in upper Harlem; on the Lower East side where I paid my dues.

I really appreciated yr not laughing out loud when Felix de Rooy showed that achingly long 35 minutes of horn as the Caribbean Christ—He's in Amsterdam now, and you were the only poet's daddy who was present, & fit right in & Adal's still photographing himself.

I wished you stayed here (not that I think you're gone) but lavished you had seen my piece with Lady Smith Black Mombazo, such singing, Daddy. And I've made a personal friend of Archie Shepp, the avant-garde sax man you liked. I know you lifted that left eyebrow and looked somewhere else if I played Cecil Taylor or if Cecil started talking metaphysics. Daddy I danced in the Tropicana in La Habana like you and Mommy before Fidel. The magic is still there but not the terror. I walked the streets of Johannesburg without a pause, swam in the waters outside Durban, jumping waves in a free South Africa, but my last weeks in Managua were also the end of Sandinista dreams. You wd have been so proud of me, riding with Comandante Tomas through the mountains realizing why the power of the automatic machine gun at my side was not yr weapon of choice. You are too gentle for some of what I know.

Oh, Papa I can't forget the night you & Mommy stayed up all night in my very bare apt in Dorchester listening to me and Pedro Pietri, all

in black with his portable coffins, read poetry. Pedro came to your service in the church where they say they funeralized you. Papa, I came to
love your friends too just because they were your friends & knew you in
a way I didn't & cdn't. Wittico, the elegant; Moose, the passionate;
J. Minor, the Cherokee chief, and Pops, your soulmate; and Tom Jones,
the dreamer, are precious to me. Even though I rarely see them I don't
see them any less than you did.

Daddy I finally got into that beaded strapless outfit you gave me & I
didn't stop lifting weights to do it, either. Somehow I grew into it. I wore
it the night the National Black Theatre Festival honored me with Ntozake Shange Day. That was in Winston-Salem, North Carolina, last
summer. Plus, I went to cocktails at Maya Angelou's and spent time
with William Marshall and Billy Dee Williams. I wish you had been
with us long enough to hear La India, she is an angelic Tina Turner.

Oh, Daddy, on the more somber side. Since you've been gone from
this plane, whenever I stay up late, like we used to, old black & white
movies starring Ronald Reagan come on. He has Alzheimer's now, so he
can't feel guilt or remorse for the plight of sick people anymore. If he had
his whole brain he still wasn't capable of experiencing compassion.
Daddy, the era of politics Reagan ushered in has outlived you and more
poor & black people are dying, suffering, homeless, violently desperate
for a vision of a world for us like you had.

Daddy do you think I could help with that? It was only a rumor that
CLR was like a father to me. I know I'm not a boy, but forgive the language, Papa. I'm one fierce muther. You did name me after you. You
know what else Daddy? David Murray, my ex-husband, my friends Cico
Freeman, Fred Hopkins, Jean Paul Bourelly, Billy Bang, even Space-
man—everyone of them could play a melody that wd make you start
swaying yr head so you cd catch every note. You were just as much a part
of our posse as Max, Milt, Dizzy, Chico H., and both Andy *and* Jerry
Gonzalez. There's no music I hear without sensing you.

Did I ever really thank you & mom for bringing gallons of fried
chicken, greens & fixins to us when we were sitting in at Hamilton Hall
in 1968? Some people's parents stopped speaking to them and cut off tuition. But you fed us. Thank you Daddy. I know how you abhor legions
of cops & militant social coups, but we were hungry.

Getting back to yr alleged grave site. *Mi novio*, Elmo, who's a Black

Puerto Rican bluesman from Chicago (I thought you'd like that!), anyway he's promised to help me lay handmade glazed bricks in a typical
Zocalo formation to let everyone know wherever you are is hallowed
ground. That you are yr own tradition & yr space is a place for spirits &
people to gather when they're in need of solace. Though Victor Cruz &
Alejandro cda blessed the place with poems in tongues & some leftover
pine spring water we found by the Russian River years ago. The sacred
never runs out, Daddy, only the profane is short-lived.

Walter Fluker

Remembering Daddy:
Strong Arms and Old Songs

Daddy made the best biscuits. Not those store-bought, spongy Pills-bury doughcakes, but big thick Mississippi, hand-sized, mouth-watering, long-lasting, *Heavy D* biscuits that sat awkwardly on the side of the plate to save space for the sausage, eggs, and Alaga (Alabama-Georgia) syrup. My best times with Daddy were those kitchen moments before the others rose, watching him bake biscuits. Even as a small child I had this seventh sense for great cuisine. My sixth sense was also for great cuisine, but I reserved the seventh for Daddy. It was special time, sacred space, unobtrusive and delightful play.

Daddy would sing one of those old songs while baking biscuits and making fresh, hot coffee. Sometimes it would be a song that he said he heard at a camp meeting in the Mississippi Delta from a "woman preacher":

Me and the Devil had a tussle, but I won.
Me and the Devil had a tussle, but I won.
  I hate the Devil, he hates me.
  Me and the Devil cannot agree.
Me and the Devil had a tussle, but I won.

Daddy struggled with many devils: devils from Mississippi, devils in Chicago, devils of fear, devils of hopelessness, and devils he could not name. The greatest of these devils was *hopelessness*. It is only in retro-spect, looking backward into the horror of those early years in Chicago, that I remember how difficult it was for him to make sense of the deep alienation and harrowing fear of transitioning from the downsouth to upsouth. *Tussling* constantly without jobs, being too old, too unskilled, and too Black to make a living for his family was a veritable hell with many fiendish imps mocking his every effort to remain sane and whole.

In the *Inferno*, Dante placed a sign over the entrance into hell. It read "Abandon hope all ye who enter here." Hopelessness reigned on the south side of Chicago and played itself out in razor fights, shootings, bad whiskey, and fantastic visions of hell that street-corner prophets spouted with great facility. Daddy didn't have much use for any of these sedatives. He would sing to himself. *Those old songs.* Yes, how I remember *those old songs* that come when hope has exhausted itself and like angelic guides they lead us into misty wanderings and quiet ways.

Early in the morning, there in the kitchen, between the stove and the table, transitioning back and forth between time and song, between downsouth and upsouth, between devils he left behind and devils that greeted him in the promised land, Daddy established his rhythm, the rhythm that would carry him through the day:

Me and the Devil had a tussle, but I won.
Me and the Devil had a tussle, but I won.
  I hate the Devil, he hates me.
  Me and the Devil cannot agree.
Me and the Devil had a tussle, but I won.

In hell, hope comes with small steps. There are no great eschatological leaps into a heaven where the streets are paved with gold—no, there are only small, calculated, carefully maneuvered steps. I understand those old songs better, now. They were melodic walking sticks that helped Daddy to stand and delicately identify safe places in the dark. He had another song that would follow the first:

Do you know Him?
Do you know Him?
Jesus Christ, God's Son?

After the coffee was made and the biscuits were baked, he would sing that song. Often it was during a morning when Daddy was making decisions about the day. I remember the times when there was no bus fare for my sister and me to go to school. Daddy would sing the song:

Do you know Him?
Do you know Him?
Jesus Christ, God's Son?

He was pondering the next step: "Do you know Him? Do you know Him, Jesus Christ, God's Son?" I dare not attempt a hermeneutical exploration of what was going on in Daddy's soul while he pondered these things, but I imagine that Gethsemane would be an appropriate metaphor.

Do you know Him?
Do you know Him?
Jesus Christ, God's Son?

Jesus, God, and the angels never show up when we beg and plead for deliverance. The sheer carnage of Black male bodies and the titanic loss of Black mother's petitions should teach us this. But it is in remembering, in transitioning, in making and baking fresh things that we make contact with the Eternal within us—it is there that the answers are provided, God dons human garments, Jesus becomes a bosom friend, and the angels just show-out in the midheavens. Somewhere between the stove and the table, between the pouring of the coffee and the sopping of the biscuits in Alaga syrup, Daddy received his answer and a new day of hope would spring forth.

Daddy made his last transition in 1984, but he still visits me in dreams and songs. Once I dreamed I was in the backyard of my house in Nashville, Tennessee, fearfully approaching two terrible Dobermans chained to a toolshed. In the dream I was a child, innocently walking into the fangs of these vicious predators. Suddenly, I felt a lift from two huge arms that gently transported me to safety. They were Daddy's arms. Daddy's arms still come to me at times of crisis when my way is lost and I am walking into dangerous territory without a map.

He also sings to me. Several years ago, I was invited to speak at a church, but for some reason, the "word" would not come. Nearly an hour before I was to present, an old song came to me in Daddy's voice: "I'm going to sit at the Welcome Table one of these days." The refrain called me back to memory. I remembered my family's flight from Mississippi. My daddy was a sharecropper. At the end of cotton-picking sea-son, his boss-man, Mr. Joe Hand, used to make the figgers do somer-saults. Daddy had an altercation with Mr. Hand and had to leave in a hurry. He later sent for my mother and three siblings to join him in the promised land. The rest of that story was written in the pain and travail of a displaced Black southerner in a hostile urban environment to which he was never reconciled. But his journey marked the meaning of Black people in America in search of deliverance from the retribution of Crusoe and acceptance into a land flowing with milk and honey. But there was never enough milk and never enough honey for us; all we had were Daddy's arms.

I sang my sermon that morning in the old way, long meters, dragging the melody until the words bled into one another and rested in the hol-low caverns of our throats.

I'm going to sit at the Welcome Table,
I'm going to sit at the Welcome Table
    one of these days.

Far beyond the inherited and distorted Anglo creeds and evangelical formulae of a salvation American-style, that melody shook up calcified memories and the Spirit walked the aisles and touched two other dis-placed southerners sitting in the congregation. They met me at the door at the close of the service and related to me their story of Vaiden, Mississippi. They reported that only a week earlier, and thirty years af-ter my daddy fled Mississippi, Mr. Hand's son—the son of my daddy's former boss-man—had set a fatal fire, killing his own wife, in the fields that my family once worked. I felt certain Daddy spoke to me in their story of cruel punishment. He wanted me to remember the suffering.

How do you remember Black fathers: their strong arms and old songs without romanticization and nostalgic wanderings into places filled with the horror of *going nameless up and down the streets of other minds where no salutation greets and where there is no place to call one's own?* I choose to remember my father as the one who never left but resides in secret places hidden from Crusoe's rage. Arna Bontemps in *Black Thun-der* says of Bundy, the slave killed by old Marse, that "You can't hurt a smoke man, can you?" Daddy is a real smoke man, now! And he is free and dangerous!

When I am most myself, that is, my Self, which has nothing to do with the illusory patterns of bondage that play out in the minds of lost boys who have never known their fathers—those mortgaged by society and sent to Never-Never Land in the urban centers of America without charming Peter Pans and sexy nymphs to defend them—but when I am most my Self I can hear distant murmurings of the "black and angry dead," who visit in dreams and songs and testify to a day of reckoning in America and the world. They say, and I pause here, that it is true that one day, "The bottom rail will be on the top rail."

To remember Black fathers is to reenter lost time, time-swept-under-the-rug, and to play in broad open spaces far from the fear of predators who lurk behind the curtains of social fictions. It is to soar in flight above the madness in ever-widening concentric patterns of freedom heralding a new day when Million Man Marches and apocalyptic gangsta paradises are moving pictures set to the rhythm of old songs with fresh meanings for struggle and redemption in a land where our fathers' bones await a new Breath of Pentecost. It is to remember that our names, our destinies, our soul journeys are in the valley of these bones and that only with the invocation of the Spirit can we see a mighty army clothed in flesh.

I await this day—better I run screaming through the valley of dry bones and challenge them to live again, to see again, to know again, to be again, to begin again. Dare we see this, my beloved who have been anointed to fly with us? Will you join us in the shout?

Bebe Moore Campbell

EXCERPT FROM

Sweet Summer

When my father died, old men went out of my life. From the vantage point of my girlhood, he and his peers had always been old to me, even when they were not. In his last years, the reality of his graying head began to hit home. I no longer boogied the weekends away in smoke-clogged rooms that gyrated all night with Motown sounds, where I'd take a breather from the dancing by leaning up against the wall, sipping a sloe gin fizz and spewing out fire-laced rhetoric of "death to the pigs." I was a mature young wife, a mother even, three rungs from thirty, a home owner, a meal planner, who marched for an end to apartheid in front of the South African embassy only often enough to feel guilty. I made vague plans to care for him in his dotage. Care for him on a teacher's salary, in the middle of a marriage that was scratching against the blackboard with its fingernails, in a two-bedroom brick fixer-upper my husband, daughter and I had outgrown the moment we moved in. That was the plan.

When he died in 1977, I suppose, a theoretical weight was lifted, since Daddy was a paraplegic because of a car accident he'd had when I was ten months old. No doubt his senior-citizen years would have been expensive and exhausting for me. And then too, I had other potential dependents. I mused about the future, fantasized about my role as a nurturer of old people, feeling vaguely smug and settled, maybe a little bourgeois.

The afternoon was muggy as only a D.C. summer afternoon can be. The humidity and my afro were duking it out on the tiny sun porch of our home, the ring being the area immediately above the base of my neck, the hair coffee-colored grandmamas laughingly call the "kitchen." It is the hair I hated most as a child. The rest of my head was

covered with a wavy-frizzy mixture that proclaimed my black ancestry
had been intruded upon. My "kitchen" has always been hard-core naps,
straight from the shores of Dahomey. Benin, they call it now. From time
to time I'd tug my fingers haphazardly through the tight web of kinks,
trying to make my recalcitrant hair obey me and separate into manage-
able clumps of curls. . . .

I remembered the sweet North Carolina summers of my childhood,
my father's snappy "C'mon, kiddo. Let's go for a ride," when life was
boring sitting in Grandma Mary's house or the yard. There was a ritual
my father had to endure before he and I could zoom away down the one-
car-wide dirt lane that led to the larger tar road. He'd roll his wheelchair
right up between his open car door and the driver's seat and hoist himself from his chair to the car seat with one powerful thrust of his body.
Then he'd clutch his leg, which would invariably start twitching with
involuntary muscle spasms. When the shaking stopped, he'd lean out of
his car seat, snatch his chair closed, press his body into the steering
wheel, pulling the back of his seat up so that he could lift his chair into
the backseat of the car. This done, he'd take out a white handkerchief,
wipe his drenched forehead and look over at me and grin. Then I'd hop
into the seat next to his and we'd take off. In those days I was his partner,
his roadie, his little minimama homegirl. In the summer he hardly went
anywhere without me. And I believed, as I engaged in my humid, sunp-
orch reverie, my probing fingers struggling inside the tangle of my
kitchen, that I would be all those things again, that when my father got
old he would need me.

The thought of our living together for the first time since I was a
child delighted me, since it was in such stark contrast to the female-
centered home I'd grown up in after my parents separated and my
mother and I moved from North Carolina to Nana's house in Philadelphia. Realistically, though, living with my father would present special
challenges. There were, of course, the implications of his paralysis, and
his lack of mobility was complicated by his size. There were over two
hundred pounds of him sitting in that chair. He was the black man's
Chief Ironside. Well, maybe Raymond Burr had a couple of pounds on
him. He tried to play it off when I teased him about his gut. Daddy
would pat his belly, grin and say, "The chippies' playground, baby girl."
Still, Daddy would be no fun to heave up and down stairs or in and out

of a bathtub, although periodically, when he set his mind on losing weight, my father dieted quite successfully and could knock off thirty or forty pounds. When he was on a diet, I don't care how many pork chops you floated under George Moore's nose, the boy wasn't eating. That kind of doggedness enabled him in his later years finally to cut loose the Winstons he had inhaled with passion when he was younger. When he set his mind on something, that was it. Nobody had more determination than Daddy. So maybe the weight wouldn't have been a problem. What would have irritated me, though, was his innate ability to run the helpless bit into the ground at times, at least with me. Maybe only with me.

The summer before he died I drove from D.C. to the outskirts of Richmond for a visit and stayed with him at the home where he boarded with an elderly widow named Mrs. Murphy. He had only recently begun working for the federal government in personnel. He was, in affirmative-action terms, a twofer: black and disabled. Finally he was beginning to make decent money. He was sick the day I came to see him, something that rarely happened to him. Aside from his useless legs, he was robust. He rarely even got so much as a cold, although, of course, from time to time he had to go into the McGuire V.A. Hospital for a stay to have his damaged kidneys checked out. The day I went to visit him he had the flu and was coughing like crazy, drinking water like a fiend, snorting, trying to let out his Big Daddy Jumbo Pasquotank County farts on the sly and rattling on and on about the stock market, his latest in a long line of plans to become wealthy. To his dying day he never saw his becoming rich as something out of the realm of ordinary possibilities. His was the American dream: to work hard and have it pay off big. "Yeah, baby. Your ole daddy's gonna make us some money." He tossed off the titles of stocks and prices per share, totally losing me amid the names and numbers. Sensing my disinterest, he said disgustedly, "You ought to listen to this, girl. I'm telling you, we can make us some money." When my only response was to shrug my shoulders, Daddy shook his head. His mood turned bossy. "Bebe, go get Daddy some more cough syrup." "Bebe, go get Daddy a big ole glass of ice water." "Bebe, go empty this urine duct for your ole sick Daddy." Which was pushing it, because I hated rinsing out his urine ducts. And he knew it. But I did it that day, holding way out ahead of me the rubber duct that contained the acrid-smelling waste he could no longer control. I turned my head in the small, cramped bathroom that held his toothbrush at one end of the sink and Mrs. Murphy's teeth in a cup at the other, as I emptied the urine into the toilet, and again as I rinsed the containers out in the special buckets Mrs. Murphy kept right next to the small commode.

When I returned to his bedroom, Daddy was laid up in the bed like some imperial royal highness, flashing me a slightly wan but still very dazzling smile as I handed him his duct; I turned my head as he fiddled under the covers, attaching the thing to himself. The room needed ten shots of Air-Fresh. He cleared his throat when he finished. Then he grinned at me.

My daddy had a killer of a smile and I think he knew it. I know he knew it. His teeth were so white, so perfectly straight they were startling. Big, white, even teeth. Chiclets. And his grin was just a little crooked, and that's what made him such a charming smiler. On that particular day, I wasn't falling for his charm. "Don't ask me to do one more thing, old man," I said, as sourly as I could.

"BebebebebebeMoore," Daddy sang out, throwing his big, heavy arm around my shoulder when I stopped fussing. I was sitting on the side of his bed, one leg under me, the other leg swinging, my big toe just brushing the floor as I looked at a magazine, my hips against his very still legs. The air had returned to normal and I thought to myself, George Linwood Peter Moore, please do not funk up this room with another one of those jumbo farts. I looked up and he was smiling that killer smile. "Don't bother me, old man," I said. . . .

The day before my father died I was a bridesmaid in my best friend's wedding and was staying with friends in Pittsburgh. My hostess awakened me around three or four o'clock Sunday morning and told me my uncle was on the phone. Uncle Norman's signature has always been brevity, an innate ability to get to the point with a minimum of fanfare or bullshit. When I picked up the phone he said, "Bebe, this is Norman. Your father died in a car accident this morning." Just like that. Then, "Did you hear me? Honey, did you hear Uncle Norman?"

A car accident, I thought, the phone still in my hand, Uncle Norman still talking, another car accident. That wasn't supposed to happen, is what ran through my mind. How did that happen twice in one life? Twice in two lives? . . .

It was cool and dim in the funeral parlor, and filled with a strange odor I'd never smelled before. There were three rooms full of caskets—bronze, dark wood, light wood, pastels. A dizzying array. The funeral director was a friend of the family. Mr. Walson had an uncanny affinity for professional solemnity. He referred to Daddy as "the body." Did I wish to see the body? Was I satisfied with the appearance of the body? Did I care for knotty pine or cherry wood? He said this, his dark face devoid of all emotion, his expansive belly heaving threateningly against the dangerously thin belt around his waist. The same odd smell that filled the room clung to Mr. Wilson. What was that smell? I leaned against Uncle Johnny and felt his hand on my shoulder. Upon learning that my grief was buttressed by a healthy insurance policy, Mr. Walson urged me to choose the cherry wood. I looked at Uncle Johnny questioningly; he has always known how to take charge. Maybe it comes from being the oldest. If he tells you to do something, you do it. "We'll take the cherry," he told the funeral director, who assured me he would take care of everything. But he could not, of course, take care of me. My grief was private and not covered.

As we left the funeral parlor, Uncle Johnny took my hand. "Do you know what your big-head daddy wanted to do?"

I shook my head.

"After I retired and moved down here next to Mama, he tried to talk me into doing some hog farming with him. Said we could make a lot of money. I told that joker, 'Man, I came down here to rest.'" Uncle Johnny looked at me. He was smiling. "Your daddy loved making money, didn't he, girl?"

"Loved it."

The cars rolled slowly up the unpaved lane that led to Grandma Mary's house, a fleet of Cadillacs, shiny, long and black, moving quietly, and stirring up dust that flew everywhere, clinging to everyone, coating shoes and suits and dresses, blowing in hair and on faces, where particles finally lodged in eyes that blinked, blinked, blinked then looked away.

It is still cool in North Carolina in April, a perfect time for a family reunion. Crowded in Grandma's yard were all the faces that looked like her face, the resemblance lying somewhere between the chin and the character lines that ran straight across high foreheads. There were others standing next to the ones who looked like her, so many people that their feet would have crushed Grandma's zinnias had they been in bloom.

The people looked up when the Cadillacs drove into the yard. They broke away from the joyous hugs of reunion, of North once again meeting South, put their cameras back into their bags and stood silently, at attention. The gray-haired old ladies fanned themselves with miscellaneous bits of paper, the backs of magazines, newspapers, napkins, even though it wasn't warm. All of a sudden there was a circle, shoulders touching, everyone's breath mingling into a giant sigh. Somebody, my daddy's first cousin, the preacher from New York, was praying, offering to the Lord brief, familiar words that the occasion called for: higher ground, no more suffering, home. The words fell around the crowd like soft pieces of flower petals. An old woman began to sing. The lyrics came back to the people who'd taken that long-ago bus ride from Pasquotank County to Philly, Jersey, New York, in heady rushes. All wiped the dust from their eyes and joined in. The last note had scarcely disappeared before Mr. Walson's assistants began calling the names of immediate family members and leading them to the limousines: ". . . Mr. and Mrs. John Moore, Mr. and Mrs. Elijah Moore." Grandma Mary gripped my fingers as I helped her into the car where my husband and daughter were waiting. I was about to sit down when I felt a hand on my back. I turned around. "How ya making out, kiddo?" It was Sammy, my Marine uncle, the hero of my childhood. Whenever I saw him I thought of starched uniforms, even though he hadn't been in the service for years.

"Okay, so far," I said. I took his hand.

He squeezed my fingers and helped me into the car. "I'm here if you need me," he said.

Later, when I was looking into the layers of expensive satin, blinking frantically as the top of the smooth cherry-wood coffin closed, it occurred to me that more than my father had passed away. Not only had I lost a treasured friend, but gone was the ease with which I could connect to his brothers, his male friends.

After he was buried, Grandma Mary's old friend Miss Lilly or Miss Lizzy, Miss Somebody, whose face had floated in and out of my childhood summers, a wiry woman with lines like railroad tracks on skin the color of a paper bag, put her hand in mine and whispered, "Baby, you sho' put him away nice. Yes you did, chile," then, even more quietly,

"God knows best, baby." She gave my arm three hard pats. Be . . . all . . . right. Don't . . . you . . . cry. Hush . . . baby . . . hush. I nodded to her, but later when I was alone I had a singular contemplation: his death wasn't for the best. The clear knowing hit me square upside my head after the last of the heavy North Carolina loam had covered the cherry-wood coffin, after Aunt Edith, my father's youngest sister, had heaved a final mournful wail that pierced through the surrounding fields of soybeans and corn that bordered my grandmother's house, then slowly faded. And what I felt wasn't even pain or grief. Just regret, gripping me like a steel claw.

In a way, it was like the end of an ordinary family reunion. I stood at the edge of the lane with Grandma Mary and watched the last of the out-of-town license plates careen down that narrow dirt road, leaving behind a cloud of dust. Pennsylvania. New Jersey. New York. Tomorrow would be another work day, regular and hard.

In the kitchen my father's mother looked tired, every one of her eighty-six years filling her eyes. She held onto the small table as she walked.

"Grandma, why don't you go to bed," I said.

"I reckon I will," she replied. I kissed her on the cheek. She stumbled and grabbed my shoulder to get her balance. "Is you gone get your daddy's car fixed?"

Her question jolted me. I hadn't given my father's Cadillac any thought since Uncle Cleat and I had left it at the mechanic's in Richmond. Soon I would be whipping around doing a "Detroit lean" out the window of George Moore's hog. Wouldn't he love to see that, I thought. "It's being fixed now, Grandma," I said.

"He sure did like that car," she mused almost to herself. "That boy loved pretty cars." She looked straight at me. "Don't bring it up the lane when you come. Hear?" I had to smile to myself. Grandma was loyal to the end. She stubbornly reasoned it was the machine at fault, and not her beloved son. I understood.

So I cleaned the kitchen, mourning my loss with each sweep of Grandma Mary's broom, each swipe of the battered dish cloth, and thought about this father whose entire possessions had fit neatly into the trunk of his yellow Cadillac, which now was mine.

I took my father's wheelchair back to D.C., even though Aunt Edith asked me if I wanted to give it to one of the old ladies in the neighborhood who was having a hard time getting around. I remember I said, "No, I want it," so fast and maybe so fiercely that Edith blinked and stepped away from me. Though why I wanted it, who knows. I put Daddy's chair in my basement and let it collect dust. Sometimes when I was washing clothes I'd look at it. The most I ever did was touch it occasionally.

In the months that followed, the fat insurance checks my father left me transformed my lifestyle, but at that moment I could feel his death reshaping my life, or at least the life I thought I was entitled to. There are gifts that only a father can give a daughter: his daily presence, his daily molding, his thick arm across thin girlish shoulder, his solemn declaration that she is beautiful and worthy. That her skin is radiant, the flare of her nostrils pretty. *Yeah, and Daddy's baby sure does have some big, flat feet, but that's all right. That's all right now. Come here, girl, and let Daddy see those tight, pretty curls, them kitchen curls.* I was all prepared to receive a daily ration of such gifts, albeit belatedly, but it was not to be. I would never serve beer and pretzels in the yard to Daddy and Tank. I would never have his company as I cleaned the dishes. He wouldn't see Maia's plays or her recitals. That was the way the cards had been dealt. I would go to my uncles, they wouldn't come to me. And the time for even those visits would later be eroded by obligations and miles. After April 1977 the old men in my life just plain thinned out.

For one thing, I got divorced and later remarried and moved far away to Los Angeles. After Grandma died, Uncle Johnny and Aunt Rena moved to Georgia near Aunt Rena's people. "You come see us," he told me before he left. "Don't forget; I'm your pop now." My Uncle Eddie finally sold his grocery store and moved from Philly to North Carolina, so I couldn't conveniently drop in at his market and chew the fat with him when I came to town to see Mom and Nana. Uncle Elijah died and I couldn't even go to his funeral, because my money was real funny that month. I sent flowers and called his wife, but what could I say? I should have been there.

My Marine uncle became a preacher. Uncle Sammy doesn't whoop and holler; his message is just plain good-sense gospel. He can even get scientific on you. When I hear his message I am thinking the whole time.

Uncle Norman and I still talk, but mostly on the telephone. My youngest uncle would call me up in hell, just to find out how I was getting treated. He is busy with his family and business. We don't see each other often.

The last time I saw Tank was a few weeks after the funeral, when he picked me up at the Greyhound bus station in Richmond and took me to get my father's car. Tank's skin is like a country night—no moon, no stars. You don't know what black is until you look in his face. Daddy always told me he wasn't much of a talker, and he's not, but he was just so nice and polite, sitting up in that big Lincoln, being my chauffeur. "Just tell me where you want to go," he said when I got into the car. We drove all over Richmond. Tank took me to where my father worked, to Mrs. Murphy's, everywhere.

Around two o'clock we pulled into McDonald's and he bought hamburgers, french fries, and sodas for our lunch; the car was filled with the aroma of greasy food. We were both famished and we ate without talking at first. All you could hear was our lips smacking against our Big Macs. Al Green was singing, "Love will make a waaay . . ." on the radio. Tank looked at me and said, "Ole Be Be," as though astonished that little girls grow up and become women. He said my name the way older southerners are wont to, two distinct syllables. I love the sound. But it was weird, because as soon as he said my name like that, I caught sight of his wheelchair in the rearview mirror and at the same time thought about Maia, whom I'd left in D.C. with a girlfriend. I was still nursing her and I immediately felt pins and needles in my breasts, and when I looked at my blouse there were two huge wet milk rings. Tank looked, he looked away, then he looked again. Then he said, as if thinking aloud, "That's right. Moore's a grandaddy."

Tank's chair was very shiny in the mirror. His words hung between us real softly for a minute before I started up, which I'd sworn I wasn't going to do. I put my head on his shoulder and I just cried and cried and cried. Tears wouldn't stop. "George was right crazy about you, Be Be. Talked about you all the time. All the time," Tank said shyly. He offered up these words as the gift they were. I just nodded.

There have never been enough idle moments really to straighten out those tight, tight curls at the nape of my neck. Untangling a kitchen calls for a protracted, concentrated effort. You have to be serious. It is not a job for weak fingers on a summer's afternoon. Still, daydreaming fingers, even those caught up in tangles, reveal much.

It has proved to be true, what I felt looking into my father's satin-lined casket: my loss was more than his death, much more. Those men who used to entice me with their storytelling, yank my plaits, throw me quarters and tell me what a pretty girl I was are mostly beyond my reach now. But that's all right. When they were with me they were very much with me. My father took to his grave the short-sleeved, beer-swilling men of summer, big bellies, raucous laughter, pipe smoke and the aroma of cigars. My daddy is really gone and his vacant place is my cold, hard border. As always, my life is framed by his absence.

Peter J. Harris

The Black Man of Happiness

1994 *kicked off* kicking my ass!

On January 26, my father died.

Pleasant Samuel Harris, Jr., sixty-nine, met his maker the day after my mother would have turned sixty-four. Like Ma, who died in 1984, Daddy died of heart failure.

He was in a hospital room in D.C. I was in my apartment in L.A.

I'm writing about happiness y'all. Believe it or not.

Oh no, I ain't happy to be an official orphan.

But I am happy knowing that despite his flaws, despite having diabetes, high blood pressure, and blocked arteries, my father had found out how to celebrate the simple things—playing cards with his second wife, tending to his yard, maintaining his pickup truck, presiding over a family barbeque in his backyard. He had found a way of making these common affairs into memorable rituals that satisfied the family in all of us.

When I spoke at Daddy's funeral, unlike when I testified at Ma's in 1984, I was a part of the official program, yet I could only speak in my most unofficial voice. Standing in the pulpit of the Ebenezer A.M.E. Church, facing a hushed crowd of over two hundred mourners, I searched for my tongue. I found it only when I forgot the body lying in the casket below me in the sharp gray suit, and remembered the man (and the best of what he stood for) that everybody had come to praise.

"I feel Southeast up in here," I began, referring to the section of Washington, D.C., me and my brothers and sisters will always consider home, despite now living in Maryland, Florida, and California. Many of the mourners were neighbors from the days we spent in the Parklands apartments during the sixties. I could feel folks letting a smile peek through their tears. "I feel family up in here y'all! I see the faces of people who know what it means to say, 'I'm from D.C. I'm from Southeast.'"

I said it meant, at rock bottom, looking out for each other, covering each other's backs. I said it meant friendships through which I still filter new personal hook-ups. I said it meant a neighborhood loveliness that shines despite Southeast being, statistically speaking, the area of D.C. most afflicted over the years with more crime, poor housing, more death, and all that. A neighborhood loveliness that recalls an era of freeze-frame moments for me and those who came to send off my father. Sledding down Radar Hill over on Stanton Road. Doowopping at the mailbox on the corner of Stanton Road and Trenton Street. Playing one-on-one games of off-the-wall baseball against the brick buildings of Parklands, where we drew a box for the strike zone. Summer days playing in the fields and in the woods across Mississippi Avenue. Winter nights playing snow-cushioned tackle football behind the buildings on Eighteenth Street. Potato salad by Miss Joyce Fox so good it should have been freeze-dried for space shuttle astronauts. Dinner tables always big enough for the child of a neighbor who had to work late or who just didn't have it all together. Enough nosiness to stay in the know, but respect, or savvy, enough to channel gossip into a daily willingness to live and let live.

Daddy was the lightning rod for my neighborhood's communion. I hated that he was dead, but I loved that I could speak about him to his friends, drinking buddies, co-workers, and loved ones.

"Y'all know Daddy as a friend and neighbor," I continued. "But y'all may not know too much about *koshies!*" That was Daddy's word for kisses when we were kids. He'd call you over to him in his best baby talk: Give me some *koshies*, he'd say. Then he'd smack big, sloppy kisses upside your cheeks. Joyous moments of tenderness from a father who often worked two jobs or more—in addition to his day gig as lead gardener with the Potomac Electric Power Company—and sometimes didn't have time to be Daddy.

By now, I had the mourners laughing outright.

My family, all sitting on the front four or five pews to my right, smiled in recognition. I could hear Glenn, my oldest brother, laugh loudest and shout, "That's right!" *Koshies*—which I acted like I hated as a kid, which I'll never feel again—soothed me as I spoke at Daddy's funeral. Allowed me to zero in on the only antidote for the pain I was feeling.

The antidote is joy. Honest focus on the plain, powerful acts of love between me and Daddy, between Daddy and his family, between our family and our neighbors, and between all of us who remember Parklands and those new lovers and mates, children and neighbors, compadres and co-workers in our lives. The antidote is trust in the purity of those acts as building blocks for living in a way that creates life-giving, life-sustaining memories we can draw on when death comes creeping, when we're under personal and social siege, when we need a cushion just because.

These are the kinds of memories that form the elemental layers of mythology. And frankly, the more I think about it, they are real insulation for my daily and symbolic life as a brother dedicated to living humanely. In a world where I can become the boogeyman in a minute—fingered out the mouths of murderers from suburban Boston to rural South Carolina—elevating my personal memories into instructive mythology might just keep me sane or calm enough to speak the magic words of self-preservation when I find myself in the center of a police flashlight, or dying while the credits roll in *Jurassic Park*, or even facing down another young brother whose brain is on cultural vapor lock.

As I add layers to my mythology—improvising on the keys to better living, gleaning the secrets I've learned from the *let's get it on* of my life—my confidence grows. I join with other men seeking to keep on keeping on. We swap our tales of families that coped, of love that lasted, of urban lives built on rural gumption, until a common body of inspiration lives and breathes, ready for freddy with a language as natural as Smokey's "Tracks of My Tears," a wisdom as familiar as Richard Pryor's Mudbone stories, and a mutual ownership as gracious as the standing dinner invitation of a favorite aunt and uncle.

This is the mythology we save because of self-love. It ain't no joke and, quiet as it's kept, it ain't no myth.

During my last visit with Pops, in the 1993 Christmas/Kwanzaa season, he glowed cause I was home, along with my teenaged son and daughter. And when it came time for that December 25th meal, he was overjoyed that my two brothers and their current wives as well as their ex-wives were home, my two sisters, one with her husband and the other with her lover were home, and all the grandchildren were home. Home with him and Pearl, his beloved second wife, who had cooked everything but the turkey and the ham. Pops himself, you see, specialized in *barbequing* the turkey and the ham on the grill in the backyard—snow and the "December Hawk" be damned!

The Harrises filled the brick house in Temple Hills, Maryland. The food made the dining room table sag. As folk laughingly fixed plates from the buffet, Daddy sat beside me on the sofa. I could smell that he'd been tasting the corn liquor his older brother supplied from our family's rural Stomping Grounds in Powhatan, Virginia. I resisted my gut reaction to dis him for drinking and affectionately palmed the back of his head, put my arm around his shoulders, and waited for my turn at the table.

"Peter," he said, his voice slurred more with emotion than the liquor, "I'm so happy that everybody could be here."

I nodded in agreement and squeezed his shoulders. He looked with pride over to men and women, boys and girls, piling homemade food onto their plates. Then he said to me under his breath, his voice this time slurred more with the liquor than emotion:

"Look at that ham! Just look at it! *Hacked* to pieces! Goddamn it! Can't nobody never carve it right."

I had forgotten this pet peeve of his; after all, I'd been a vegetarian since '79. But as long as I'd known him, he really did get pissed if you cut chunks, rather than slices, off a ham or turkey. Especially if he'd been tasting.

But this wasn't the time nor place for his Gemini-ass to trip off into his growling, evil twin.

"It ain't nothing but dead meat, no way," I cracked, playfully punching his shoulder. "Go head over there and cut it up right, if it's messing with you so much."

"Naw, naw, it's too late now. It's already been fucked up. I'm leaving it alone," he said.

He gazed once more at the sacrificial ham. Checked out his loved ones enjoying themselves and settled back into the sofa with an expression of simmering contentment.

In the end, the pull of our ritual was too hip to resist. He was satisfied with having spoken his piece—which was only right, according to the psychic *Man of the House Manual* he lived by. But finally he was, I believe, glad to just groove on the sounds of enjoyment after a life of work and raising a family. Sitting pretty for a country boy with no formal education and nothing saditty about him. He had reached sixty-nine the hard way—one anonymous day at a time.

He was happy.

That's what fuels the happiness at the core of my sadness over his death. The advice I gave my father over the ham was the kind of thing he would say to me when I was tripping.

You got to have a understanding, he liked to say, something simple, full of proverb, but always focused on the bottom line, the basic concern. *Sometimes, you got to do what you gotta do.*

Now I gotta do this:

Live every day with heroic sincerity, revolutionary courtesy, and militant self- and cultural-affirmation as the polyrhythms fomenting the personal timbre that alerts everybody I meet to the priorities and principles my life embodies. On the interpersonal tip, these rhythms have certainly been the pulsating mortar holding me together during an adulthood of divorce, physical and emotional distance from my children and family, bankruptcy, blended families, and under- and unemployment. The strength of these rhythms it goes beyond the personal, though. On the social level, I believe when I amplify the percussion of these qualities with a democratic willingness to meet folk eye-to-eye and work with folk shoulder-to-shoulder, we become the downbeat for movements that challenge us all to change the world for the better.

I am accepting the challenge of being a man of the twenty-first century. Modern, confident in the usefulness of my personal journey . . . Traditional, grounded in the validity of the wisdom of my forerunners . . . Dedicated, energized by the unsung genius I find in the unexpected meetings with Black men of change . . . Humble, educated by the inevitable blues that come with love, fatherhood, individuality, and the turning of seasons.

I face the millennium happy. With this understanding:

I am the world. I got the whole world in my hands. I got my life in my hands. I got the lives of everybody I meet in my hands. I meet a lot of Black men. I am a Black man. We are the world. We got our lives in our hands. I am the Black man of happiness. I risk saying that we don't need to fret over dead meat no more. I refuse to be dead meat no more. I risk joy and I act on my faith.

I risked my faith at Daddy's funeral and I was rewarded with amens and hugs and confirmation of my deepest, most powerful memories. I am convinced that happiness is not only an essential ingredient in the antidote against pain. It is *the* enzyme we need to be the catalyst for galvanizing the relationships between Black men and Black men, which will enrich the relationships between Black men and their loved ones. A contagious, generous happiness—politically charged to *throwdown* against white supremacist notions of Black male inclinations—can indeed be our new currency of exchange, electrifying our communications and interactions, as we build on the common historical memories and mythology we share of struggle accomplishment, and high style. Replacing imposed celebrations of the so-called standards of male behavior with standards we cultivate ourselves. Allowing our own definitions of happiness to marinate us, keep us thinking with the cultural flexibility that defines the best of what it has meant to be a Black man.

My father, my most intimate symbol of what it has meant to be a Black man, tried to be happy all his life. I know this because he told me himself. He drank Smirnoff Vodka to be happy. He bought a Cadillac to be happy. He ate candy and ham and fried chicken to be happy. He struggled forty years to love his first wife and ten years to love his second wife to be happy. He grew vegetables and roses to be happy. He even accepted personal weight for his wrongs and apologized to be happy. And when he died, hundreds of people were moved by this complicated, cranky man full of generous happiness and braved one of those cold January days in D.C. to come honor him. Now, I am living simply, Daddy's number-three son, yes. But jacked up a notch by relentless testimony because the lessons from his proud, anonymous life should not remain anonymous. They are necessary to my living a satisfied life as an African-American man. I publicly insist that those lessons (along with others I learned from Ma and my other teachers) be a part of our mythology and any of our discussions about freedom and the pursuit of happiness.

I am a caretaker of the lessons of my father's life. I am the Black man of happiness. I got a big mouth. I plan on walking the walk that back up the talk, too. *You better bet it!*

Alice Walker

"Good Night, Willie Lee, I'll See You in the Morning"

Looking down into my father's
dead face
for the last time
my mother said without
tears, without smiles
without regrets
but with *civility*
"Good night, Willie Lee, I'll see you
in the morning."
And it was then I knew that the healing
of all our wounds
is forgiveness
that permits a promise
of our return
at the end.

5

Gifts

We remember the hugs and kisses, the songs and stories, but most especially the "dates." Daddy would take each of us, away from the house, out "on the town," for bonding time, fun time, father-daughter bonding time. Sometimes he took us to a movie, other times out to dinner (to a real sit-down-and-eat restaurant) and still other times on picnics, car rides, or shopping sprees. Each time we left home, prettied for our date with Daddy, we knew we would return home with gifts he would purchase for us: books, a collector's beautiful black doll, journals, or a piece of jewelry that reflected our family's Africentric identity. He made us feel so very special and so very loved.   AKOUSA, HIARI, AND SALA IMARA

By his good example, Papa instilled in me a number of qualities by which I have attempted to govern my life. His tireless energy in working more than sixteen hours some days and the honesty of his endeavors gave me a work ethic based on the adage "an honest day's pay for an honest day's work." I began working at the age of eight in the home of a neighbor for the experience, for I did not receive a salary for my efforts. Papa taught me the value of the family unit. His love and devotion to Mama exposed me to fidelity in marriage and respect for womanhood. My marriage of forty-nine years is testimony to the influence that I received at home regarding that institution.
REV. NORMAN HENRY RATES

I remember as a young girl holding pins and paint at the ready for the windmills, little cities, and an octagonal dog house my father made just for me. Like an eager apprentice, I studied every step in the process, marveling at the magic of my father's hands and taking seriously his imperative for the making of craft: "Take your time, Vita, and do it well." It was this apprenticeship that took me to graduate school as a student of design, that guided me, step by step, to the completion of various projects, and that now sustains me in my work as both teacher and illustrator. With each fold of origami, Exacto cut, watercolor stroke, and fibre manipulation, I feel my father's creativity moving in my wrists, and I am determined to take my time and do my work well. My father and I do not hear the same music in a number of arenas, but our hands and neural networks synthesize into a marvelous symphony called love.   V I T A   J O N E S

Letters from my father are pressed with love in my book of family memories. One in particular speaks to his role as nurturer, friend and counsel with intuition. It was written in 1971 when I was in my final semester of college and considering marriage immediately after graduation. It reads:

> This is just a little note, you see. I'm in the post office and it's about 5:00 and I'm in a hurry. So just deposit this check to your account and you won't have any trouble cashing it. . . . Don't get all excited about our bills. Relax sometime, and take it easy, be sure to eat enough. I don't worry much. I just wonder do you eat enough, and are you going to let some young man fool you or rush you into something you are not ready for. What I am trying to say is you are suppose to get married, . . . but don't get rushed into anything unless, that's what you want. How can I pay for your summer school without it being in a slump? When is the first payment? I have the money, but might have to bother my savings account. I would like to come over there next weekend, but don't look too hard.

I didn't take my father's advice, but I should have.

H E L E N   S P E N C E R

Pearl Cleage

daddy

i have always been
focused on my father

when i was four
my sister six
we hid behind
the bathroom door

to peek a peek

my father
innocently naked
turned to find us
red-faced and giggling
our curiosity overwhelmed
by our surprise

i can close my eyes
and see it all again

the steamy billows
through the shower's
open curtain

our small flushed faces
and my sister's
panicked flight

my father calmly
reaching for his robe
to shoo me out

the joy i felt
at finally *knowing*.

Lionel Arnold

Snatched from Nothingness

Memory is not simply a matter of retrieving information
aimed at empirical truths; it is an act of imagination, a
creative process of crafting meaning from the remnants of
time.   THOMAS R. COLE AND MARY G. WINKLER,
                    THE OXFORD BOOK OF AGING

What is remembered has been saved from nothingness.
What is forgotten has been abandoned.
    JOHN BERGER, THE USES OF PHOTOGRAPHY

My earliest remembrance of my stepfather whom I called Tom is associated with the first house we lived in after he married my mother. I must
have been about four and still had not learned how to tie my shoes. After
my mother, sister, and he had shown me several times how to tie a knot,
he instructed all of them not to tie my shoes any longer and said that if
I were ever to learn that I must do things for myself, I would have to begin now. It may seem like an insignificant little thing but behind it lay
instruction in self-reliance. This was but one instance of his way with
children.

With his head full of curly black hair, muscular build, and a ready
broad smile, it was easy to understand why mother was deeply in love
with him. There was also an ease about the way he talked and moved
that made children and dogs take to him immediately. It was perhaps his
love of children that made him willing to accept a ready-made family.
On more than one occasion I have seen him take a toddler in his arms
and establish instant empathy with the child—white children as well as
Black. The bond would be strong enough that when he would have to

leave, the youngsters would cry to go home with him. In order to pacify the crying child, he would promise to come back at a later time.

Pertinent facts about Tom's family, aside from the daily information we lived with, were something of a mystery. Only when he was drinking did we learn that his father was a schoolteacher in North Carolina; his mother and father had Indian ancestry; there were eight children; Tom was the second born; and he resented the fact that his father had chosen to send his older sister Bert to college instead of him. He had to leave school early because his father had died and he had to work on the farm to help feed the younger children.

By the mid-twenties, the family, along with uncles and cousins, had moved to Greenville, a small town in western Pennsylvania north of Pittsburgh. Tom's uncle, Robert Torrance, a barber, must have been about the first of the family to migrate northward but to this day no reason has been given for the move. A cousin, Cy, who was a plasterer, and Tom joined together to enter the plastering trade. At that time, before the widespread use of Sheetrock, the walls of most houses and public buildings were plastered. Where and how each learned the trade I have never learned.

There was a very close family tie between Tom and his brothers and sisters. During the depression when we had to move to the country about five miles from Greenville, to secure cheaper housing no doubt, Tom's sister Ann, her husband, and their three children moved in with us, Tom, my mother, my sister, and me. The house had only four large rooms and one can imagine the tensions the lack of space may have caused the adults, but the children had a wonderful time playing together. On numerous other occasions during his lifetime, Tom came to the rescue of members of his family.

Perhaps the real reason Tom continually talked about his lack of education was that he felt he had missed out on something that would have given him self-assurance in his ability to calculate bids on plastering as well as a background for advancing in his business.

As far as work was concerned, Tom was not lazy and worked hard the greater part of his life. The nature of his work demanded that he work long hours. Many times a job would be an hour's drive from our home and often he would have to work late to finish a job so that he could move on to the next one. Although he may have talked a lot about taking a vacation, he seldom did because winter meant that there would be a period when it would be too cold to plaster. Deer season was the one time of year that he did take time off.

For miles around, Tom was known as one of the best plasterers. He took great pride in his work. In the forties and fifties, it was quite fashionable to put intricate, swirl designs in the plaster. The symmetry and beauty of the pattern required a skill developed by years of practice.

When we were growing up, Tom's brothers, nephews, and myself all wanted to go to work with him. Usually he would promise to take us but never did. Children do get in the way no matter how much they may want to help and they also have to be watched constantly. This he knew.

During my college years I used to work for him mixing and carrying the mud. Once the board was full of mud I'd try to learn how to plaster. More often than not because I did not know how to handle the trowel, the mud ended up on the floor. But under his guidance I finally learned how to flick my wrists in a coordinated way to make the mud end up on the wall.

Tom's southern upbringing determined his taste as far as food was concerned. Alaga (Alabama-Georgia) syrup with hot buttered biscuits, pinto beans cooked with ham, cornbread, fried chicken, watermelon, cantaloupe, sweet potatoes—candied or baked, collard greens, and pickled pig feet were his favorite foods. He was also very fond of oyster soup. Whenever we had oyster soup, he always insisted on skimming out the oysters for himself. Mother took us aside and explained to us children that he was entitled to do this because he was, after all, the provider.

Like any housewife who reads about interesting recipes to vary the diet, my mother was always trying new dishes, such as chicken à la king, rhubarb cream pie, banana cream pie, and popovers, on the family. Under protest he might try some of it, but he always managed to have a bedtime snack of sardines or another one of his favorites. Amusingly, he was so fond of pinto beans that he often ate those for a late-night snack. Constantly he reminded my mother that she could not cook southern foods like his mother.

No doubt the fact that he worked inside every day contributed to his love of the outdoors. Part of this outdoor spirit might also be traceable to his early years in North Carolina on the farm and the quail and coon hunting experienced there because Tom loved tramping through the woods hunting deer, rabbits, pheasants, and quail. There were always a couple of hunting dogs about the house—a beagle for hunting rabbits and a pointer or two for hunting quail and pheasants. He was an excellent shot with a shotgun and high-powered rifle. In the living room there was a mounted trophy of a ten-point buck with its hooves turned upward to hold a rifle. In the depression, during the thirties, he supplied the table with rabbits, ring-necked pheasants, quail, squirrel, and venison. For my birthday one year he bought me a twenty-two rifle and taught me how to use it. I remember sighting a sitting rabbit and hitting it with a bullet from the rifle. Somehow the love of killing never rubbed off on me. I had read Schweitzer, and his reverence for life put a damper on it. But the love of nature stuck and is still with me.

Gardening may have been another expression of his love of the outdoors and nature. On the other hand, it may just have been necessity that led to his gardening because money and food were scarce during the depression. We always had a huge garden. The onion shoots had to be weeded carefully in order not to pull out the onions. Tom loved to watch things grow and every evening when he returned home from work he would check on the garden. Of particular interest to him was the growing of watermelons and cantaloupes which he planted in mounds. He taught us kids not to step on the ends of the vines so as not to kill them, and showed us how to tell when they were ripe by smell, "thumping," and "plugging." One of his favorite crops was Kentucky wonder beans which he liked cooked with ham and white potatoes.

If Tom could be said to have one weakness, it was for alcohol. Regularly on the way home from work he would stop at the Roadside Tavern for a drink or two and arrive home late for dinner. Mother would always wait to eat with him but if he were too late she would let us children eat without him. At the week's end, he usually got "plastered." We kids knew that was the time to hit him up for change because he was always very liberal when under the influence. With a few drinks under his belt he frequently reached for the guitar and tried to plunk out his favorite sentimental tunes, "Silver Haired Daddy of Mine" and "Springtime in the Rockies."

When he had had too much to drink, he would also shock us kids by sucking raw eggs. He would tap a tiny hole in one end of the egg and put salt and pepper in it. Then he would cut a small hole in the other end and—zoom—suck out the egg leaving an empty shell.

Often when he was drinking Tom would get into fights. On one occasion during the winter, he got into a fight and was so drunk that he thought he was hitting his opponent when he was hitting the frozen ground instead. His hand was swollen for weeks and had to be bathed in Epsom salt water and treated with a salve.

Sometimes he would get so drunk that his stomach couldn't take it and he would vomit again and again. While groaning during such episodes, he'd moan, "ooooh—oooh—oooh, I'm a sick woman." But none of this seemed to cure him because he always went back to drinking.

Religion was not one of the areas Tom was attracted to or interested in. His attendance and participation at the services of the A.M.E Zion church in Greenville were sporadic to say the least. He had no close attachment or dedication to the church. Once I remember he and my mother joined with another couple to form a quartet which sang at the church. They rehearsed for some time in order to perfect the harmony and their efforts were appreciated by the small group of Afro-American parishioners. Tom did not seem to appreciate sermons. However he was not averse to my sister and me attending Sunday school regularly.

In spite of the fact that in the twentieth century most people talk openly about sex, I show that I belong to another age by the reticence with which I approach it. Already I have alluded to Tom's hair and physique which made him extremely attractive to women. It was indeed a source of tension in the marriage. Tom had fathered an illegitimate child before his marriage to my mother, and apparently he and my mother had reached an agreement that with the financial settlement made to the unwed mother there was to be no more contact between them. Any time a single woman known to be fair game sexually appeared, there was sure to be an argument usually begun by my mother.

During the depression, the family did not have sufficient funds to buy a license for the model T. Since my sister had to go to high school and Tom had to go to work, the car had to be driven with or without a license. To avoid arrest Tom drove the back roads. It was during such a trip that Tom tried to rape my sister, but she fought him off and told

Mother about it. A big argument ensued. Eventually my sister went to live with our father and grandfather who took her in.

In his final days I visited him in the hospital or at his home. With calmness and without complaining, he bore his illness and the loss of his leg from gangrene which had set in from a lack of circulation. He did not fill his last days with regrets. On one visit to the hospital I remember his introducing me to his roommate as, "This is my son." He seemed quite proud of our relationship.

There are always many more people who have influenced us profoundly than we are permitted to fully recognize. Biographies we have read and ideas we have discovered affect us more than we can ever put our finger on. By the same token, I can probably describe only a few of the ways that Tom may have influenced my life.

Tom never shirked work, took pride in his work, and tried to be his best in what he did for a living. Even at an advanced age, I still don't mind working as I have all my life. His love of his family and his loyalty to them, although he never said much about it, has undoubtedly had its influence on me.

Because of the example he provided in drinking, after one experience in drinking too much, I have always managed to drink in moderation if at all.

In matters of race, Tom was a true integrationist. Seldom if ever was the term "racism" used in my home. Whites were in the majority in the small community in which we lived and never felt any threat in competition for jobs from African-Americans. Tom related to persons as persons and never thought in Black and white terms. Couples and their children moved freely in and out of each others' homes, card parties, and gatherings without any stigma attached to being of a different color.

In no sense of the word was Tom stingy. He shared freely with his family and my sister and me. In giving me a watch when I graduated from high school and a ring on my finishing college, he seemed to be saying he was proud of the choices I had made.

At no time was he concerned about being an example, he was just himself and made no apologies for it. I suspect that the best example is the natural one. Nothing staged.

Like many adults, I enjoy eating foods I grew up with. Pinto beans, green beans with ham and potatoes, watermelon, cornbread, and bacon are favorites. Tom's southern taste still appeals to me although bacon is now on the *verboten* fat list.

Although Tom's surname was Clark, he never insisted that I take his name. Perhaps he was so unconsciously insistent on his own identity and individuality that he was not about to deny another person his identity.

André Malraux once said that "the rarest thing in the world is a mature person." Certainly Tom embodied many of the qualities of a mature person, but one would have to bear in mind a bit of advice: "Be patient with me. God isn't finished with me yet."

Anthony Dorsey

Remembering, but Judging Not

At twenty-nine, my mom (Barbara Ann, I call her) was her own person, a Black woman with an Afro, a B.A. from Fisk, an M.A. from Ohio State, and a bright idea. She made a conscious decision to have a child. Mind you, a child, not a husband. For her, a woman liberated long before it was politically correct (and deemed healthy) to be so, "choice" meant the right to choose single-parenthood. When I was born on January 25, 1971, she had no apologies, no regrets, no explanations, only happiness. I was her first born, and she gave me her name.

It was just the two of us—Barbara Ann and Anthony Crosby—until, after a brief courtship, she married a radical Puerto Rican from the "Boogie Down" Bronx. The number in our family changed, and so did our name. My mom's husband became my dad. He adopted me and gave me his name. I became Anthony Dorsey. Not knowing about the "bright idea" and my mother's "choice," I grew up believing that my dad was my father which means that I considered myself half African American and half Puerto Rican. As far as I knew, I had the same parents as my sister Tashamee, who was born in 1973. We were two half African-American and half Puerto Rican children living in a nuclear family in Roselle, New Jersey.

I was entering the fifth grade when my dad moved to D.C. to work on his dissertation, a decision that eventually led to my parents' divorce. The move and the breakup of the family did not change my identity. I continued to believe that I was half African-American and half Puerto Rican. Not until I was twenty-one did I learn the truth about my identity.

I found out on Mother's Day in 1992. I had just graduated from Hampton University in Virginia and was ready for an extended stay of fun away from home. No way. My mom Barbara Ann wanted my "not-quite-grown butt" home in two days. She had something to tell me. "Something important," she said. Something I had earned the right to know and the maturity to process.

I went home to New Jersey with a number of what-is-it questions in my mind. Almost as soon as I walked through the front door, my mom made the disclosure. I remember her exact words: "Anthony, there is someone who is not exactly who you think he is." I thought for a minute, in silence. She froze. I reviewed my last twenty-one years and said, "You mean my dad is not really my dad?"

I could sense my mother's relief and her surprise at how quickly I solved the riddle. Somehow, deep inside, I had always known, and it was not all that difficult a riddle. My dad stands five feet and nine inches tall. He is distinctly Hispanic in appearance, with oily skin and wavy brown hair. I am six feet, two inches tall and African-American in appearance. I have never had oily skin and my hair is black. My father has a very fragile disposition that explodes in anger. I am calm and tend toward excitement, not anger.

The disclosure did not cause me to rewind the tape of my years with my father. I did not think, "He left us because I am not his biological son." I did not give normal/natural father-son arguments of the past a different reading—as in, "It would have been different if. . ." The truth is, my dad loves me, he loves my sister, and he loves his eldest son from his first marriage. But as the saying goes, "Love don't pay the bills." The truth is, my father is an alcoholic, he is verbally abusive, and he is irresponsible.

I have never seen him in a drunken rage, but I have seen him drunk and I know that he has a history of driving under the influence. It was because of his problem that I learned of his infidelity to my mother.

I remember it well.

When I was eleven years old, my mother sent me to live with my father in suburban Maryland. On my first day with him, I asked my father if he had ever cheated on my mom. He said, "No!" Well, that same night he came home drunk. I was asleep, but was awakened when he used the telephone. He called his lady friend and proceeded to discuss their past, their future, and how things would change because of me. Because of me!

I knew after hearing that conversation that my dad was a liar. No love lost, just the facts. From that moment on, I believed he would lie to anyone at any moment. My dad was a liar and also a coward. Why couldn't he just own up to his business? Why did he have to lie? Why did he feel the need to lie and then drink?

The verbal abuse peaked when I was in college. He would call me once a month. Once a month with the same threat. "Anthony, I am not paying any more tuition," he would say. At first I patronized him, but later I ignored him. The tuition continued to get paid. It was paid on time and I graduated on time.

Unfortunately, my sister did not handle the threat as well as I did. She would call me from college in Atlanta and cry, "Anthony," she would sob, "what if Daddy stops paying tuition?" I would tell her the same thing every month. "Don't worry, Tashamee, Daddy will pay the tuition and everything will be fine." It pained me to know that my sister suffered this way and that my father knew he was hurting her. When I graduated from college, I told my father that I would never speak to him again if he continued to hurt my sister. The stress was too much for her. For a number of reasons, principal among them my father's cruelty, she became clinically depressed and had to withdraw from school. I did not speak to my father for four years.

I do not understand why he never hit me and why he never stopped paying my tuition. After all, I was defiant, I was tuff-talking, and I was adopted. But what I really cannot understand is why he did right by me, his adopted son, and continued to do wrong by my sister, his biological daughter?

For the sake of my sanity, I broke all emotional ties with my dad years ago. He sends me a card on my birthday and on selected holidays. I never initiate correspondence with him because of the pain and the discomfort he has caused my mom and my sister. I love my dad for the efforts he made to be a good father. I have faith that he did the best he could. I do not hate him. Actually, I pray for him. Pray that one day he will do right by his biological daughter and, as well, his biological son. Pray that one day he will be free of all demons.

That is the same prayer I have for my biological father. Barbara Ann says he came to visit me one time before we left the hospital. She says he called me a "handsome child." That was the last time she ever spoke to or saw him. Animosity? I have none. Feel sorry for myself that my father could see me, flesh of his flesh, and choose to walk right out of my life forever? No. I feel sorry for him. He could have known me. He missed the joy Barbara Ann experienced—my laughter, my smile, my first steps, my first days of school, my accomplishments, my growth into a man.

I confess, though, that I now wonder what he looks like. I wonder if I resemble him and sound like him. Do I walk like him? Do I think like him? Sometimes I wonder whether or not I should try to locate my biological father, but quickly decide against it. I actually enjoy the mystery and fun of playing the wondering game. I have made my family proud of me. My father can't be proud. He doesn't know me. He has missed my evolution into a young, proud Black man.

I am grateful to my biological father for his abundant genetic gifts. I am grateful to my dad for adopting me and giving me some semblance of fatherhood. From both of them, I received the greatest lesson a son must learn in order to become a whole man: how not to fail as a father. Because of their un-example, I know I could never/would never abandon my child or be unfaithful to their mother. Realizing that Black men have historically had difficulties handling the pressures of fatherhood, I will not judge the two fathers in my life harshly. I will love them unconditionally and I will forgive them.

My mom, who has never wavered in her support or been stingy with her trust, I will always idolize. I am the proud product of a female-headed, single-parent household. I am happy that I am Barbara Ann's son.

Don Belton

My Father's House

When I was a child everything in my father's house had a name and everything had a place. If something wasn't given a place or a name in my father's house, it didn't exist. I grew up yearning for the unnameable, the unplaceable. Later, I would learn names for what was missing, but back then I lived in a hard Eden, sensing something was buried in the kingdom of my father's house, something hot and unspeakable.

There was a way to speak to adults, my father taught me. A way to ask. A way to speak on the telephone. A way to eat. To be excused from the table. To stand. To sit. To behave when company came. A way to play so as not to disrupt the entire house. So as not to get my clothes dirty. Not a right and wrong way. There was one way: the way my father taught me. I was constantly corrected and reproved. I was rehearsed in his rules. I was policed and inspected. This color socks only goes with that color trousers. Use this fork for salad and that fork for meat. Only girls laugh: tee hee. Boys must laugh: ha ha. I took my rest at my precise bedtime, and my day began at exactly the same hour each morning. My evening and morning prayers were meticulously recited like incantations for an easy sentence in the prison of my father's house. I was not allowed to break a rule—ever. There was always something to say I was sorry for, something for which I knew I would never be entirely forgiven. Even at an early age, I learned to keep my sins a secret.

My father's Bible sat, big as the Book of Life in a DeMille epic, on the glass-topped coffee table in our living room. His Bible was bigger than the TV screen in the cabinet Magnavox he owned until the late 60s (when the Civil Rights Movement, riots, and the murder of Martin Luther King, Jr., had won consumer credit in giant downtown appliance stores for upstanding members of the Negro middle class like my father. It took all that before a nineteen-inch color television set, full of the mass cultural phantasmagoria, was installed in our North Philadelphia row home). But back in the late 50s and early 60s, when I was a baby and toddler, the Bible lay, as if in state, as the presiding shrine and oracle of my father's house.

As far back as I can remember, I was carried back and forth to church, by my father and various other relatives. I was taken back and forth as though I were receiving treatments for a persistent ailment. During my childhood, we attended various churches, all of them Black and all of them Sanctified Holiness. Although there were often prayer meetings in our home, where the Black saints would gather, transforming themselves as they sang and spoke their quiet supplications to God, church provided a mode of expression that was forbidden in my father's house. Church was a spectacle. The members of the congregation not only prayed and sang. They "shouted." They danced the holy dance and walked the floor of the church in otherworldly syncopation. They beat their hands and jangled tambourines in double time. They screamed and cried. They fainted. The services at these churches were emotional extravaganzas so feverish that a small battalion of white-gloved ushers were dispatched to administer fanning, blankets, and smelling salts to soul-struck worshipers.

I learned about the Bible in the churches we attended. When I was two or three years old I started Sunday school, where I was indelibly imprinted with religion, indoctrinated through songs and stories. I sang with the children's Sunday school choir: "The B-I-B-L-E / That is the book for me / I'll stand alone / on the word of God / the B-I-B-L-E." My favorite song, however, was "Jesus loves me / This I know / for the Bible / tells me so." I sang it in and out of church. I sang it with the plaintive sincerity and hunger to be transported that children possess.

Perhaps I was so wrapped up in this song because even then it seemed to offer a paradigm that could subvert the power of my father's religion, his house, even as I used it to make a show of submitting to its power.

I was obsessed with Jesus, though, truly, I had no idea who or what Jesus was. Perhaps my obsession stemmed from my early recognition that Jesus was a sign of ambiguity in a house where everything else seemed hard and fast. The images of Jesus available to me were of a beautiful young white man, adapted, I now realize, from the Christ images of Italian Renaissance paintings. Recently I made a brief tour of muse-

ums and cathedrals in Italy. I was struck by the homoerotic force of the
Christs painted by Giotto, Michelangelo, and da Vinci. The images of
Christ that emerged during the Renaissance celebrated spiritual princi-
ples at the same time that they celebrated the male body.

The Christ images of *my* early childhood were the earliest images I
can remember where there was the clear association of maleness with
beauty. The depictions were from a standard repertoire and many
quoted one another: Christ crucified, the Last Supper, the Good Shepherd, Christ praying in the Garden, Christ expelling the money lenders
from the Temple, Christ with the bleeding heart. Of course the Christs
of my early childhood, unlike the Christs from the Italian Renaissance,
were two-dimensional, for the most part; the work of hack colorists and
copyists. Still, they retained some of the flavor of their sources and
passed along intimations of the power of those sources to me. I recall,
very early, being fascinated by a drawing in a book my father owned of
Samson straining his perfect body between two pillars, toppling the
palace of the Philistines. This picture was like a door for me into which
I escaped for hours from the resoluteness of my father's house. I lived in
a suspended state of enchantment, poring over that picture, captivated
by its tricks of proportion and light, its representation of the beauty of
harmony in the male body. I assumed, until I learned to read well
enough, that this was merely another picture of Jesus.

What these pictures of Jesus bore in common was the picture of an at
once consequential and pregnable male youth—a god—wearing scant,
diaphanous clothes, clothing that parted strategically to provide voyeuristic focus on beautiful limbs, a naked heart. The only thing I had to
compare these pictures to back then was the provocative, but by today's
standards tame, pinup girl calendar photos hanging in the office of an
uncle's gas station and the neighborhood barber shop, where my father
and I went for our weekly haircuts—both aggressively male and secu-
lar spaces.

The calendar pictures of thinly clothed young women were profane,
not sacred. They were visual confections. But so, in a sense, were the
pictures of Jesus I knew from my Sunday school textbooks, the illustrations in my father's Bible, funeral parlor fans, and decorative household
notions. This seemed especially true of pictures of the crucified Christ
wearing nothing more than a loin covering. Even as a child, the image

of the exposed, undressed Christ made these pictures available to me for erotic readings. Both the image of the pinup girl and the image of Jesus were sentimental, populist cultural productions. Both were idealized and eroticized through their vulnerability to the gaze of the viewer.

I remember once looking at a picture of Jesus, painted on a plate, that hung on the wall in our kitchen and asking my father, "Is Jesus a man or a woman?" The picture showed Jesus standing outside a small house knocking at the door. He was holding a shepherd's hook, which I recognized since it had been identified for me by my father in another picture where Jesus was among the lambs, The Good Shepherd. If he was a man, I had no idea what sort of man. Certainly, no man I knew had long hair. My father had told me many times that the Bible maintained that it was a shame for a man to wear his hair long, and so he and I went ritualistically to the barber each week to have our heads shorn and sprinkled with bay rum. It was not only the hair, however, that made me suspect Jesus might be a woman. It seemed he was always doing something a woman rather than a man did in terms of the gender vocabulary I understood then. He suffered. He healed. He wept. He provided care. He was a kind of male mother, I thought.

In the picture in our kitchen, I was told in response to my questions, Jesus was knocking at the door of my heart, asking to come in. But I could plainly see Jesus was *not* knocking at the door of a heart. He was knocking at the door of a house, my father's house. This was even stranger, because Jesus was white.

In the neighborhood where I lived, whites did not socialize with Blacks, though we had one or two white neighbors and there were several white merchants along our avenue. No white person ever entered our home when I was very young. When a caterer came, or a carpenter, or the florist or a furniture delivery man, these were Negro men. In those days, we lived and socialized in an authentic Black community. Moreover, images of white men in my father's house were rare and exotic. Television, newspapers, and magazines had not yet come to dominate our virtual lives. And we didn't know any white men, though at the family New Year's Eve party held annually in our home the gathered men told white man stories. In these stories, white men embodied evil and power. The white man was worse than the Devil, because, according to my father's religion, the Devil had been put under the subjection of God. The white man was godless and was subject to nothing and no one. The white man lied and seduced, jailed, ravaged, and lynched.

Yet, for all the white man's evil deeds since time immemorial, I knew that my uncles and my father smiled in the faces of white merchants and white policemen. They were gracious when a white man summoned them to a counter or a desk in a downtown bank. They deferred to white men on the sidewalk, especially at night on dark streets far from home, and spoke to no Negro or family person in the same tones of high regard reserved for a white man: "Yes, sir," and "No, sir," and "Thank you, sir." My mother bore my father's children, kept his house, cooked for him, and he never once thanked *her*. These black men loved their wives and children. I knew this. I knew they were good men. They dreamed, worked, and sacrificed. Through my childhood and adolescence, each of them exhausted themselves to build a legacy out of their bodies in factories, shipyards, metal yards and, rarely, office buildings—selling second-hand, driving trucks, shining shoes, hauling, hammering, and serving. Many of them worked two or three jobs concurrently. In their time, each would destroy his body with work and strain. Once or twice a year, he might seem to weep as he prayed a desperate prayer in church. Or take down a guitar in a living room and sing a song that was like a letter from "down home." Or sit among each other in a kitchen laughing, telling drawn-out, mercurial stories. I always suspected their public deference and private hatred for white men belied a preoccupation with a white man's power to subvert or corroborate their own claim to Western manhood.

And there were the pictures of Jesus, white, lordly, and ravishing, on the walls of my father's house. It is a simple matter to say that my father, in his persistence in "white" Christianity, was only a victim of the histories of colonialism and slavery. But that version denies my father's agency and his subjectivity. After all, my father was a man, thinking and willing. *He* put that Bible in a place of prominence in his house. *He* framed and hammered those pictures to his walls.

I never asked why Jesus was white. Perhaps his "shameful" hair balanced out the social currency of his racial whiteness. I *wanted* him to be white. He needed to be white. I read Jesus' whiteness as a queerness, like the whiteness of a ghost or the queerness of the white peacock I'd once seen at the Philadelphia Zoo—a manifestation of the world's erratic side that had not yet been spoken. This whiteness was strange, not hateful. Something strange was at the gate of my father's house, knocking.

I had to wait to become a man myself to understand that my father's coldness was his gift to me. By teaching me to become regimental and unbreakable, my father taught me to safeguard my heart from the same world that would, so shortly after the announcement of President Johnson's New Society, mock my father's dreams and destroy the neighborhood that had been his Canaan, the son of Georgia peasants. My father would work himself to death by the time I reached the age at which he fathered me.

Jesus was a queer token between my father and me, a sign of paradox. The paradox, I now understand, is that love is its own safeguard. When I reached adolescence, our house had grown noisy with phantom TV, stereo, and radio voices. My father's house was heavy with things. Fine, second-hand furniture and the carpenter's handiwork were replaced by plastic-covered creations from giant factories. We hid away from one another inside that house. I, in my room, listening to music and reading books. He, in the basement, alone down there for hours, when he wasn't hiding in sleep on the living room sofa before the ghoulish light of the TV. The community outside my father's house was no longer the model Black community of the late 50s that had been his pride. The neighborhood was under siege. A chapter of the Black Panther Party had moved in down the street from us in 1969, and with the Panther headquarters had come a heavy and menacing police presence on our avenue. In 1970, Philadelphia police raided the Panther house. My father's neighborhood awoke to gunfire. By the late afternoon, the Philadelphia police chief strode down our avenue, declaring through a megaphone that all the dirty bastards living in this hellhole should be shot. Only a decade earlier, John Fitzgerald Kennedy had flashed by our sycamore-shaded house, smiling and waving in a motorcade on his way to the presidency of the United States, trailing hope.

In 1970, I was attending a Quaker boy's day school on an academic scholarship. There, I was isolated and admired in a world of affluent white boys. At home, I missed my father terribly, although I could not ever remember being close to him or hearing him tell me he loved me. I was lonely for my father. At the same time I hid from my father, I began to track him. I sneaked and went through his chest of drawers. I looked in his closets, his shoe boxes, fishing tackle boxes and toolboxes for the secrets of his heart. I went behind him, fingering the filters of the cigarettes he had smoked and left in ashtrays, hoping to finger some secret thought. Once I steamed open and read a letter he had written to the grandmother who raised him, hoping I would learn my father's true identity.

One day when I was eleven or twelve years old, and my father was out of the house on an errand, I made a fine, strange discovery. I found, hidden beneath a floorboard in our basement, his money box. The box was unlocked. There were several rolls of half dollars and dimes, and twenty dollars or so in old bills. Beneath the money box, however, there was a bundle of photographs wrapped in a brown silk scarf. The photographs were male physique photos—a series of white male nudes, well-made men standing in a sun-washed forest. I looked at each photograph of each man, carefully, as if each picture was a letter from some distant homeplace of the soul. My hands felt as if they were vibrating. When I was done looking at the photographs, I wrapped them as I had found them and replaced everything beneath the floorboard. I never mentioned the pictures to my father or anyone. Still, I always felt he knew I'd seen them after that day and that even before I'd seen them I'd felt them buried in his house. At times, I thought he left them there for me to find. Perhaps I am wrong, but I believe my father died waiting for me to unearth his softness. Somewhere inside the furnace of work he turned himself into, my father was a man crying for love between men, love that risked and healed the contradictions.

Kiini Salaam

A New Understanding

Sometimes every note I hear in my father's voice is a new one. Simple things that I should know about him are like a foreign language to my ears. Sometimes it is a language I delight in learning, like reading the autobiography he eagerly sent to me in the mail and discovering he was a sergeant in the army. Other times, it is a language that mocks me in my ignorance, laughs and curses boldly in my face like the first time I walked into my father's apartment (at the age of seventeen) and saw the shoes of Nia (his significant other) at the door and had to conclude on my own that they lived together. But my moments of delight and shock are just the accent that characterizes the exchange. What matters most about my conversations with my father is not what language they're in or who surprises whom, but that they are and that we keep having them.

In some ways, I know my father quite well, and in others, I don't know him at all. Ours is not quite a personal relationship. I couldn't tell you what his favorite food or favorite color is (or if he even has one). I don't know what type of music or which musician he's currently fascinated with. I don't always remember his birthday, and when I do, I don't always remember to call him. I will never know the tiny, personal details about my father and his everyday life. The time has passed for that type of relationship. But it isn't too late to cultivate a new type of a relationship based on my knowledge that the next conversation outweighs the last.

In the personal statement I wrote to accompany my application to Spelman College, I commented that my mother had given me a sense of self and my father had given me an appreciation for all types of music. Because he's a writer, I gave it to him to read and he said "an appreciation for music!" as though stung. I imagine it must have hurt him to see me reduce our relationship to an appreciation for music, but at that time, that statement was all I could write about my father. My child-like equation "out of sight=out of mind" convinced me that music was all I knew about him. But, as an adult, I can clearly see that all of the things my father went away to do when I was a child are the exact same things that have allowed me to get closer to him as an adult, and that have afforded me security, direction, and clarity in my life.

My father is a writer, a traveler, a contact-maker, and a businessman. As I began to draw on his contacts and meet people he knew, he and I began to talk. "My name is Kiini Ibura Salaam. I am Kalamu ya Salaam's daughter," I would tell someone. Then they would proceed to tell me who my father was to them. Armed with this information, I would go back to my father and talk to him about what this man said about him, ask him who that lady from Texas with all those sparkling bracelets was, and what he was doing in Atlanta to meet the director of that company. Through my father's friends, I got to know his comings and goings and began to understand what he did when he sped off in his little blue Toyota away from us into the world. I even began to see him perform, which I don't have any clear memories of having seen before my high school graduation. I knew he was a poet, but I never realized he was a performer—a preacher poet.

That our true person-to-person interaction began through long-distance telephone lines between New Orleans and Atlanta when I moved away is no longer surprising. One of my parents' agreements upon separation was that until high school graduation, my mother would be their children's primary caregiver and that when we entered college, my father would become primarily responsible. In hindsight it was an ingenious agreement. As human resource theory dictates, it is better to take someone's assets and match them with the right job, than try to mold them to fit a job that doesn't suit them. Well, my mother was good at raising us—good at taking care of children, instilling values, making food stretch, watching us tear each other's hair out during childhood and go crazy as adolescents—but after we were formed and needed not so much daily care, but infrequent long-term care, her financial resources could not stretch to meet our needs, neither could her contacts or knowledge of other cities and situations. My father, on the other hand, was not very good at relating to us as little people, but now that we are older, I am most comfortable with him guiding me as I move out into the world, and he is more comfortable relating to us as young adults. His ideas, understanding, and matter-of-factness are often my salvation in sticky situations.

Presently, I am on the tail of a unique twelve-month traveling fellowship. I traveled to four countries, and I did it fearlessly, partly because I know that my father is sitting in his office on 2218 Brainard Street, just one little collect call away. He is a constant, an anchor. I am now in my eleventh month abroad and the separation from home has begun to weigh heavily upon me. The homesickness that was nonexistent for the first six months has ballooned into a constant companion waking me up in the morning and laying down with me when I go to sleep at night. My father, it seems, has sensed this. In the past two months, he has called me more times than he's called over the course of the entire year. Whereas before, the majority of our phone calls were straight-to-the-point business calls—"I sent you such and such in the mail, did you get it? I need this much money, can you send it?"—our phone calls are becoming more and more conversational. Now, they are more like life reports.

I can now step back from my criticism of my father's participation (or lack thereof) in my childhood upbringing and see him for what he is—a role model, a strong and powerful man, a loving father, and a friend. I can now see that his leaving us, leaving his job and forcing us into financial straits, impacted me more than just economically. He didn't just leave his job, he left his job *and* opened his own business. A business that put his children through college and gave me a marked vision of my own self-owned business and, consequently, a self-owned life. His record collection (of mostly jazz, but also reggae and world music) that covered the walls of our living room when I was a child formed the mainstay of my music appreciation. His status as a community artist kept me surrounded by people with artistic impulses and alternative visions of a way of life. He and my mother were seriously committed in every way to our upbringing and I have the self I am to thank for it.

If all this praise and appreciation isn't enough, my father was also instrumental in developing one of my most important selves—my writer self. I wrote my first short story in 1991 as a first-year college student at Spelman. I read it to my class; then I sent it to my father. Not one to exaggerate truth or throw out compliments where they aren't deserved, he expressed excitement and interest. Beyond simply liking it (which was enough of a boost for my ego), he encouraged me to do something I hadn't even considered, sent it out for publication. I know that having my story accepted for publication was key to me considering myself a writer today. I don't know if, back then, my father's praise would have been enough. Today, it is.

When my father and I talk on the phone, we discuss our work. He tells me about the 50,000 projects he's working on (simultaneously) and I tell him about the three pages I wrote to further my (one) project. Anytime I write something new, I put it on disk and send it to him. Likewise, when he completes projects, he puts them in a padded envelope and sends it to me through the post. As my editor, he reads my work as soon as I send it to him, then he gives it to me straight. What I like most is hearing his excitement and his analysis. I have, at times, become too dependent upon his praise, but I shall work on that dependency as I continue to hone my craft.

After reading an interview that my father did with me for the Third World Press' *Why L.A. Happened*, a male reader contacted a friend of the family and expressed his joy. He said the interview was inspiring. It encouraged him to have hope for the relationship he wants to foster with his own daughter. I too say that I am inspired. Every time all five of the Salaam siblings are in New Orleans (usually in the summertime), my father comes down to 1708 Tennessee Street and takes a family picture. Although we don't exchange "I love you's" and he's never shown us one of these photographs yet (I'm not so sure he's ever developed the film or if he even knows where the rolls are), it is the idea that matters. It is his interest in us, our development, and the love his interest implies that makes my heart sing.

Tayari A. Jones

My Daddy, the Pregnant
Warrior Woman, and Me

My father filled my early childhood with puzzling images. One was a poster of a beautiful woman with an Afro who was wearing shiny bullets. The caption read: Think About It! Another was a silhouette of my older brother sandwiched between portraits of W. E. B. Du Bois and Malcolm X. The image that has remained with me most is of the pregnant warrior woman who carried a small boy strapped to her back. Both of them peered at me from a poster tacked on the door of my father's makeshift basement study. She was a dark woman whose hair was cut close to her head like some of the mothers of my playmates. She was looking directly into the camera, but smiling. One hand was touching her swollen stomach and the other was clutching a rifle. Even as a young girl, I knew somehow that the pregnant warrior woman, my daddy, and I were on the same side in the struggle for liberation for people of African descent. My name, chosen by my father, says it all: Tayari Acio Jones. First and middle names straight from the motherland, last name directly from my father's northern Louisiana home. I was Tayari, which in Swahili means "she who is prepared."

To be prepared for the politically aware life my father wanted for me, I went to a small preschool called the Learning House, where, with the other African-American pupils, I chanted before eating my lunch: "We will eat all of our food and drink our milk to make us strong to fight in the struggle for liberation for all African people." I didn't know how different my upbringing was. In fact, I thought all children chanted for liberation and that all of them knew about the pregnant warrior woman who "fought for the freedom of Azania." I also thought they knew that

"Gulf Gas finances the other side" and therefore would never consider sitting passively while some adult filled his tank at a Gulf station.

I learned that my family was different only when I graduated from the Learning House and attended a traditional school. The first clue was that I was surrounded by children whose names were LaShaun, Tracey, Mark, John, and Audra, and who thought my African name was the funniest thing since Saturday morning cartoons. The next clue was that I was not allowed to say the "plegaleence" or morning devotional then required in all public schools. When I asked why I couldn't, Daddy said, "Because we don't believe in that." When I pressed further, he pointed to a strange picture on the wall in his basement study of an old man in a tall hat and a curious uniform surrounded by the faces of four little girls. The caption read: "The Shame of Uncle Sam." I understood that those girls, whom I later learned died in a Birmingham church bombing, were like the pregnant warrior woman.

There were many other things we didn't do that made my family different. We didn't go to church; we never flew a flag on the Fourth of July; we never stood for the singing of the national anthem; and we did not use straightening combs or perm kits. Both my mother and I wore our hair natural. And going way across town to a recently integrated school was out of the question for my family. My brother and I traveled several miles each morning to a school located less than a mile from a public housing project.

Six years after I left that school, I found myself, once again, living within walking distance of this same housing project. This time, however, I was a student at Spelman College. When my classmates walked through the area, they purposely avoided eye contact with the people whose neighborhood we were invading. I did the same, at first, but one day something happened to remind me of who I am. I remember strolling back to campus with several friends when one of them said, "Don't look." Of course all of us quickly glanced where we were told not to, as much in sync as a marching band. Then, all together, we quickly looked away.

"She's wrong to wear so much make-up," one of my friends said.

"I think it's a he/she," another whispered excitedly.

Then it was I heard my name called.

"Tayari. Tayari."

The person looked familiar, but I couldn't tell who he was through all of the make-up.

"It's me. Robert Johnson." He held his arms out for a hug.

"Girl, don't you remember me?" he asked.

Of course I remembered him. Johnson came right before Jones, so I usually stood behind him in the lunch line. To the shock of my friends, I walked into his arms and returned his hug. That night, I called my father and told him what had happened so that I could hear the praise he saved for those special occasions when I demonstrated how well I was wearing my name and how well I remembered the pregnant warrior woman: "You're my mule if you never win a race."

During my last two years of high school, my daddy moved to Washington, D.C., to teach at Howard University while I stayed in Atlanta with my mother. Not having him in the house filled me with an anger I found difficult to articulate or suppress. I had always considered him to be my advocate. When my mother would say that I could not have, say, a slice of cake, Daddy would say, "Oh, Barbara, let her have a little piece." I took incidents like these as proof that my daddy loved me ten times more than my mother ever could. When he left, I felt as if I had been discarded.

When I left home for college, I didn't feel the loss as keenly. As a matter of fact, I felt closer to him than I had in years. This is probably because many of my professors knew him. When I would turn in a well-written paper or speak out passionately in class, they would say, "She is so much like Mack." This positive reinforcement bolstered me and I began to strive to be more Mack-like. I even found myself working into conversations my identity as his daughter, his *only* daughter. That I worked hard to be Mack-like and to live up to the name my father had given me is in no small way responsible for my graduation from Spelman College with *magna cum* honors. With a sense of accomplishment under my belt, I headed to the University of Iowa for graduate study. Pursuing a Ph.D. and becoming a college professor seemed so very right for me. After all, both of my parents earned their doctorates and both were college professors. But as I packed my bag for Iowa, I was more excited that two of my short stories were to be published than I was that I had earned a fellowship to such a prestigious university. In retrospect, I know that more than anything I wanted to be a writer.

My daddy remembered his graduate school days with great fondness, and for good reason. That was when he met the love of his life, my mother. He would tell my brother and me about how she made him feel so warm that he didn't notice the sting of an Illinois winter. I was hopeful that a similar experience was waiting for me in Iowa. What I found instead was disappointment. I sat in classrooms listening to teachers interpret my favorite novels in ways that were completely contrary to my worldview and my politics. Using all of the lessons I learned from my father and the pregnant warrior woman, I challenged syllabi that didn't include a single Black author. I would not accept invisibility. After each battle, I would call home for consolation and support from my daddy. My daddy's response surprised and disappointed me.

"It is naive," he said, "to think that those white people are going to reward you for challenging everything they believe."

This was not what I called home to hear. I wanted to be reminded that I was my daddy's mule if I never won a race.

"You need a long stick," he said. "Everything you do to improve yourself lengthens your stick."

I was in no mood for metaphors. Nor was I interested in lengthening my stick in a program that had nothing to do with my first love—becoming a writer. When I told my daddy that I wanted an M.F.A. in creative writing rather than a doctorate in English, he thought for a few seconds and then responded. "A master's in creative writing isn't much of a stick. It's more like a switch."

The man urging me to "let some things slide" could not be the same man who made me walk a picket line on behalf of sanitation workers when I was a toothless six-year-old. He could not be the man who gave me the image of the pregnant warrior woman. I knew he had my best interest at heart, but this felt like betrayal. The conversations between us become more bitter until I wrote him a long tear-stained letter about my passion for writing and my determination to be a writer. He promptly replied in a longer letter. His position remained unchanged: "I accept the fact that you want to become a writer. Clearly, a Ph.D. is not a prerequisite for becoming one. But having one may allow you to make a more independent life while you struggle." I rejected the advice he offered in the letter of eleven pages bearing his distinctive left-handed scrawl and expected him to live up to his promise to love and support me no matter what.

When I gave my parents the date of my graduation from Iowa—with a master's—neither made plans to attend the ceremony or asked what I would like as a graduation gift. I was a quitter. Failure does not deserve celebration. When I informed my godmother Cousin Doll that nobody was coming to my graduation, she responded with shock in her voice. "You're telling me that you are getting your master's and nobody is going up there to see you get it?" She went into action. Everyone was in attendance at my commencement. I was in a state of joyous disbelief: My relationship with my father survived my going against his wishes. The day was special for me and the graduation luncheon even more so. My daddy lifted his glass. "I have something to say to my child."

I looked up at him.

"You're my mule if you never win a race."

Rosalyn Terborg-Penn

Jacques Arnold Terborg, Sr.: Our Beacon

My father, Jacques Arnold Terborg, Sr., began life in 1909 in Suriname, a multiracial nation located on the Caribbean coast of South America. He was born in Paramaribo, the capital, the only child of Creole parents, Adrian Wilhelm Jacques and Delia Bierman Terborg. After one year in Suriname, his parents moved to Brazil and shortly thereafter to Barbados, where they remained until moving to their final destination, the United States. Like other immigrating Caribbean families, they chose to live in Brooklyn, New York. Because my father was stricken with pneumonia when he was in the second grade, he and his mother returned to the tropical climate of Suriname. Even though this was the country of his birth, Jacques was virtually a foreigner there. The native language of Suriname was and still is Dutch, but my father was able to speak only English and a little Portuguese.

My grandmother, Delia Terborg, realized that socialization and education were the keys to my father's survival. It was decided that he could not return to the cold climate of the United States until his respiratory problem was under control, so she made certain that he was enrolled in school in Paramaribo. Delia felt that a musical education was just as important as an academic one, and so she enrolled her son in violin lessons. Within a few years, by the time he was thirteen, Jacques had learned to play all types of stringed instruments. When he was still a teenager he formed his own orchestra, and they were sought after to perform for Paramaribo's Creole elite. Eventually, Delia returned to her husband in New York City while Jacques stayed on in Suriname to complete his studies and to play his Caseco-style music, which is similar to the Brazilian bossa nova. During this time, my grandfather often sent his son sheet music of the latest jazz arrangements from the States. As a result, Jacques' band was the first to introduce this music to Paramaribo audiences.

In 1928, Jacques left Suriname to join his parents in New York City and in that same year began matriculating at New York University. There he became a student of W. E. B. Du Bois and, inspired by Du Bois's teachings, my father and fellow classmate Dorothy Height formed the Rameses Club. In additional to this club, he joined Phi Beta Sigma fraternity and the Talisman, a New York African American men's social club.

During the first half of the depression, Jacques lived in Brooklyn with his parents, doing little. He feels today that this was a very unproductive period in his life. However, by 1936 he had returned to playing music. Although he could play any stringed instrument, his primary love was the guitar. He began playing locally in the percussion section of Joe Alston's Band. Once Tiny Bradshaw heard the band, however, he took it over and Jacques toured with the orchestra up and down the east coast and in the Middle West. He had an opportunity to meet and socialize with a number of famous entertainers, among them "Bojangles," Louis Armstrong, Duke Ellington, Cab Calloway, Lena Horne, and the Mills Brothers. He kept in touch with bass player Milt Hinton, who played with Dizzy Gillespie in the late 1930s, and maintained a close friendship with the late Charlie Fowlkes, baritone saxophone player in the Count Basie orchestra. Today, Jacques Arnold Terborg, Sr., is the last surviving member of the original Tiny Bradshaw Band.

My research of the life and times of my father began when my daughter Jeanna asked me questions about his life and wanted me to read an essay she had written about her grandfather for one of her college courses. I filled in gaps in the story we had learned from him, and from my mother, and I began to examine my life for the various ways in which he had influenced my personality and my politics. I remember his passionate recounting of his position on the dropping of the atomic bomb on Japan rather than on Germany. In my father's eyes, the act was racist. The Japanese were yellow, he said. The Germans were white. And the Americans were racist.

Because my father had been active in politics all of his life, I was not surprised that he fully supported my involvement in the Civil Rights

Movement of the 1960s. He left Queens, where he was living at the time, to go south and work in the Southern Christian Leadership Conference (SCLS). Nor was I surprised that he worked to send two buses full of members of our church to the 1963 March on Washington. Of course, he was among the hundreds of thousands assembled at the Lincoln Memorial when King moved the nation with his "I Have a Dream" speech.

In his eighties, my father continued his activism, this time working in various ways to dismantle the Reagan administration. It was the "Evil Empire," my father said, and America, in his opinion, was a "nation of sheep" blindly following evil.

The 1990s brought illness and fear to my father and to all of us in the family when the respiratory problems he had as a child resurfaced. Fortunately, he overcame the bout that hospitalized him in January of 1991 and was strong enough to attend functions where he was recognized as a walking repository of knowledge on the Big Band era of the 1930s.

Jacques Arnold Terborg, Sr., deserves the attention and praise he has received. He is a former jazz performer, a witness to significant cultural events in the history of our people. More significantly, he is an impassioned race-man whose fervor for freedom for African Americans has not diminished with age. My father is a beacon for generations to follow.

Judy Scales-Trent

Gifts

There was a day, that fall, when I could believe it wasn't true—not true that my father was now old and failing, not true that he would soon die.

It was a cool sunny day in October during a visit to my parents' home in North Carolina. The sky was blue and clear. Mom was outside working in the garden, coming in every now and then to get something from her potting room next to the back door. Dad and I were in the TV room: he was watching a football game and I was reading. It was a comfortable, companionable time. The droning voice of the sports announcer, all of us at home engaged in our individual projects—it reminded me of Saturdays in New Rochelle when I was a teenager. Back then, Mom would be in the kitchen cleaning and putting away the groceries, while Dad worked outside in the yard, listening to the Brooklyn Dodgers' game on his portable radio ("... there goes a hi-i-i-gh pop fly to center field ..."). And we girls hurried to finish our Saturday chores so we could go out with our friends.

But it was years later now, more than thirty years later.

Dad got up from his chair, slowly, carefully, then left the room, and returned wearing a jacket and cap. He had decided to go for a walk, and asked me to button his jacket for him: his arthritic fingers could no longer do this. "Can you believe it?!" he asked, amazed that a task once so easy had become so hard. After he left, I went looking for Mom: did she know Dad had gone out for a walk? Was this all right? Was he that strong? I was afraid he might lose consciousness and fall, as he had many times recently; I feared his legs might simply fail him once more. She told me that she had been encouraging him for some time to get out of the house and visit with neighbors while they worked in their yards. A few minutes later, still worried, I checked with Mom again. This time she asked me to take the car and see if Dad wanted a ride back home. As

I drove to the end of the block, I saw Dad standing at the corner, talking with a neighbor who had stopped raking leaves for a moment. It was such an old, familiar sight—my father outside on a walk. Yet it was something I hadn't seen in years. The neighbor laughed when I explained why I was there: "Your father just started his walk! He doesn't need a ride!" So I left. But I took the long way home, driving slowly around several long blocks, then looked for Dad once more. He was still standing at the same corner, one block from home. This time, however, he was alone. And he was happy to see me: "I'm so glad you came back. I didn't know *how* I was going to get home! My legs are just so weak."

Later that afternoon, I went to a bookstore and bought a poetry anthology. For the first time in a long time, Dad wanted to see what I was reading. He took the book, and leafed through it, excited. In the introduction, he found a stanza that he recognized, and read it out loud:

"Friends, Romans, countrymen, lend me your ears;
I come to bury Caesar, not to praise him . . ."

It was an old friend he recognized, and he read with pleasure. But his joy didn't last long. For within a few minutes he became upset, confused: "How can there be poems by different people in one book?" He thought someone was doing something wrong, cheating. I tried to explain the idea of anthologies to him—to this man who had dozens of anthologies on bookshelves in that very room. He listened carefully, but didn't quite trust my explanation.

It was also during this visit, in the fall of 1993, that I finally brought home some of his books. Dad had offered them during my spring visit: "I probably won't read them again," he said. But I didn't take them in the spring. I knew what his offer meant. And if I accepted the gift, then it would be true, wouldn't it? True that he would never read them again, true that things would never be the way they had once been, true that he would soon be gone. By fall, though, I had gotten more brave. So I went through his bookcases—rows and rows of books, books mashed together, books stacked on top of each other. And as I sat on the floor going through them, I realized that these books were well used, sometimes marked. He often noted where and when he had bought the book and read it; sometimes he wrote comments in the margins of the text, or at the end. I could see the years pass as he changed from a ballpoint pen to a yellow high-lighter. And I saw, in a way I had never noticed be-fore—in the way that children never really notice their parents—how my father had focused his reading. His collection included a good selec-tion of literature on civil rights, biographies of important Black Ameri-cans, popular novels, opera librettos. This is what I remember as a child. But now there were also shelves and shelves of Greek and Roman classi-cal literature, mythology, and art; there were analyses of classical texts. I had forgotten that, after he retired, Dad started auditing classes in classical literature at a nearby university and continued until he had taken them all. There were also books and books of poetry, and books of poetics. And I remembered that after my son was born, Dad sent me Gabriela Mistral's poem "If You'll Only Go To Sleep"—the perfect poem for new parents. So as I packed for my return home that October, I included some books of classical Greek and Roman literature, books of poetry and poetics, and opera librettos, some thirty or forty librettos from his many trips to the opera.

That was the last time I ever saw my father alive.

A few weeks later, he died.

I have received many important gifts from my father—a good name, a respect for hard work, an understanding of work as mission, a sense of caring for family and friends, a love for our people. There are other gifts I am sure I don't recognize yet. But the gifts I have been thinking about since his death are the love of books and the love of music. I think about how he shared these treasures with me as a child and how they teach me, nourish me, bring me comfort today.

I know that Mom read to us kids all the time. Many years later, when she heard me read *The Runaway Bunny* to my son, she told me that I had made her read me that same book some two thousand times! But I have no recollection of this. My sole memory of a parent reading to me is of the time when Dad read *Black Beauty* to me and Kay at bedtime, one chapter at a time, and this is probably because Mom was there with us all the time, and Dad was not. I remember that Dad used to write short stories for us too. And I recall that there were always stacks of books everywhere—in the living room, in Dad's study, in boxes on the third floor. Evenings would find us all in the living room reading: there was no television in the house. Way back then the *New York Times* often published a poem on its editorial page. And sometimes, as we were sitting and reading together, Dad would be moved by a poem and read it out loud. (As a teenager, I found this mortifying: how easily are children embarrassed by their parents!) Later, when I went away to college, Dad told me that he would pay for any book I wanted from the Oberlin College bookstore. We were not wealthy, so this felt like quite a luxury to me.

My first memories of music with my father are from church, where we sometimes shared a hymnal and sang together. Dad often sang the tenor line, and, as I got older, I would try the alto. (When the church service got too long, he was the best companion, for he would pass notes with us kids, and play paper and pen games too.) I started piano lessons quite young, and loved it from the first. It was a language I recognized; it created a place where I could speak. Year after year, before I could go by myself, Mom took me on the bus through Harlem—across 125th Street, down Seventh Avenue, to Mr. Lawrence's apartment, for my piano lessons. She waited during my lesson, then we rode home together, my tired head leaning against her shoulder. When my parents decided to buy me a serious piano, Dad asked Altona, his adored elder sister, to come up to New York City and help us select it. Altona had played piano as long as Dad could remember. As an adult, she taught piano at the college level and gave piano recitals. So the four of us—Mom and Dad, me, and my aunt Altona—spent one whole day going from store to store. Altona sailed into each store majestically, then sat at piano after piano, playing thrilling fragments of music on each one, before declaring it not quite up to her standards. I still have the piano we picked out that day. Even now, when the piano tuner comes to my house, he never fails to comment on the beauty of the tone.

Music had been important in Dad's life—both in church and at home—since he was a child, and he shared his love of music with us. It must have been wonderful for him to be able to explore music in a new way, once we moved from the South to New York City, to the less-segregated North. And I have so many recollections of hearing music with him. I have memories of trips to the WQXR recording studio downtown, where a few guests were admitted free to watch the string quartet record its concert; I recall sitting outside at night on the hard concrete seats at Lewisohn Stadium for concerts for the New York Philharmonic (55¢ a ticket!); and I will never forget my tenth birthday gift from him—an evening at the Metropolitan Opera to see *Madame Butterfly*—just me and my dad alone. On Saturday afternoons, it didn't matter that there were two adults and three children in a four-room apartment: it was time for Milton Cross and the opera on the radio, and we children could only listen, not speak. Dad had stacks of records of spirituals by the choirs of the Black colleges, choirs we heard in concert on their annual trip to New York City. I played these records over and over, along with his records of sermons by the theologian Howard Thurman. I didn't like the modern chamber music we went to hear at Sarah Lawrence College, but I loved riding out into the snowy countryside to hear Christmas music at Sacred Heart Convent. And I especially enjoyed those rare summer Sundays when we would all get on the subway early in the morning, ride from Harlem to Penn Station, then take a train to Lenox, Massachusetts, where we arrived at the Tanglewood Music Festival just in time for the afternoon concert of the Boston Philharmonic. We ate our picnic lunch on a blanket on the lawn, basking in the sun, the greenery, and the music, then returned home by train that evening, tired and content.

So, now, after many years, during that last visit with my father, I brought home some of his books and some of his music. A few weeks later, on Thanksgiving Day, Mom and Dad went to the home of their friend Carrie for dinner. I have eaten at her home, so I can assure you that she served a feast, and that the food was delicious. Mom told me later that Dad ate a lot, and enjoyed both the food and the fellowship. The next day, he complained about feeling bad and said he wanted to go to the hospital. But Dad complained a lot those days, so Mom wasn't sure whether he really did need medical care. In an effort to distract him, in an effort to comfort him, she put on a video I had sent him earlier, a video of Jessye Norman and Kathleen Battle in concert, singing spirituals together. Finally, she took him to the hospital.

He died the next morning.

Dad would have enjoyed his funeral. He always liked a good party or family get-together: he loved to hug the women and tell stories with the men! And there was a lot of hugging and storytelling that day. There was also wonderful music. The Bennett Belles, a choral group from

Bennett College, sang first. Oh, how my father loved recalling his first
teaching position at Bennett, and how he loved the Bennett women!
Then his Omega brothers gathered around his casket and sang the
Omega hymn. They were all so beautiful, so dignified in their dark
suits, hands clasped behind their back: my heart broke in two at that moment. And, in between the eulogies, in between the stories that his
friends and colleagues told about him, we sang his favorite hymns—
"Amazing Grace," "Precious Lord, Take my Hand," "There Is a Balm
in Gilead." If it had been the funeral of one of his friends, he would have
wept, as we all wept. For he loved many people, and music touched him
deeply, opening him to his sorrow.

I wish I had recited a poem for my father that day, a poem which I
found later, marked, in one of his treasured books, *American Negro Poetry*. In that poem, James Weldon Johnson's "Go Down Death," Dad
had drawn a line around these words:

And Death took her up like a baby,
And she lay in his icy arms
But she didn't feel no chill.
And Death began to ride again—
Up beyond the evening star,
Out beyond the morning star,
Into the glittering light of glory,
On to the Great White Throne.
And there he laid Sister Caroline
On the loving breast of Jesus.

Six weeks after Dad's funeral, I packed two suitcases, mailed two
boxes of files, and flew to San Antonio, Texas, for a semester-long visit
to another law school, a visit I had planned many months earlier. I would
have to rent an apartment, furniture, and a car; learn my way around a
new town; make new friends. I had planned this visit because I felt a
need for adventure in my life, and I had been looking forward to living
in a part of the world where I would see new plants and birds, hear a different language, try new foods. But this was the wrong time for an adventure: the earth was shifting dangerously under my feet.

A colleague had warned me about the hazards of leaving home for
four months. "Visiting a strange place for a long time can be hard," she

said. "So take a picture from home with you, something beautiful, and familiar." I knew she was right. But instead of bringing a picture from my living room in Buffalo, I chose two books of poetry—one of Dad's books, *American Negro Poetry*, and one of mine, a collection of poems by Lucille Clifton. I also took a CD of Jessye Norman singing sacred music. And there in my two-room apartment in San Antonio during those four months, and still now, today, I played that sacred music again and again, and I read the poetry out loud, again and again. And I finally understood that without ever saying a word, my father had been telling me this all my life: "Cherish the music. Keep reading the books. They will see you through."

And they did.

Lurma M. Rackley

My "Real" Daddy's Girl

A month before my seventh birthday, my mother, my nine-year-old sister, and I got married. We stood in my grandparents' living room and joined our lives to a man I'd met three years before. At our wedding, he gave us each a ring. The ones for us girls held dainty, radiant birthstones standing high in their settings—aquamarine for my sister, diamond for me. They seemed the most precious gift in the world, at the very least equal in importance to Mama's plain gold band.

My sister, Jamelle, and I could hardly contain our excitement that day. Grandmother had not been as gleeful over the prospect of her daughter taking on a husband again and moving us to a town three hours away. So we had tried to subdue our joy in the weeks preceding our big day. But now it was done, and we bubbled over. We had a new last name, because our new daddy was legally adopting us, and we had our rings, making everything official. Yes, indeedy, we were on our way.

But not yet. We were in for a shocker less than an hour after the ceremony when Mama and Daddy gave us great big hugs and kisses and headed off *alone without us* to a honeymoon at Atlantic Beach, where Black people owned property and vacationed, on the other side of South Carolina's segregated Myrtle Beach. We stood, stunned, beside grandmother, mentally checking off the minutes before they would return and we could start our new life.

My new daddy was six feet, six and one-half inches tall, with smooth black skin, extremely dashing, and sharply dressed. All the little girls in our new elementary school wanted his attention. "Jump us up, Uncle Jack," they'd squeal in delight whenever he came to the small school on South Carolina State College's campus to drive us home. He'd oblige, tossing each one high in the air and catching her by the waist in a smooth motion that floated her back to earth. I'd watch with a mixture of pride and jealousy. They all loved him, but not as much as I did by then.

It hadn't always been that way. When I first saw him, I was four years old and crazy about my mother. Mama was attending Claflin College in Orangeburg, South Carolina, on weekdays and home with us at my grandparents' house on weekends. This week, she'd brought me back to school with her for a visit. She and I were sitting across from each other in a booth in a small café not far from campus one afternoon when the tallest man I'd ever seen walked in.

He walked right over to our booth and started kissing Mama from her fingertips right up along the arm she casually rested across the back of the booth. Like the Flash, I leaped from my side of the booth and in one motion, pushed the man's face away and snatched my mother's arm down, shoving it into her lap. "Now you keep your arm here," I demanded, and flounced back up into my seat, casting an "I dare you" glare at the stranger.

He laughed in a high-toned giggle I'd later come to cherish, and sat down next to Mama, but not too close. For Mama's sake and mine, he respected my jealousy and fear and need to protect her. He talked to me and studied me, as though he wanted to know me for me, not just because I was her daughter.

From that day on, he established himself as a loving adult who cared about me, who recognized my strengths and weaknesses, my faults and assets. And throughout my years with him, he found ways to create special bonds . . . routines for each person to share that tacitly excluded others.

After we moved to Orangeburg as a family, on Saturdays he and I were the two who got out of the house early to drive over to the campus to check the mailbox. Though my legs were too short to reach the pedals, he took delight in my interest in driving and would let me sit between his legs to steer when we reached our street; then, back at home, we'd wash the Pontiac and shine the chrome with a "shammy."

And when he noticed my penchant for holding onto a dollar, he started to be short on cash every now and then. "Hey, Puddin'," he'd call to me, walking into the bedroom I shared with my sister and our doll collection. "Could you lend me a dollar? I'll pay you back in one week, and if I don't, you add on a nickel for each day I'm late." He'd watch me mark the transaction on the calendar inside my closet door, and he'd purposely let the deadline slip so I could collect interest on the loan.

For one lesson though, I almost thought I'd never forgive him. He, like so many other fathers, took on the task of teaching me how to ride a bicycle. As I pedaled along the gravel road in front of my grandmother's house on a weekend visit, Daddy balanced the bike in back and listened to my nervous chatter.

Every few seconds, he'd grunt a response or throw in a word or two of encouragement. That is, until he decided I could do it without him, and he let go—but he didn't tell me! I was pedaling along quite well alone and jabbering away until I realized he hadn't answered me in more than a minute. I turned to look for his steadying hand and saw him about twenty feet behind me.

By the time he bounded over to the ditch I'd toppled into, I was screaming hysterically, a host of crickets and mosquitoes chirping noisily in the muddy rainwater around my ears. I spent the rest of the day sulking in my mother's lap; and this time, he did not insist that a big girl like me shouldn't whine and cling to her mother all day long. I forgave him when I mounted my bike the next day and discovered he was right: I *could* ride by myself.

As the years passed, Daddy taught us lessons that shaped our politics, our personalities, and our expectations of men. He washed our hair much more gently than Mama did; and he unquestioningly joined in the household chores. His Saturday routine was waxing and buffing the floors while Mama did the washing and we did the vacuuming and dusting. He'd inspect our work with a set of eagle eyes. "Ah, you didn't dust up here," he'd lightly scold, running his finger across the top of something like a doorway that I thought surely only a man of his height even knew existed.

My sister says she takes pride in her ironing to this day because Daddy praised the job she did on his shirts and took time to show her how to do them even better. I learned to polish and buff my shoes from sharing that chore with him. And from Mama and Daddy, I learned what an honor it was to be a woman.

The two of them prepared us for the changes that would occur in our bodies with frank talk, and discouraged premarital sex by discussing the serious consequences faced by girls we knew who'd had babies in their teens or had chosen abortion, which was illegal at the time. In fact, they made coming into womanhood such a grand notion, I could hardly wait to start my menstrual cycle. And when I did, at thirteen, I ran to tell Daddy the moment he returned home from a business trip. "Guess what happened while you were gone," I grinned, swinging a new sanitary napkin like a pendulum before him.

To my utter embarrassment, I found out a few weeks later that he'd shared that silly episode with his psychology class, as a way of showing how close fathers and daughters can be. He wanted his class to know that there was nothing about a girl's nature that should make her Daddy uncomfortable, and that she should know she could share all her secrets with him.

Typically, my sister and I have measured the men in our lives against the memory of the romantic love Daddy displayed unabashedly for Mama in those days. Even in the parking lot outside church after Sunday services, he'd kiss her sweetly on the lips before opening her door and seeing her seated inside.

Sometimes he'd put his hand on her legs or say something about her ample bosom in a code that was supposed to be above our heads. But we knew, and he didn't mind our knowing that he appreciated her in the way a man in love appreciates his woman. I never heard him say anything degrading about her, and when they disagreed on how to raise us, they discussed it in the privacy of their own bedroom. When we saw them, they presented a united front.

Sometimes people who knew us before Mama and Daddy married would ask us if we ever heard from our "real" daddy. I thought they were crazy. This was my *real* daddy. No other man could have, or did, love me more; no other man could have, or did, teach me better lessons, or show me a better model for a man-woman relationship.

Mama and Daddy divorced when I was fourteen, and he feared he would lose his relationship with us, I suppose because we had not been born to him. But it was a groundless fear. The bond he began with me from the moment we met has strengthened with each passing year.

Although my fifteen-year-old son understands the biological relationships in our family, he, too, knows who is my "real" daddy. So he's
planning to "take after" Granddaddy Jack and be at least six feet, six and
one-half inches tall. I'm hoping he also inherits my daddy's compassion,
loving spirit, and inherent gentleness . . . in case he's one day blessed to
have a little girl.

Beverly Guy-Sheftall

Confessions:
Remembering Walter P.

There are many roads to feminism. The path I chose was significantly affected by family experiences, something I came to realize long after I'd left home. While I have been aware of my mother's profound influence on my evolving gender consciousness for many years, it has taken much longer for me to see the connection between what I observed among my grandfathers, uncles, and father, most particularly, and my later involvement in efforts to empower women. At a time when gender relations within the African-American community are often fraught with difficulty, it is important to remember different narratives about growing up female within an extended family in the Deep South.

I was reared in Memphis, Tennessee, in the Jim and Jane Crow era, surrounded by hard-working women—very different women—and decent, hard-working men. My traditional, maternal grandmother, Etta Carmichael Varnado,* was a housewife who never worked outside the home. She reared five children with her Baptist minister husband, Willie Louis Varnado, who lived to be ninety. He was the patriarch of the family whom everyone respected, so much so that even when my mother's adult friends came to visit, they left their cigarettes in their purses. My paternal grandmother, Sadie Savage Guy, a grand old lady, taught third grade in a low-income Black neighborhood, cooked the best Sunday dinners, and taught me and my two sisters that life could be comfortable, even sweet. What we most looked forward to each year was an envelope on our birthdays which included a check matching our

---

* Seeing the 1996 movie *A Time To Kill*, which was set in Canton, Mississippi, my maternal grandparents' home, reminded me of my southern heritage and the centrality of race in shaping my worldview early on.

years written in the most beautiful handwriting by our grandfather, Walter Peabody Guy, Sr., a tailor and businessman. Grandmother was proud of her father, Fred Savage, a shoemaker with a business on Beale Street and a member of the Memphis Board of Education in the 1880s.*

My mother, Ernestine Varnado Guy, an accountant, left my father, Walter P. Guy, Jr., a schoolteacher and commercial artist, when I was in the eighth grade, moved back with her parents, never remarried, and raised her three daughters to be self-reliant and resourceful. I am sure that living with a single mother who got inadequate financial support from my father, though he was available for pick-ups and loved his daughters in his own way, had much to do with the kind of adult woman I would become.

My mother's three sisters were an important part of the circle of women who surrounded us as well; in retrospect, I now realize how much they defied easy categories. Lillian, my mother's best friend, was a housewife and considered motherhood a woman's most important responsibility (she reared six children with a husband whose work as a college president was his life). She was sturdy, in control of her household, and had a mind of her own. Growing up, there was nothing I liked better than visiting Aunt Wynn and Uncle Levi's house, eating hot dogs and navy beans on Friday evening, and watching her take care of business, efficiently and with compassion. Her six and my mother's three were taught to be responsible, excel in school, and that we could always depend on family. Aunt Pearl, my mother's oldest sister, taught in a poor, rural segregated school in Meridian, Mississippi, worked very hard, lived in an extended family with her husband's (Uncle James's) family and daughter, and understood at a profound level the ravages of racism in the Deep South. Aunt Doris was married to a sweet, nurturing man (all the nieces fantasized about having a husband like Uncle Frank when we grew up); she worked alongside him in his family business in Jackson, Mississippi, lived comfortably, and convinced me, vicariously, that marriage was a viable option—if you could find someone like Uncle Frank.

My journey as a feminist began rather abruptly when I was eleven

---

* I've learned from Paula Giddings, who's completing a biography of Ida Wells [Barnett], that my great-grandfather was also a close friend of Wells in Memphis and that he was also an outspoken political activist.

years old, I now realize. On a particular day in 1957, my two sisters, Carmella and Francine, father, and I arrived back home from school to find an empty house. My mother had moved us around the corner with her parents without informing any of us. Memories of that traumatic day are still painful, but also a reminder of my mother's courage during a time when there was a stigma attached to being middle-class, female, and divorced.* Though I revisited through the years the conversation my mother would have with her three daughters later that evening after my father deposited us at our new home, I did not think much about what I learned from my father's response that day. He was calm, did not express any anger, and arrived dutifully the following morning at my grandparents' home, as he would until all of us left for college, to drive us to school where he also taught. My father never engaged us in a conversation about that day as we were growing up, but years later (my mother was sixty-two and he was seventy-three and suffering from kidney disease), when I informed him that Mama had succumbed to breast cancer, he cried (this was the first time I had seen him shed tears) and recalld how painful it had been to "lose" us in that way.

Though I would have preferred growing up in the kind of two-parent household which all my cousins and most of my childhood friends experienced, what I remember about Walter P. (as he was affectionately called at Manassas High School) was his devotion to his work and his easy temperament. He was uncontrolling, never raised his voice at home (even when he was probably angry), and insisted that men, even fathers, had no right, under any circumstances to be physical with females. All the spankings we got as children, therefore, came from my mother. A particular incident stands out in my mind with respect to his abhorrence and intolerance of men who hit women. One afternoon while we were in high school, my father was informed by another teacher that Carmella's boyfriend had hit her, at which point my father ran like a bolt of lightning to where they were and proceeded to pounce on the young man and scream at him that he was totally out of order. The young man attempted to restrain my father by explaining that my sister had angered him by talking to another male and that his punishment was justified, at which point my father informed him that he had

---

* My parents actually never divorced. Instead, my mother filed for a legal separation.

never "laid hands" on any of his daughters even when they needed discipline and that there was nothing any woman could do that would justify her being hit.

When I became aware of the reality of domestic violence much later, I was shocked because I had grown up in two households (my father's and my grandfather's) in which I hadn't even heard men raising their voices at woman, not to mention striking them. This was also the case in the homes of my aunts and uncles. I was utterly unprepared, therefore, for my first and only experience with abusive behavior which culminated in violence when I was forty-one, divorced, and deeply involved with feminism. It included the theft and burning of my car, stalking, assault, burglary, and, perhaps worst of all, putting my name and phone number with a lewd message in public telephone booths throughout the city. A year of terrorism—during which I was in and out of court with this seemingly passive and harmless college professor who was finally convicted of arson—forced me to confront at a very visceral level the possibility that I might not, in fact, survive. For the first time in my life, I understood what it meant to be vulnerable and in danger. Throughout the year, I thought about my gentle father constantly, and why I couldn't share with him what I was experiencing. I was afraid that he might come to Atlanta and do something terrible to his daughter's friend turned enemy. Because of the way my father had always dealt with me when he was displeased, I assumed that people who cared about each other dealt with their problems rationally. I remembered one time in particular when I cut some classes in school that instead of scolding me, he told me calmly that I was only hurting myself. He reminded me that thousands of people throughout the world would give almost anything to get an education, and that I was only throwing away a precious gift. I felt very bad, worse than I would have felt if he had chastised me, and as a result I never cut another high school class. Men who bothered to notice came to understand that appealing to my analytical bent was the way to negotiate differences.

Though my father had many flaws (as we all do), he didn't expect his daughters to see the world as he did. He didn't require blind obedience from the three of us or deference from my mother. He was not manipulative or obtrusive, nor did he expect us to take care of him. He didn't dote on us. We were not "Daddy's girls." When we were young, he required very little of us—that we obey our mother, do well in school, and refrain from chewing gum and wearing red lipstick! Though later in his life he was disappointed that none of his daughters had children and two of us were divorced, I overheard him bragging to the nurses at his dialysis unit that we had degrees instead of husbands and babies.

Because I embrace feminism, I am often assumed to have had negative relations with men. On the contrary, feminism has been an easier road to travel, for paradoxical reasons, because of my father. Because he was not domineering, I've always known that men are not inherently controlling. There was also much I didn't have to unlearn. For example, because my father was stingy—he never remembered our birthdays or gave us very much—I didn't expect to be taken care of by men. Over time, I forgave my father for being irresponsible in the provider category, though he worked very hard, and finally came to realize this was probably why my mother left him. The house we lived in was delapidated but not because my father was poor. I begain to understand that he was a free spirit who probably should not have married in the first place. He spent several summers working on the railroad in Canada and was there when one of us was born; I loved to hear him speaking French and telling "on the road" stories, and hoped that I would grow up and travel around the world too. He owned a neighborhood sundry store and left school everyday to work there, including weekends, which he clearly enjoyed better than coming home. He also expressed his creativity by decorating houses during the Christmas season—but not ours.

Because his strengths lay elsewhere, I came to appreciate him for other reasons. His greatest gift to me was what I came to admire in him as a teacher. He taught art for over forty years in the same public school classroom and never missed a day! Never ambitious, he believed that the greatest satisfaction one can get out of life if helping someone gain knowledge. During my first year at Spelman, I wrote an essay for a composition class entitled "People I Remember," in which I paid tribute to my father and voiced my desire to become a high school teacher. I indicated that when I grew up, I wanted to be as devoted to my work as he had been. I also came to judge my father less harshly when I caught glimpses of him as a surrogate father to many of his students. After he died, one of his students, Wiley Henry (also an artist), wrote "Homage to Walter Guy" which was published in the Memphis *Tri-State De-fender*. He captured the role at which my father was best—not husband or parent, but teacher:

> The first day in art class, a short, stocky framed yellow man stood at the head of the class to announce his presence as a serious instructor who sought to help those who were willing to follow his lead. From my view he stood tall as a mighty oak. He said his name was Mr. Guy— Walter P. Guy, Jr. . . . The first year in Mr. Guy's class was quite rewarding. The creativity I felt inside me was running over . . . with little control. . . . Mr. Guy recognized my budding talent and began to develop and cultivate it. All the doodling and drawing I had done was not enough to please this stern instructor. He worked closely with his students on a variety of projects day after day, after school and even during a much needed lunch period. . . . and held his ground as a fair, impartial art teacher whose genuine concern was to set his students on their journey to new heights in the art world. He gave me insight and direction. All that was in me was rechanneled and redirected. . . . for he knew that many Black artists came to recognize their talent, but fell short of the mark that inevitably caused their failure. Mr. Guy's shoes are too large to fill. . . . Thanks, Mr. Guy, for being there when it mattered the most. . . .

At age fifty, I now realize that I am my father's child, though we are also different. Teaching, though not always in the classroom, is probably what I do best. It is difficult for me to express anger even when I am very upset. I have wanderlust, a free spirit, and resist being controlled. I probably should not have married. I love art and people who are creative.

Now when I am asked what led me to feminism, I say it was my mother and my father.

devorah major

A Line of Storytellers

I could fall asleep anywhere when I was a child. If I was tired I could curl up in the corner of a stranger's sofa, doze off leaning against an overstuffed armchair, catnap in the back seat of a car, or snooze, chin couched in hand, at my school desk. Sleeping, then or now, was rarely a problem for me. That is, I could fall asleep anywhere if I was tired. If I wasn't sleepy, my eyes stayed open, and my mind concocted all kinds of tales. I saw mythological beings in the cracks on my walls, and landscapes in the shadows on the ceiling. Most of the time I could amuse myself with the scenery of darkness until, minutes or hours later, I dozed off to sleep. But for some reason, on this particular night, I would not fall asleep.

My father ran our house. What he said, went. My mother was ever present and certainly had some skill as a negotiator, but my father's temperament, or more accurately temper, my father's height and the lightening way his growl could catch you at your throat and squeeze tight your windpipe before that sass you were planning to say got all the way out of your brain and onto your tongue, as well as my father's undeniable intelligence, which over the years has mellowed into a wide swath of salt and pepper wisdom, made him the absolute ruler of our domain. When my brother and I suggested that the democratic principles which he espoused should be a part of our household, my father explained the idea of a dictatorship. Then he put the notion of benevolent in front of the idea of dictatorship. Then he put his name in back of that to complete the thought. The world needed democracy, but our home was a dictatorship and he was the dictator. There were no votes. There was only the possibility of getting a hearing. I believe this is where the idea of benevolent came in.

Which is to say that bedtime was bedtime. You didn't pout. You didn't whine. If you had anything negative to say about it, you could scream your head off, as long as it was inside your imagination. If you wanted to stay up more than five minutes longer, you could forget about it. Bedtime was bedtime.

This night it was past bedtime. It was way past bedtime. I went to bed as told, without voiced complaint. I had been in bed for hours. I had gone over my day and planned the upcoming weekend with several variations in the way it could go. I had spent time reconsidering the possibilities of finding a real pathway to Oz, the imaginary land I went to live in whenever San Francisco realities left me feeling lonely and abandoned. I had gone over some of the characters I would meet were I to find the particular sewer cover, windstorm, or hot air balloon that would carry me to that wonderland. I decided that even though Tic Toc had a nice sense of humor, he still didn't seem to be all that warm a friend. I definitely felt like Ozma had a lot more going for her than the very rotund and obviously recycled tin man. I had tried, unsuccessfully, to transform a particular paint crack in the wall from a foreboding witch into any number of more peaceable ideas, an upside-down flower, a tree by a river, a horse. The crack obstinately insisted on remaining a scary witch. I turned my back on her and looked at the slats under my brothers bunk. I counted them frontwards and then backwards and then frontwards again. I counted up the number of friends I had, less than five, and then the number of almost friends. I counted the people I wanted to be friends with until I realize that I was still wide awake. My older brother was fast asleep, but my parents were not. They were playing jazz albums in the living room. Someone was visiting and all the adults were laughing and having a good time, a much better time than me, laying in bed, eyes opened, toes wiggling, and heart racing. I had dilemma. I was bored, a painful hazard of childhood. I was bored and ready for action. It was time to get up! But then, bedtime was bedtime. Bedtime was absolute. Bedtime was inviolate.

What could I do? I got up. I mean I had done everything I could do to make myself fall asleep, and everything had failed. I got up and went into the living room. I was depending on my little girl cuteness, and the presence of company, to save me from too harsh a rebuke. I was a sickly child and my getting up because of problems breathing or a low-grade fever was not unusual. As soon as I reached the living room door my mother began to make a fuss over me. Was I sick? Did I feel alright? What was the matter? The matter was that I could not sleep. Being awake seemed more fun. Being up very late, which was then and remains today one of my favorite pastimes, seemed full of enticing possibilities. "I can't sleep," I muttered hoping that my soft voice and doe eyes would charm my father once again. "I'm not tired. I tried to fall asleep." I kept the stream of words trickling out of my mouth as I crawled into my father's lap. It worked. He did not rage. Instead he held me gently expecting, I am sure, that a few minutes resting against his rumbling chest would cause me to doze off and get my "sweet little girl" reward of being carried back to my bed.

But I stayed awake, wide awake. Time passed and I was still wide awake. This would not do. Bedtime was bedtime. It was way past my bedtime. My father carried my very awake, and quietly protesting self back to bed. Then he sat on the edge of the bed and began to tell me a story. It was a story about a little girl who wouldn't go to sleep. I began to join in the story telling. It wasn't just one night that she wouldn't go to sleep. No it was a lot more, it was days and days. She wouldn't go to sleep for weeks. My father added details. I added color. He created plot turns and turned her mischief into drama. Finally, I believe, the little girl fell into a dead sleep right in the middle of the sidewalk on her way to or from school. I don't remember how she escaped her predicament, but I remember being relieved that my father and I had gotten her home safely. She found her bed and from that day on she went to sleep when she was supposed to go to sleep. In fact, she looked forward to bedtime and sometimes went without being told. When we finished telling each other the story my father leaned down and gave me a kiss and told me it was time for me to go to sleep. Our smiles were moonlight on the shadows in the room. The witch on the wall turned into a starburst as I snuggled under the covers and he stood up.

"But what about our story?" I remember asking.

"I'll type it up," he answered hovering in the doorway, well aware that I was trying to stall his exit.

"Really?"

"Goodnight," he laughed and closed the door behind him. I must have fallen asleep a few minutes after that.

Now the promise to type our story was a serious promise. After all, my father was a real writer, a real writer. He had a room with a desk, a big black Royal typewriter, and shelves and shelves of books. Sometimes people paid him for his words, which proved to outsiders that he was a *real* writer. He shared his workroom with my mother who had an easel, never quite dry oil paints, and finished and unfinished canvases all over the walls. My mother was a *real* painter. I was an ordinary child. I drew for fun. I wrote in school and it was fun. I wasn't a painter and I certainly wasn't a writer. A few days later, as promised, my father showed me our story. He had typed it up and added even more details. It was wonderful, and it was written by him and me.

After that we didn't write together. He went about in his very adult world which included working, battling with the world and his family, and writing until close to dawn more days than not. I was in my child's world which was often lonely and full of the quiet pains that many children, especially colored children, carry and do not share with their parents. I mean why, what can adults do about it anyway? I grew into dance and drama. I was going to be one of the great Negro actresses of the stage. I was going to be one of San Francisco's first Negro prima ballerinas.

My father continued to write, publishing a story here and an article there. My head became incredibly hard at the same time as my body became quite shapely. In that period I also mastered the act of not hearing what I did not want to hear. I became a teenager, and an inevitable gulf came between my father and me. He bridged the gulf with letters. When I protested his decisions over *my* life, my father wrote to me. He wrote his reasoning, he wrote his concern, and he wrote his love. I can't truly say I appreciated all of his logic at that time. But I appreciated the work, the effort of page after page after page of thoughts pointed at me, crafted for me.

In time I began to write too. I left home and wrote long letters back. I had lovers and wrote letters full of gush and passion and poems full of sugar and thorns. I got into arguments, and when I couldn't get through to someone else I wrote. I remembered the power of words. I remembered the magic of language. I remembered my father's letters. And when I had a little girl, I remembered the story that he and I wrote together.

I never planned to be a writer. I planned to be a dancer and actress.

My mother was the painter. My brother the photographer, and briefly, filmmaker. My father was the writer. Years later writing swallowed me up like the ocean taking a cast-off soda bottle, breaking it into pieces, and smoothing out the edges until it became jewels to return to the sand. Years later I learned to swim in words, learned to breathe under the water of their weight. Years later I became a writer too. And now, I am my father's daughter, a storyteller come down from a line of storytellers.

Carolyn M. Rodgers

For Our Fathers

The wind blew my father from the south to the north.
He came with a heart as deep and as wide as a tunnel—
he came with a dream and a hope for a beautiful harmonious future.
He came, Daddy was a prayer, a jitterbug hymn and a collard /
cornbread sweet potato / green country psalm . . .

    the city sifted him like wheat from chaff
    like corn from husks, and the wind that blew
    him here blew him down, blew him around, while
    the flashing lights glazed his eyes and rechanneled
    his heart in a new direction. He became a new dimension.

He learned how to lock and close doors and bar windows. He bought dogs
not for love, but for protection. He learned to carry guns not for harmless
hunting but for restraining men. He learned how to be cool, not country,
to be stiff and serious and silent. Laughter was reserved for home and
homebodies, home folk. He was a tree, with cautious and displaced roots,
walking the streets with feet that hurt, with feet too big for computerized
shoes that tapped the rhythm of concrete, and not the loving crush of
green grass.

2.

    ever since my father been
      here wid me
    his feets has hurt him
they been tired and flat wid a crop of corns
      feet kept daddy out of the wars
    and he was glad
      when he went for his examination
    he say the white man told him everything was wrong wid

his feet
they was in such bad shape.
my daddy say he told the white man "ain't nothin wrong
wid my feets, except they 'smart' a lot
they was born hurting and tired and flat.
cause they knows so much history . . ."

The history, the root, the strength of my father is the strength we now
rest on.

Like rocks, our fathers and their brothers came and sweated
in factories, prowled the streets for day labor and pennies for their
expensive food. They stayed with their children or pawned them
out to loving Big Mamas or Big Daddys and their card-playing
and drinking was their balm in an evil Gilead. They had a sense of
a portion of honor in them, their God was their strength, their
pride, their purpose, their faith . . .
And no one had to tell them they were Black/they graced their
mirrors every morning . . . and did what they could
to retain some love, some dignity, some honor, while they lost
their sons to wild city streets and wars, their women to white men's
kitchens and corners.
They gave to us a portion of their grace, they gave to us
a legacy of hope, they pushed us out, us kicking and screaming,
through rapacious schools, hoping that somehow an education
for us would right the wrongs for them.
And we grew loud and bold and stupidly brave and taught
ourselves with Marx and Mills to call them weak and useless, as the
holocaust of the sixties began.
We blamed them for surviving, we blamed them for living as
best they
could, we blamed them for what history did not allow
them
or even us to do — never remembering that the
love
we had for ourselves was the love they gave us.

3.
When I was a child my father was the fix-it man
everything that went wrong in our house my father could fix
I thought my father could fix everything.
           I grew and learned sorrow . . .
    I had a puppy, and because we had rats in our house
           my mother laid poisoning on our bare part-dirt, part-
    linoleum floors. And my puppy, being animal, being curious,
           being stupid, ate the poison and died.
Was the poison really for the rat, was it for the dog, or was it
           for us . . . the Black niggers caught in the dirty
                misery constrained ghetto?
    The puppy died; and mama tried to throw him out.
But I was a child, a child who believed in daddy, big Black daddy,
           the fix-it man, and I would not let mama throw my puppy
           away
     because *I believed that when my daddy came home*
           from work he could fix that dead dog.
I was a child, a Black child who believed in a Black man.
                the sixties stripped us of such a love and trust.
    and we ran naked in the streets, changing our hair, our food,
our God, our dress, condemning our elders and screaming obscenities
           at each other and others—in the name of "revolution," in
the name of positive change.
                we stripped ourselves of our heritage, of tradition,
of the strength of old wise men who were our cushions of love,
                who gave us extravagant care, who were our rocks
in this weary land.

4.
           Now, I am no longer a child, I have tasted sorrow.
                only, in these last few hours, these last immutable days,
    I have seen my father's son, my brother, shot down in the night
           by Blackmen, wearing naturals no doubt, Blackmen molded in
                the model of Shaft.
    And I have seen my father's heart, that funnel of love turn into a
                sieve of dust . . .

And at my brother's graveside I watched my father, your father,
   all our fathers sit, stiff and strong, brave and proud and
   ramrodded in grief, I saw our sons and brothers . . .
     I saw the Jesus in my father's hands, saw the wino in his
feet turned out like shuffle, saw the doctor, lawyer, preacher
     in his face, saw the construction worker in his back,
   saw his actual hair turn white and gray, saw him fold into
     himself his body limp like some autumn leaf opening
and closing in the beating rain I saw him and all our fathers
    and knew. We must look at our old men, look to them
for strength, for knowledge, for direction and learn what they have
   always known. That love and *respect is our*
beginning. Love and respect is our end. We must learn how
   to love, to protect, to cherish, our young, our old, our
     own.

Credits

Excerpt from *Notes from a Native Son* by James Baldwin. Copyright 1955, renewed 1984 by James Baldwin. Reprinted by permission of Beacon Press.

"My Father's House" by Don Belton. Reprinted from *Wrestling with the Angel,* edited by Brian Bouldrey. Copyright 1995 by Brian Bouldrey. Reprinted by permission of the author.

Excerpt from *Report from Part I* from *Selected Poems* by Gwendolyn Brooks. Copyright 1972 by Gwendolyn Brooks. Reprinted by permission of the author.

Excerpt from *A Taste of Power* by Elaine Brown. Copyright 1994 by Elaine Brown. Reprinted by permission of Pantheon Books, a division of Random House, Inc.

Excerpt from *Sweet Summer: Growing Up With and Without My Dad* by Bebe Moore Campbell. Copyright 1989 by Bebe Moore Campbell. Reprinted by permission of The Putnam Publishing Group.

"forgiving my father" from *Good Woman: Poems and a Memoir* by Lucille Clifton. Copyright by Lucille Clifton. Reprinted with the permission of BOA Editions, Ltd.

"A Little Bit of Soap" from *You Don't Miss Your Water* by Cornelius Eady. Copyright 1995 by Cornelius Eady. Reprinted by permission of Henry Holt & Co.

Excerpt from *Laughing in the Dark* by Patricia Gaines. Copyright 1994 by Patricia Gaines. Reprinted by permission of Crown Publishing Group, Inc.

Excerpt from *Wayward Child* by Addison Gayle. Copyright by Addison Gayle. Reprinted by permission of Marie Brown Associates, Inc.

"The World According to Claude" by Anthony Walton first appeared in *Reader's Digest*. Reprinted by permission of the author.

"Eulogy" by Cornel West. Reprinted from *Faith of Our Fathers* edited by Andre C. Willis. Copyright 1996 by Andre C. Willis.

Excerpt from *Fatheralong* by John Wideman. Copyright 1995 by John Edgar Wideman. Reprinted by permission of Pantheon Books, a division of Random House, Inc.

Contributors

OPAL PALMER ADISA is a poet and novelist whose works have appeared in numerous journals in the United States, Canada, and Jamaica and in several anthologies. She is the author of *Tamarind and Mango Women, traveling women,* and *Bake-Face and Other Guava Stories.* She has taught at San Francisco State and the University of California, Berkeley.

LIONEL ARNOLD, who earned degrees from Thiel College, Harvard University, and Drew University, worked for many years at LeMoyne College, where he was professor of philosophy, college pastor, and dean, and later at Oklahoma State University, where he was professor of humanities and religion. Since his retirement, he has participated in work camps in a number of countries, among them Germany and Ethiopia; traveled extensively in Europe, Asia, Africa, South America, and Latin America; and worked with Habitat for Humanity in Paris County, Oklahoma.

HOUSTON A. BAKER, JR., is a nationally recognized scholar whose many articles and books are considered major contributions to scholarship on Black literature and culture. His most recent books are *Black Studies, Rap, and the Academy* and *Blues Journey Home,* a volume of poetry. Baker is director of the Center for the Study of Black Literature and Culture at the University of Pennsylvania.

JAMES BALDWIN, who gained national prominence in the sixties and seventies for compelling essays on race in America, is one of the most studied of African-American writers. In addition to essays, he wrote plays, short stories, and novels. A prolific writer, he authored nine books, most celebrated among them *The Fire Next Time* and *Nobody Knows My Name* (essays); *Go Tell It On the Mountain* and *Another Country* (novels); and *Blues for Mister Charley* (a play). Baldwin died in Paris, where he spent most of his life as an expatriot.

DON BELTON, a native of Philadelphia, is author of *Almost Midnight* and editor of *Speak My Name: Black Men on Masculinity and the American Dream*. A former reporter for *Newsweek*, he has been a fellow at MacDowell, Yaddo, and the Rockefeller Center in Bellagio, Italy. He currently teaches at Bennington College and is working on a new memoir.

GEORGENE BESS teaches English at Georgia Southern University in Statesboro, Georgia. She is currently completing her doctorate at the University of Maryland in College Park.

GAIL BOWMAN, a graduate of Harvard Law School, practiced law in Washington, D.C., until she received the call to ministry. An ordained minister with a masters of divinity from Howard University, she is College Minister at Spelman College.

CHARLIE R. BRAXTON is a poet, playwright, and free-lance journalist who lives in Hattiesburg, Mississippi. His poetry has appeared in various magazines and journals, among them *Catalyst*, *Drum Voices*, and *Black American Literature Forum*.

FLORA WILSON BRIDGES, who teaches religion at Spelman College, is the founding pastor of the Amistad United Church of Christ in Atlanta, Georgia. A doctoral candidate at Vanderbilt University, she is writing a dissertation on systematic theology with a concentration in African-American spirituality.

GWENDOLYN BROOKS was the first African-American woman to receive a Pulitzer and the first to be named Consultant-in-Poetry at the Library of Congress. She is a prolific writer, having authored over twenty books, including many volumes of poetry, a novel, and two memoirs.

ELAINE BROWN is the author of the controversial and celebrated autobiography, *A Taste of Power*, which chronicles her rise to leadership in the Black Panther Party. She lives in Atlanta, where she is raising funds for a school for Black children.

DILLA BUCKNER earned her doctorate at Rutgers University and has been actively involved as a planner and participant in conferences, programs, and projects that advance excellence in English at historically Black colleges. Currently chair of the humanities division at Tougaloo College, she is conducting research on representations of the South in Black autobiography.

BEBE MOORE CAMPBELL is the author of the very popular autobiography, *Sweet Summer: Growing Up With and Without My Dad*, and two novels, one of which, *Your Blues Ain't Like Mine*, won the NAACP Image Award for fiction. She is a contributing editor at *Essence* magazine and a regular commentator on National Public Radio.

REBECCA CARROLL is the author of *I Know How the Red Clay Feels: The Voice and Vision of Black Women Writers* and *Swing Low: Black Men Writing*. A W. E. B. Du Bois Fellow at Harvard University, she is currently at work on a social theory book on the politics of Black American beauty.

CHERYL CLARKE is a poet and educator whose works have appeared in a number of publications, among them *Home Girls: A Black Feminist Anthology*, *This Bridge Called My Back: Writings by Radical Women of Color*, and *Persistent Desire: A Femme-Butch Reader*. She is the author of four volumes of poetry, the most recent of which, *Humid Pitch*, was nominated for the 1994 Lambda Award for Poetry.

LUCILLE CLIFTON is Poet Laureate of the state of Maryland and author of four volumes of poetry and one prose memoir. Her many distinctions and awards include the University of Massachusetts Juniper Prize, a nomination for the Pulitzer Prize in poetry, and an Emmy Award from the American Academy of Television Arts and Sciences.

KATIE LEE CRANE is an ordained Unitarian Universalist minister who lives and writes from "The Ark" in Somerville, Massachusetts, where there are two adults, two children, two cats, two TVs, two toasters and, more often than not, a flood in the basement.

MIRIAM DECOSTA-WILLIS—a daughter and mother, teacher and writer, feminist and racialist—is professor of African-American Studies at the University of Maryland, Baltimore County, where she teaches African, Caribbean, Afro-Hispanic, and African-American literature. She has edited or co-edited six books, including *Blacks in Hispanic Literature*, *Erotique Noire/Black Erotica*, *The Memphis Diary of Ida B. Wells*, and the forthcoming *Singular Like a Bird: The Art of Nancy Morejon*.

TOI DERRICOTTE is a well-known poet whose works have been widely anthologized. She is the author of four books of poetry, including *Captivity* and the highly applauded *Natural Birth*, and the recipient of many honors and awards. She is tenured associate professor of English at the University of Pittsburgh.

ANTHONY DORSEY, an honor graduate of Hampton University, Hampton, Virginia, and a teacher in the city of Atlanta, recently earned a master's degree in educational administration at Georgia State University. He is a native of New Jersey.

MARCIA DYSON is president of Speak Easy, Inc., a national lecture manage-
ment agency and editor-in-chief of *Voices* magazine, a forthcoming publication
for young African-American women. She makes her home in Durham, North
Carolina.

CORNELIUS EADY is the author of several volumes of poetry. He teaches English at S.U.N.Y. at Stony Brook.

ELLEN FINCH, the mother of seven children, is an independent scholar of
Kemetic culture with an emphasis on women's rituals and spiritual powers.
With a bachelor's degree in premed from Mount Holyoke College, she is enrolled in the College of Health Science at Georgia State University where she
is preparing to embark on a career in midwifery.

WALTER FLUKER, an ordained Baptist minister, is dean of Black studies and
the Martin Luther King, Jr., Memorial Professor of Theology at Colgate Rochester Divinity School/Bexley Hall/Crozer Theological Seminary in Rochester,
New York. A featured speaker at churches and universities, he is the author of
*They Looked for a City: A Comparative Analysis of the Ideal Community in the
Thought of Howard Thurman and Martin Luther King, Jr.* and editor of the forthcoming *The Sound of Genuine: The Papers of Howard Thurman.*

PATRICE GAINES, a journalist at the *Washington Post*, is a member of a team of
reporters nominated for a Pulitzer Prize in commentary. She is the author of an
autobiography entitled *Dancing in the Darkness: From Colored Girl to Woman of
Color: A Journey From Prison to Power.*

ADDISON GAYLE was a leading voice in the Black aesthetic movement of the
seventies and a recognized scholar on the Black American protest novel. His
books, chief among them *The Black Aesthetic* and *The Way of the New World*, are
frequently referenced in today's scholarship.

THADDEUS GOODAVAGE (a pseudonym) is a free-lance writer whose complete
essay "Are You My Father?" first appeared in *Faith of Our Fathers: African-
American Men Reflect on Fatherhood*, edited by Andre Willis.

SANDRA Y. GOVAN is a poet and critic whose work has appeared in *Erotique
Noire, Sexual Politics, Langston Hughes: The Man, His Art and His Continuing Influence*, and *My Soul Is a Witness*. An associate professor at the University of
North Carolina at Charlotte, she is completing a book on the fiction of Oc-
tavia Butler.

BEVERLY GUY-SHEFTALL is a nationally recognized Black feminist scholar
who has pioneered studies in several areas. In the late seventies she was coeditor

of *Sturdy Black Bridges*, the first anthology of Black women's literature; in the early eighties, she was founding director of the first Women's Resource and Research Center housed at a historically Black college, and founding co-editor of *SAGE: A Scholarly Journal on Black Women*, the only journal in the world devoted exclusively to the experiences of women of African descent; and in 1995, she edited *Words of Fire*, the first anthology ever published of African-American feminist thought. The author of three other books and many articles, she is the Anna Julia Cooper Professor of English and Women's Studies at Spelman College.

PETER J. HARRIS, a graduate of Howard University, is a poet, teacher, and writer of short fiction. He is the author of *Hand Me Down My Griot Clothes, The Autobiography of Junior Baby*, and *Whenever Dreams Live*, a book of original Kwanzaa folktales. He is founding editor of *Genetic Dances*, a magazine on Black fatherhood and editor/publisher of *The Drumming Between Us: Black Love and Erotic Poetry*. Harris lives in Los Angeles.

JENNIFER HICKS, a graduate of Meharry Medical College, is a practicing gynecologist in Vicksburg, Mississippi.

LANGSTON HUGHES, who began publishing during the Harlem Renaissance, wore many hats as a writer. He was columnist, playwright, editor of anthologies, poet, novelist, and creator of Jesse B. Semple, a satiric character. He was a prolific writer, producing several volumes of poetry, eight anthologies, and two autobiographies.

THEODORE JENNINGS, a native of St. Louis, is a second-year student at Oberlin College, where he majors in economics and Japanese.

TAYARI A. JONES, a graduate of Spelman College and the University of Iowa, is a free-lance writer whose forthcoming book is *Am I the Last Virgin? African-American Women on Race and Sexuality*. She lives in Texas, where she teaches first-year composition at Prairie View University.

DOLORES KENDRICK, a nationally recognized poet, is the author of three volumes of poetry, *Now Is the Time to Praise, Through the Ceiling*, and the highly celebrated *The Women of Plums*, which won the Anisfield-Wolf award and which inspired the opera *The Killing Fields*, two theatre productions, and a CD. Kendrick is the recipient of fellowships and awards from the National Endowment for the Arts, the Yaddo Writers' Colony, and the Fulbright program. She lives in Washington, D.C.

JAKE LAMAR is the author of a memoir, *Bourgeois Blues*, and a novel, *The Last Integrationist*. He is a well-known journalist who writes for the *New York Times*.

PINKIE GORDON LANE is a prolific poet whose writings earned her the distinction of Poet Laureate of the State of Louisiana. She has served as artist in residence at the University of Northern Iowa and as a Du Pont scholar at Bridgewater College, Virginia. She is the author of four volumes of poetry.

AUDRE LORDE, one of the most anthologized and quoted of contemporary Black women writers, authored thirteen books, among them *The Black Unicorn*, *Cancer Journals*, and *Zami: A New Spelling of My Name*. Founding member of Kitchen Table Women of Color Press and active participant in various movements for justice, she has been recognized as a pioneer in Black feminist lesbian thought.

DEVORAH MAJOR is an actress, a dancer, and a writer whose poetry and short fiction have been widely anthologized. She is the author of *street smarts*, a volume of poetry, and *An Open Weave*, a novel. She resides in San Francisco, where she performs in clubs, theaters, and cultural centers. She is currently working on her second novel.

MANNING MARABLE is professor of history and director of the Institute for Research in African-American Studies at Columbia University. He is the author of four books, among them *How Capitalism Underdeveloped Black America* and *Beyond Black and White: Transforming African-American Politics*.

LEE MAY is a feature editor at the *Atlanta Constitution* and author of the memoir, *In My Father's Garden*.

Before his sudden death in October of 1996, SCOTT MINERBROOK was an *Emerge* contributing editor and *U.S. News and World Report* associate editor. His book, *Divided to the Vein: A Journey into Race and Family*, will be published by Harcourt Brace in 1997. He was the father of two sons.

LENARD D. MOORE, a native of North Carolina, is founder and executive director of The Carolina African American Writers' Collective and the founding publisher of *Earlobe*. While he is best known for his book *Forever Home*, his poems, essays, and reviews have appeared in a number of magazines, newspapers, and anthologies.

ITABARI NJERI, journalist and poet, is the author of *Every Good-bye Ain't Gone*, which won the National Book Award.

BETTYE PARKER-SMITH, an educator, lecturer, and critic, is recognized for her pioneering work in scholarship on African-American women writers. In addition to being published in a number of journals, she coedited *Sturdy Black*

Bridges: Visions of Black Women in Literature, the first anthology of contemporary Black women writers. She lives in Tampa, where she serves as vice president and senior program officer for the Florida Education Fund.

ALBERT RABOTEAU is Henry W. Putnam Professor of Religion at Princeton University and is former dean of the graduate school at Princeton. He has received honorary degrees from Loyola College in Baltimore, the University of Notre Dame, and Loyola Marymount, and is a member of the American Academy of Arts and Sciences.

LURMA M. RACKLEY, a graduate of Clark Atlanta University, has had rich experiences in the fields of journalism and communication, earning awards in both areas. She is currently completing a book on a well-known radio and television broadcasting legend in Washington, D.C. She lives in Alexandria, Virginia.

CAROLYN M. RODGERS has published widely in major journals and anthologies, among them *Jump Bad Anthology*, *Natural Process*, and *Breakthrough*.

NOLIWE ROOKS, a native of San Francisco and a graduate of Spelman College, is currently coordinator of Black studies at the University of Missouri—Kansas City. She is the author of *Hair Raising: Beauty, Culture and African-American Women*.

PATRICIA ELAM RUFF, an attorney in Washington, D.C., is a free-lance writer whose works have appeared in *Essence*, *Emerge*, and the *Washington Post*. The mother of three children, she is a regular commentator for National Public Radio and CNN. Ruff recently completed her first novel.

KIINI SALAAM, a graduate of Spelman College, recently earned a master of science degree in publishing from Pace University in Manhattan. Her poetry, essays, and short stories have been published in journals and anthologies. She is currently completing a novel.

JUDY SCALES-TRENT is professor of law at S.U.N.Y. at Buffalo, and the author of *Notes of a White Black Woman: Race, Color, Community* (1995). Her father, William J. Trent, Jr., was the first executive director of the United College Fund. He served in that position from 1944 to 1964.

NTOZAKE SHANGE, poet, novelist, and playwright, is a nationally known writer whose choreopoem, *For Colored Girls*, ushered in the Black feminist movement of the seventies.

BRENT STAPLE is an award-winning journalist and author of the highly acclaimed autobiography, *Parallel Time*.

DOLORES STEPHENS, a native of Virginia, is chair and professor of English at Morehouse College. Her research focuses on post-colonial women's prose and fiction. She is the mother of two daughters, but the surrogate mother of many Morehouse sons.

ROSALYN TERBORG-PENN is the author of several books and articles on African-American and African Diasporic women's history. She is professor of history at Morgan State University and founder of the Association of Black Women Historians.

DOROTHY PERRY THOMPSON is a poet and a critic whose works have appeared in a number of anthologies. Her first volume of poetry, *Fly with the Puffin*, was published in 1995. She is an associate professor of English at Winthrop University.

TONI VINCENT is a Unitarian Universalist minister who was ordained at the Howard Thurman Church for the Fellowship of All People. A social worker and teacher, she lives in San Francisco.

ALICE WALKER, one of the most celebrated of contemporary Black women writers, is the author of three collections of essays, four volumes of poetry, two collections of short stories, and four novels, most acclaimed of which is *The Color Purple*, which won the Pulitzer Prize for literature.

ANTHONY WALTON is a poet and essayist whose works have appeared in *Callaloo* and the *New York Times*, among other publications. He authored *Mississippi* and, with Michael Harper, coedited *The Little Brown Book of Contemporary Afro-American Poetry*. He recently worked with Al Sharpton in the writing of Sharpton's autobiography.

MARY HELEN WASHINGTON pioneered as a scholar of Black women's literature with the publication of *Black-Eyed Susans* in 1975. Since then her name has been synonymous with scholarship on Black women writers. Other publications include *Midnight Birds* and the acclaimed *Invented Lives: Narratives of Black Women, 1860–1960*. She is chair of the department of English at the University of Maryland, College Park.

JOHN WIDEMAN, a major contemporary Black writer, is the author of several works, including *Philadelphia*, a collection of short stories, and *Fatheralong*, a memoir.